T0360547

THE POLITICAL ECONOMY OF

DENG'S *NANXUN*

Breakthrough in China's
Reform and Development

THE POLITICAL ECONOMY OF
DENG'S *NANXUN*

Breakthrough in China's Reform and Development

John Wong

East Asian Institute, National University of Singapore, Singapore

World Scientific

NEW JERSEY · LONDON · SINGAPORE · BEIJING · SHANGHAI · HONG KONG · TAIPEI · CHENNAI

Published by

World Scientific Publishing Co. Pte. Ltd.

5 Toh Tuck Link, Singapore 596224

USA office: 27 Warren Street, Suite 401-402, Hackensack, NJ 07601

UK office: 57 Shelton Street, Covent Garden, London WC2H 9HE

Library of Congress Cataloging-in-Publication Data
Wong, John, 1939–
    The political economy of Deng's *Nanxun* : breakthrough in China's reform and development /
John Wong.
        pages cm
    Includes bibliographical references and index.
    ISBN 978-9814578387 (alk. paper)
    1. China--Economic policy. 2. China--Economic conditions--Regional disparities. 3. Economic
development--China. I. Title.
    HC427.92.W65494 2014
    338.951009'049--dc23

                                            2013048376

British Library Cataloguing-in-Publication Data
A catalogue record for this book is available from the British Library.

In-house Editor: DONG Lixi

Typeset by Stallion Press
Email: enquiries@stallionpress.com

Printed in Singapore

Contents

v

Introduction

China's Dynamic Growth in Transition

Thanks to its successful economic reform and the open-door policy that started in 1978, the Chinese economy has since experienced spectacular growth averaging at 9.9% a year for over three decades. By 2012, China's total gross domestic product (GDP) reached 52 trillion yuan, about 125 times more than in 1979 and slightly more than half of today's US GDP at current exchange rate. In the process, China has also achieved highly impressive social progress in terms of satisfying people's basic needs, employment, healthcare, education, life expectancy, and other social objectives, with rising income inequality being the noticeable exception. More significantly, as recognized by the World Bank, over 600 million Chinese people had been lifted out of absolute poverty between 1981 and 2005, a truly "crowning achievement in the history of global poverty alleviation".[1]

No economy can keep on growing at such breakneck rates for such a long period without running into various problems and constraints. This is as much a philosophical as a technical question. Technically speaking, as an economy has experienced high growth for a prolonged period, its original growth-inducing forces would inevitably weaken, simply as a result of the working of the market forces.

---

[1]China's official poverty line started at a very low level, at 200 yuan per head per year. Since 1885, this base line had been raised five times to 1,196 yuan in 2009 (while GDP had grown 42 times during the period). By the end of 2009, the number of people below the poverty line thus fell to a mere 27 million. In 2010, the government revised the base line to 1,500 yuan, which by one stroke had raised the number of the poor three times to about 100 million. In 2011, the standard was raised to the current level of 2,300 yuan, which is still below the World Bank's current standard of US$1.25 per day, or 3,000 yuan per year. ("China to raise poverty line to 1,500 yuan", *China Daily* (April 12, 2011). Also "China's rural poor population declines", *China Daily* (February 27, 2013).

On the supply side, the growth of an economy is fueled by the growth of labor force and productivity increases. For a developing economy at its early phases of development, growth occurs when surplus rural labor is transferred from the low-productivity agriculture to the high-production manufacturing, i.e., industrialization. For over three decades, China had made use of its demographic dividend to successfully promote its labor-intensive manufacturing activities with such abundant surplus rural labor.

In 2012, however, China saw its working-age population decline for the first time, an indication that China's labor supply is approaching what the Nobel economist Arthur Lewis called the "turning-point" — the "Lewis turning point", meaning no more "unlimited supply of labor". In China, this has been manifested in the increasingly tight labor market (particularly in its coastal regions) and the rise of minimum wages in recent years.

Historically, the other high-performance East Asian economies had all experienced a shorter span of high growth than China. Japan chalked up strong growth for about 25 years, through the 1950s and the1960s and part of the 1970s. South Korea and Taiwan had about 20 years of high growth, mainly in the 1960s and the 1970s. Hong Kong and Singapore had even shorter periods of high growth. In terms of sustaining long-term growth, size obviously matters. Singapore had quickly run into serious labor shortages after over 10 years of hypergowth.

China has already sustained hypergowth for almost 35 years in a row. This is because it has much greater internal dynamics for sustaining such continuing dynamic performance. The case in point is that just over half of China's population today are urbanized. China may still have plenty of room for growth in the medium term. Still, as an economy grows more mature, its growth rate is bound to come down. China therefore must also start adjusting itself to the inevitable transition from the double-digit hypergowth to the more sustainable lower growth.

What many commenters have often overlooked is that demographic impact on growth is usually long-term and gradual in nature. China's declining population growth will not translate into real labor shortages until after 2020. China's immediate concern is the gradual disappearance of its past "demographic dividend", i.e., easy availability of abundant cheap labor that had fueled China's past massive industrial expansion. In the years to come, China will see the slowly shrinking of the labor pool at age 20–35, who are most in demand for labor-intensive manufacturing activities.

This means that China will be losing its comparative advantage in labor-intensive manufactured exports. It also points to the urgent need for China to rebalance its economic growth pattern on the demand side by reducing its dependence on external demand (i.e., exports) and promoting greater domestic consumption.

In the meanwhile, China will also face mounting pressures in keeping up with its high rates of productivity growth of the past, because it has exhausted easy sources of productivity gains associated with market reform and institutional improvement. After the initial catch-up phase, future productivity growth has to come from more investment in human capital, more expensive R&D, and more thorough-going market reform.

All these would add up to an overall potential of lower growth for the future. In any case, China today is the world's second largest economy with total GDP of US$8 trillion (2012), already exceeding half of the US level, even though China's per-capita GDP, currently at around US$6,500, is still low. With such a huge base, China's economy just should not be growing at double-digit rates any more. Further high growth would further aggravate social tensions and environmental problems. Continuing high growth would simply be too disruptive for both China and the world.

Adjusting to More Stable Normal Growth

Actually, the central government in Beijing had all along wanted lower and stable growth. Premier Zhu Rongji had spent enormous efforts fighting economic overheating throughout the 1990s. Premier Wen Jiabao had done the same in reining in over-investment and property speculation in the 2000s, In mapping out their various Five-Year Plans, China's policy makers regularly targeted growth at only 7–8%. But these official targets were invariably over-fulfilled each time in implementation, with actual growth often over-shooting into double-digit rates, partly because local governments had wanted higher growth for themselves.

Beijing is therefore happy to embrace the "new normal" of lower but more sustainable growth so long as low growth is not so low as to lead to the "middle-income trap". The 2011 growth projection by the World Bank shows that China's average growth through most of this decade would still be at 7–8% and then down to 6% or 5% in the 2020s.

This may be a little optimistic; but both the internal and external sources of China's economic growth in the medium term are still fairly stable. Even if China's economy were to grow at only 5–6% for the next 10 to 15 years, it would still be on course for China to become the world's largest economy by 2030, with its per-capita GDP likely to more than double to US$17,000–20,000. This is the per-capita level of Japan in the late 1970s, and Singapore or Hong Kong in the 1990s. China in 2030 will no doubt be a developed economy, though it is still far from an affluent society. More significantly, this means that China is likely to follow the footsteps of its dynamic East Asian neighbors of Japan, Korea, and Taiwan, which had successfully avoided falling into the "middle-income trap".

It is sufficiently clear that what is "low growth" for China is actually *not low* in regional and global contexts — the lackluster 7.8% growth of 2012 was still a highly respectable growth performance amidst global slump. China's economic growth for 2013 is slated to come down further to be around 7.5%. But the other prominent emerging BRICs (Brazil, Russia, India, and China) are expected to plunge even more: Brazil's and Russia's growth for 2013 is projected to be 2% while India's is 5%. China's growth performance is still a showcase in the context of the global deceleration of economic growth.

Furthermore, the new leadership under Xi Jinping actually sees lower growth as an opportunity to achieve better quality growth and build a more inclusive society. In Xi's view, lower growth is no obstacle to the realization of his "Chinese Dream".

Suffice to say that China's expected lower growth in the years to come will continue to make waves, both regionally and globally. Policy makers, business houses, students, and academics will continue to pay close attention to the ebbs and flows of China's future economic growth. Given China's economic size, even a lower growth of 6–7% will still significantly affect regional and global economic growth.

From the standpoint of economic development, China's growth performance has been unquestionably a success story. How and why China's economy was able to sustain such a strong growth momentum for such a long period? These are the issues that will also continue to engage the interests of scholars, practitioners, and policy makers, particularly those from the emerging world. Many developing countries are especially interested in how China's successful development experiences could be instructive for their own development.

Furthermore, as the heyday of China's double-digit high growth and dynamic changes is over, China is entering a new period of economic consolidation and political and social adjustment. China's policy makers under Xi's new leadership are in the mood of looking back at the past and doing some stock-taking, so as to prepare the ground for the next phase of reform and change. It is also high time for China scholars to re-visit some of China's important landmark events in the past and, with the benefit of hindsight and new information, take a closer look at the crucial factors that were instrumental in making the change and transformation.

Nanxun the Critical Reform Breakthrough

For China, economic reform and economic growth are actually one and the same process. Such is the reform–growth nexus, which interacts in the way that the two feed on each other. Reform leads to growth, and growth begets more reform. A reform breakthrough in each period would bring about a development breakthrough. In fact China's past three decades of development can also be seen as one big reform–growth nexus. China's phenomenal growth performance over the past three decades was actually the outcome of the successful working of the reform–growth nexus.

It will throw a lot of interesting light by dissecting China's past growth-cum-development process of 1979–2012 into four discrete sub-periods: (i) 1979–1988; (ii) 1989–1990; (iii) 1991–2001, and (iv) 2002–2012, as shown in Fig. 1. Each of these four sub-periods denotes different growth rates and different growth patterns.

Economic growth in the first sub-period of 1979–1988 was sparked off by reform and the open-door policy, with annual average growth rate of 9.8%. The growth process was accompanied by a lot of fluctuations. But high growth was brought to an abrupt end by the outbreak of the Tiananmen incident. In the aftermath of the Tiananmen, growth plummeted to 4% for 1989–1990, as reform came to a halt.

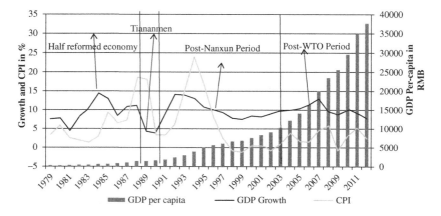

Figure 1.   China's GDP, CPI, and economic growth, 1979–2012.

Source: National Bureau of Statistics.

The third sub-period of 1991–2001 marked the second spurt of China's of even stronger growth triggered off by Deng Xiaoping's *Nanxun* (tour of South China) in early 1992, averaging at the double-digit rate of 10.4%. This may be called the *"Nanxun* effect" because the main source of growth stemmed from a sleuth of reform measures that were unleashed by the *Nanxun* in line with Deng's call for building the "socialist market economy". Looking back, this dynamic post-*Nanxun* reform–growth nexus also laid the preconditions for China's subsequent economic takeoff.

The fourth sub-period of 2002–2012 marked the third spurt of China's high growth, averaging at 9.9%, which was associated with China's accession to the World Trade Organization (WTO) in November 2001. This may be called the "WTO effect", which enabled China to capture the mechanism of the international capitalism to achieve sustained high growth as a result of China's greater integration with the global economy.

China's past three decades of reform and development were actually not a smooth-going but a dynamic process of fluctuating growth. The underlying political and economic factors that were responsible for the transition from one sub-period to another were therefore highly significant. In particular, the political and economic changes in the intervening years of 1990–1996 that interfaced the first two sub-periods of high growth, i.e., from 1979–1988 to 1991–2001 were the most crucial. This was Deng's

Nanxun phase, which gave rise to the critical reform breakthrough, creating a new round of dynamic reform–growth nexus. This, in turn, sparked off double-digit economic growth through the 1990s. This is in fact what this book is all about: the political economy of Deng's *Nanxun* and how it brought about a breakthrough in China's reform and development.

The Political Economy of the *Nanxun*

It is well known that China's economic reform bears many distinctive Chinese characteristics or more precisely, the "Dengist characteristics". Instead of taking to a big bang approach, economic reform by Deng Xiaoping was to be a gradual process, by trial and error or through learning by doing. Such is Deng's celebrated reform strategy of "crossing the river by first feeling the stones". The reform first started with agricultural reform based on household responsibility system, which was an immediate success, giving rise to the first spurt of high growth in the early 1980s.

After this, the reform focus shifted to industrial reform in the urban areas, which had proved to be an exceedingly complicated undertaking. The government introduced a dual-tracked price system to deal with numerous "relative prices". For agricultural reform, it would need to deal with the relative prices of only a few major crops. But industrial reform had to tackle thousands of commodities. As happened in the other transitional economies, the dual-tracked price system was apt to give rise to corruption and rent-seeking activities as well as a high inflation, which, in the case of China, led to the outbreak of the Tiananmen incident in June 1989.

The immediate aftermath of the Tiananmen event marked the low point in China's reform and development, with average economic growth during 1989–1990 plummeting to 4%. Much more serious was the fact that many government officials (the cadres) in Beijing had lost faith in the kind of economic reform that they had witnessed. Among China's top leadership, there was intensive ideological debate between the reformists and the conservatives. Reeling from the shock of the violent Tiananmen crackdown, many senior leaders in Beijing were indeed in favor of taking a more cautious approach to reform. China's reform was initially at crossroads; but it had soon come to a halt.

To break out from such low doldrums of reform and development, Deng Xiaoping made a historic tour of South China in the spring of 1992, popularly known as *Nanxun*. In Shenzhen and other places, he made several speeches, openly attacking the leftist ideology and their conservative economic policy stand that dominated the post-Tiananmen leadership in Beijing at that time. Instead of pulling back from the market reform or slowing down the process, Deng cogently argued that the only sensible way out was to speed up economic reform and further open up China's economy to the outside. Deng boldly introduced the concept of the "socialist market economy" as the country's new ideological orthodoxy.

The fact that Beijing, originally as a strong bastion of the Party's conservatives, should have so quickly and easily swung toward the reformist side, underscored not just Deng's high political preeminence and prestige in China, but also the popular support for continuing market reform outside Beijing, particularly in the coastal region that had been the forefront of economic reform. After the Tiananmen, the Chinese people did not want to go back to the old system, and most people would just want to see a more market-oriented economy and a more open China. The door, once open, can no longer be shut again.

As it happened, Deng's *Nanxun* immediately put a new reform–growth nexus into action by sparking off a new wave of economic growth, fueled by increasing trade and rising foreign direct investment (FDI). The total FDI of the four post-*Nanxun* years was almost six times that of the previous 12 years. The cumulated FDI from 1979 to 2011 amounted to US$1.2 trillion, and 97% of it came after the 1992 *Nanxun*! The massive influx of FDI also led to a sharp rise in domestic fixed investment. Hence, China's rapid investment-driven growth through the 1990s.

With the market reform now having a clear direction and carrying a strong mandate from Deng, the Chinese government immediately set out to tackle the important reforms in earnest, including the important foreign exchange reform and the fiscal reform in 1994. This is truly the period of breakthrough for China's economic reform, which in turn sparked off an instant hypergrowth for three years (1992–1995) averaging at 13.6%. But such relentless growth also created serious economic overheating, with double-digit inflation. The CPI (consumer price index) hit an all-time high of 24.1% in 1994.

Thus, China's first brush with a truly open market economy was market chaos and macroeconomic overheating. Subsequently, it took Premier Zhu Rongji several years to refine his techniques of macroeconomic control to stabilize the economy and consolidate the reform and development that was sparked off by *Nanxun*. Having stabilizing the economy, Zhu then proceeded to push for more reforms such as the state-owned enterprise (SOE) reform and the financial sector reform. In the process, Zhu was also preparing China for the eventual accession to the WTO and the transition toward the second spurt of even higher growth after 2002, which was triggered off by China's increasing integration with the regional and global economies.

Taking the whole period of 1978–2012 into consideration, it is of course obvious that high growth was due to Deng's economic reform and open-door policy that was formalized by the Third Plenum of the Party's 11th Central Committee in December 1978. But one policy decision, however path breaking, just could not bring about a nation's development success for over three decades. Deng's reform decision in 1978 merely set the nation on a reform course. Not enough. It was his second shot, the *Nanxun* that led to the subsequent realization of the market economy for China.

It may further be argued that what Deng had personally suffered in Mao's Cultural Revolution made him realize that there was something fundamentally wrong in the Chinese system. Hence his determination to open a new chapter in China's modern economic history by launching economic reform and the open-door policy. In this sense, the Cultural Revolution was the mother of Deng's economic reform.

Having realized the problems of a half-reformed economy that led to the outbreak of the Tiananmen event and post-Tiananmen deadlock over the reform, Deng was determined to launch the *Nanxun* to prepare the political ground for China's final march toward the market economy. In this sense, the *Nanxun* was the mother of China's transformation into the market economy.

*****

The chapters selected for this book were written by the author when he was Director of the Institute of East Asian Philosophies (IEAP), which later became the Institute of East Asian Political Economy (IEAPE). Still later, IEAPE was renamed in 1997 as East Asian Institute (EAI) to become an autonomous research organization within the National University of Singapore. The Institute was originally set up by Singapore's first Deputy Prime Minister, the late Dr Goh Keng Swee as a think tank for "China watching". These chapters were originally written for circulation to the Singapore government as confidential reports to Cabinet Ministers and Permanent Secretaries only. As "China watching" in Singapore in those early days were politically sensitive, these chapters not been formally published before.

Apart from this Introduction, which provides a broad background from today's perspective for readers to understand what was happening during this *Nanxun* period, the author has written a lengthy abstract to each chapter. These abstracts not just highlight the salient points and arguments of each chapter, but also explain how those issues and problems can be seen in retrospect, based on additional research. The abstracts to each chapter thus constitute additional intellectual value-added to this volume.

The chapters were written based on whatever information that was available at the time, in addition to capturing prevailing political mood of the day. The abstract also serves as an ex-post evaluation of the past events based on additional new information, and shows how those events have evolved over the years. In combination, these chapters piece together a reasonably realistic picture of the political economy of the crucial *Nanxun* period.

*****

Chapter 1, on China's per-capita GDP at the beginning of economic reform, and Chapter 2, on Deng's entrepreneurial approach to economic reform, can serve as basic introductory chapters to provide a useful background for readers to understand China's reform and development in this period. Before the reform, China's GDP measure was the "Gross Social Product", based on the socialist concept of NMP (net material product) mainly by excluding service activities. This is much out of line with the conventional GDP accounting (standardized by the UN as SNA) that was used in all market economies. Initially, China's policy makers and its many home-grown economists, without proper training in basic neo-classical economics, had problems understanding the concepts of GNP (gross national product), GDP, and PPP (purchasing power parity) based GDP. But economic progress or economic growth is based on yearly increases in GDP. China's GNP accounting therefore had to adapt and gradually be revised over the years to meet international standard.

China's successful reform translated into double-digit rates economic growth, which in turn resulted in the doubling, doubling, and doubling of China's per-capita GDP over the past three decades. When Deng Xiaoping introduced reform in1978, China's nominal per-capita GDP was estimated to be around US$230 and it was still only US$350 in 1989. By early 2013, it was over US$6,000 or around $9,000 in PPP terms. By 2012, China's had already overtaken Japan as the world's second largest economy with China's total GDP slightly over 50% of the US level. China's economic growth performance over the past three decades is truly remarkable.

China's approach to economic reform, as discussed in Chapter 2, bore much of Deng Xiaoping's wisdom, especially his well-known pragmatism. Deng started off reform by complaining that he could not find any textbook to teach him how to go about in converting a planned economy into a market economy. So he had to plan the reform progress slowly and gradually, through learning by doing, as manifested in his oft-repeated dictum: "Crossing the river by feeling the stones first". Such an approach to reform is necessarily opportunistic, unstructured, and flexible; and hence dubbed the "entrepreneurial" way of carrying out reform.

This was a far-cry from the "Big Bang" strategy that was adopted in the former Soviet Union and other Eastern European socialist countries. Instead of Chinese gradualism, they went for a "shock therapy". The comparative reform performance between the "technocratic approach" of the former European socialist countries and the "entrepreneurial approach" of China is sufficiently clear. China's success was borne out by its rapid economic and low inflation, as compared to low growth and hyperinflation in the other transitional economies. Economic reform everywhere is full of risk and uncertainty. In this sense, Deng's gamble had paid off.

Chapter 3 is about the 7th Party Plenum, held in December 1990. This was the single most important Party meeting in the immediate aftermath of the Tiananmen event. By that time, political stability was restored and the economy was also gradually back on track. But the Party unity was still an outstanding issue, with the top leadership clearly divided over the speed as well as the direction of reform. The pro-Deng reformist group put up the reform-oriented platform at the Plenum, calling for the reform to be carried out "faster, better, and more effectively". But such reform advocacy was blocked by the conservatives led by the influential Party elder Chen Yun, who had argued for a more cautious approach to reform, or even putting reform on hold for the time being. The Party's top leadership was thus in a stalemate over the reform issue.

Most people in Beijing were still reeling from the shock of the Tiananmen that was still fresh in their memory. They were naturally in favor of stability, and they wanted to see the consolidation of the past reform first before venturing into a new round of reforms. Deng had himself realized that a lot of problems that led to the outbreak of the Tiananmen such as high inflation and rent-seeking activities were due to the operation of a half-reformed economy. To Deng, the only way out for China was to break out of the past low reform trap by completing the march to the market reform. Apparently, such a radical reform idea did not go down well with most top leaders in Beijing at that time, despite Deng's supreme power and prestige.

Deng was soon aware that Beijing had become the stronghold of the anti-reform conservatives. He had to go out to Shanghai and Guangdong to appeal to the more liberal reform supporters there. Such is the origin of his *Nanxun*. In retrospect, the 7th Plenum was of great historical significance in the sense that it catalyzed the *Nanxun* and its subsequent reform breakthrough.

Chapter 4 is about the post-Tiananmen ideological debate on reform. As the top leadership in Beijing was divided over the ways and means of going about further reform, this originally "technical issue" soon turned into an ideological battle between the two groups of advocacy. It started off with two pro-reform newspaper articles in Shanghai bearing the title if one's surname was Mr. Socialism or Mr. Capitalism, implying that if the reform should be fundamentally socialist or capitalist in character. It is in the very nature of the Chinese Communist Party that once things had become ideological, they would politically get very complicated. The Party's past political campaigns were full of such insinuations or innuendoes. This is how Mao started his Cultural Revolution, with the first salvo being fired from Shanghai.

The *"she* vs *zi"* debate clearly pointed to the political struggle between the two factions at that time: (i) the conservatives and (ii) the pro-reform liberals. China scholars were then much puzzled over the origin of this debate. It was only 20 years later, on the 20th anniversary of the *Nanxun,* that the full political background of these two articles came into light. The author of these articles was Zhou Ruijin, who was then the editor-in-chief of Shanghai's *Jiefang Ribao* (Liberation Daily). He wrote the articles with support from Deng. These Shanghai articles provided the first voice of Deng's *Nanxun jianghua* (talk). It is also of great historical interest that the first shot of Deng's *Nanxun* was actually fired in Shanghai, not in Shenzhen.

Chapter 5, on the immediate *Nanxun* effect, shows how Deng's trip to Guangzhou, Shenzhen, and Zhuhai in early 1992 (around the Chinese New Year) had produced dramatic results, virtually in a matter of just few months. During his trip, Deng made no bone about China's need to move toward a market economy as soon as possible. His radical views on economic reform, informal, impromptu, and often very blunt, touched off immediate political reverberation in Beijing, much shaking the conservative camp led by Chen Yun. More importantly, General Secretary Jiang Zemin quickly changed tack and jumped over to join Deng's new reform bandwagon.

The market moved even faster. Within weeks of Deng's first appearance in Shenzhen, Deng's straight-talking remarks (*Nanxun jianghua*) about the reform were soon leaked into the Hong Kong media. Hong Kong businessmen had quickly grasped such a radical shift of the political climate in China and flocked to South China to seek new business opportunity. In a matter of just few months, China witnessed an unprecedented FDI boom, as FDI rose 250% in 1992. Consequently, China ended 1992 with 12% growth — later adjusted to be even higher, at 14%. Such roaring economic growth was the immediate endorsement of Deng's *Nanxun* by the market.

Chapter 6 discusses the most remarkable post-*Nanxun* reform progress that was accomplished in 1994. The immediate economic upsurge of the *Nanxun* provided a strong precondition for Beijing to put up a comprehensive reform package that was adopted at the Third Party Plenum in November 1993, for implementation in 1994. This included the most crucial tax reform (tackling the historical issue of revenue sharing between the central and local governments), the foreign exchange reform (abolishing the dual-exchange system), and the banking reform (making the People's Bank of China as a real central bank for the nation, and commercializing the four specialized state banks).

Indeed, 1994 went down in Deng's reform history as the single most important landmark year, next to the rural and agricultural reform in the early 1980s. The reform breakthrough in 1994 was indispensable for the development of the (socialist) market economy while it also laid the foundation for China's dynamic economic growth in the following two decades.

Chapter 7 shows how the Chinese economy in 1995, fueled by rising FDI and rapid growth of fixed investment and exports, had become overheated within a short span of two years, with inflation soaring to the record high of 24% in 1995. Zhu Rongji, then first Vice-Premier, was in charge of the country's economic affairs. Zhu had to employ some tough macroeconomic control methods to rein in the economic overheating and finally brought economic growth in 1995 successfully to a "soft landing".

As China's economy at that time was still not fully marketized, it had no built-in macroeconomic stabilizers as found in a normal market economy. Economic growth was therefore often accompanied by a lot of ups and downs. Through most 1990s, Zhu had to deal with such macroeconomic instabilities, mainly with administrative measures. He could not rely mainly on indirect economic levers to fine tune the economy and smooth out the fluctuation.

Chapter 8 discusses China's 9th Five-Year Plan, 1996–2000. The 8th Five-Year Plan, 1991–1995, presented by Premier Li Peng at the 7th Party Plenum in 1990, was already overtaken by events and rendered irrelevant by Deng's *Nanxun*. This 9th Five-Year Plan was put up along with a long-term vision for 2010 was supposed to address some potential challenges China would be facing in the run-up to the 21st century. In concrete terms, China would quadruple its per-capita GDP in 2000 from the 1980 level — *fan-liang-fan,* so that China would develop into what Deng called a moderately affluent (*xiaokang*) society by the turn of the century.

This chapter also discusses the problems faced by China's various "Five-Year Plans", which were the product of central planning. As China's economy was increasingly marketized due to ongoing market reform, it would also become increasingly "unplannable". In fact, China's subsequent Five-Year Plans, ritually put up from time to time, provided only a rough indication of the leadership's long-term vision, which was often overtaken by actual events, including external shocks.

Chapter 9 turns to the topic of *Xiangzhen qiye* or township village enterprises (TVEs), which were uniquely the Chinese experience of rural industrialization, having no parallel in other transitional economies like the former Soviet Union. TVEs cropped up in the 1980s, and were still growing in the post-Tiananmen period of the early 1990s. As collectively owned business enterprises, TVEs operated outside the state economic plan. They had to be more competitive in order to survive. In this sense, they were commercially more dynamic than the state-owned enterprises (SOEs).

However, as China's economy became more extensively marketized after the *Nanxun*, the collective sector would soon lose ground, and TVEs had to adjust and transform. Many had grown up to become export-oriented and then incorporated or privatized. Others were dissolved or absorbed by SOEs. By 2011, collectively owned enterprises accounted for only 1.3% of all enterprise units in China. Under the impact of continuing industrialization and urbanization, the rural sector had indeed been fast shrinking and the demise of the TVEs was therefore inevitable. Nonetheless, TVEs had played an important role at the transitional phase of China's reform and development.

Chapter 10 explains why Deng was so concerned about agriculture. It may be remembered that Deng's first shot on economic reform was fired in the countryside. After his *Nanxun*, reform was intensified in the urban sector, which led to a big industrial boom in urban areas. It so happened that China's agricultural growth, particularly grain production, was slacking in this period. Per-capita grain production in the early 1990s was slightly declining. But China's top leadership started to get worried. The situation was aggravated by an alarming article by the famous American agronomist Lester Brown, who had openly declared that China had started to "lose the capacity to feed itself".

Deng was particularly concerned about the state of the Chinese agriculture. He belonged to the first generation of communist leaders who had a strong "peasant mentality" and a deep-rooted rural background. He had also been much influenced by Mao's economic policy: "Agriculture is the foundation of the Chinese economy, with grain as the key link in agricultural development" — *Yinong weiben, yiliang weigang*. Thus, during the heyday of the post-*Nanxun* economic boom, Deng was reported to have cautioned his colleagues by stating, "Should China encounter problems in the 1990s, it would happen in agriculture".

It had subsequently turned out that the small dip in grain production in the early 1990s was partly due to bad weather and partly because wrong government policies for grain acquisition. But China's top leaders had ever since made efforts not to ignore agricultural and rural development. Throughout the 1990s, the Number One Central Document issued every year was invariably about agriculture and rural development. As a result, China's grain production growth for the next two decades had outstripped its population growth, i.e., China has throughout not lost its ability to feed itself.

Chapter 11 is about progress in foreign trade reform in the *Nanxun* period. To Deng, economic reform and the open-door policy always go together and reinforced each other. Consequently, "reform and open policy" (*gaige Kaifeng*) had ritually become one single phase in all official statements. The *Nanxun* was supposed to speed up domestic economic reform, but this had immediately triggered off a trade boom, which in turn called for more reforms in the foreign trade sector. The foreign exchange reform is the case in point. Throughout the 1990s, the main thrust of the government's foreign trade reform efforts was aimed at preparing China to join initially the GATT (General Agreement on Tariffs and Trade), and later the WTO.

Chapter 12 is about China's efforts to join the GATT so as to be a formal participant of the multilateral trade negotiation (MTN) process, which would in turn provide institutionalized protection to China against protectionism and discrimination. As China was originally a founding member of the GATT, it initially applied to "restore" its membership by invoking the "Grandfather Clause" of the US law. After the Tiananmen incident, the United States subjected its trade with China to the annual review of the MFN (most favored nation) clause and also put up a major stumbling block to China's accession to the GATT. This made China all the more determined to join (or rejoin) the GATT; and this had turned out to be a political tug-of-war between Beijing and Washington.

Chapter 13 is about the politics and economics of China's continuing efforts to join the international trade body, first the GATT and then the WTO, which officially superseded the GATT in 1995. China failed to become a founding member of the WTO when it was first formed, mainly due to the continuing US blockage. Officially, the US opposition to China's WTO membership was based on the technical argument that China's trade regime was not sufficiently open and China's economy was not sufficiently marketized. As China's foreign trade throughout the 1990s was growing at 17% a year to become potentially a foremost trading power, the US wanted to pry open the vast China market as wide as possible by making China to make more concessions first. This raised China's "admission price" to the WTO.

China finally acceded to the WTO in November 2011. China's total trade turnover in 2001 amounted to only US$510 billion, as the world's 5th largest trading nation. Ten years later, in 2011, China's total trade rose seven times to reach US$3,642 billion to become the world's leading trading nation. Of even greater importance, China's economy after its WTO membership was growing at double-digit rates. Such is the WTO effect on China's dynamic economic growth that was discussed earlier.

Chapter 14 winds up the book by discussing the business involvement in China of the ethnic Chinese from Southeast Asia. The common term for these ethnic Chinese is "overseas Chinese" (*huaqiao*), which is politically and technically difficult to define or identify. These Chinese had long ceased to treat Southeast Asia as a sojourn while the governments in Southeast Asian countries were no longer treating them as foreigners or "overseas Chinese" in the original sense of the term. At the same time, it is well known that China's success in economic reform and the open-door policy had owed a great deal to the capital, technology, and entrepreneurship of the ethnic Chinese from the "Greater China" (Hong Kong, Macau, and Taiwan) and Southeast Asia. But there are no systematic data and information for a detailed analysis of this subject.

Instead of identifying which ethnic Chinese groups from which place had invested in China, this chapter has captured some prominent business conglomerates investing in China but originating from the Chinese diaspora in Southeast Asia (now ASEAN). They include the Salim group from Indonesia, the Lion Group from Malaysia, the banks from Singapore, and the CP group from Thailand. Together, they had made important commercial presence in China, operating as part of what Western media had dubbed the "Bamboo Network".

xxiv   *The Political Economy of Deng's Nanxun*

Even more significant from historical perspective is the fact that three decades later, China's economic relations with the ASEAN region have not only rapidly grown, but their patterns have also changed. As the world's second largest economy with capital surplus, China has become an important player in the FDI scene of ASEAN. Capital and technology are now steadily flowing from China into ASEAN. The table has turned.

*****

Ezra Vogel's recent book, *Deng Xiaoping and the Transformation of China* has dealt with the politics of the *Nanxun* period, but not the reform and development aspects. In fact, few China scholars today are going back to this period.

China's reform–development nexus is indeed a continuing and yet a complex process. To understand its present complexity, the past will always be useful and relevant. Sure enough, in early December 2012, as Xi Jinping was about to take over the helm from Hu Jintao, Xi made a special tour of Shenzhen, much in the spirit of Deng's *Nanxun*. Xi's Shenzhen tour was meant to signal his similar determination to carry out with the unfinished business of reform for China. This should sufficiently underpin the importance of revisiting the *Nanxun* period.

As China's economy is getting mature and slowing down in growth, the main thrust of China's future development focus will be increasingly more on political and social reform, which has yet to achieve a significant breakthrough. China's officials and China scholars should find Deng's experience and his struggle for reform during the critical *Nanxun* phase highly instructive. That is probably what Xi had in mind.

Part I
Background Chapters

Chapter 1

China's Per-Capita GNP at the Beginning of Economic Reform

Introduction

This chapter was circulated in 1990 under the title "What is China's Per-Capita GNP?" "Economic growth" means increases in a country's GDP (gross domestic product) or GNP (gross national product) over a certain period of time. "Economic development" is conventionally defined to mean increases in per-capita GDP/GNP over a sustained period along with concomitant socio-economic changes. The original idea for circulating this chapter to the Singapore government was to ascertain China's per-capita GNP level when it first started economic reform and the open-door policy, as compared to its neighboring economies; and what the Chinese economy had achieved in the first decade (the 1980s) of economic reform.

This had turned out to be a very complicated exercise. First, the conventional GNP accounting that was standardized in the early 1950s by the United Nations into the commonly accepted "System of National Accounts or SNA" for all market economies, was not wholly adopted by China's National State Statistical Bureau. Before the start of economic reform, China's national income was based on the concept of "Net Material Product or NMP", which was generally adopted by all the Soviet-type socialist economies. Typically, NMP excludes the service sector and other similar activities, which were considered unproductive under the Marxist definition.

Throughout the 1980s, China's own system of national accounts was still in the process of adjusting to the international SNA format for definition and computation. By 1990, China's National Statistical Bureau had not completed its transition as it continued to publish statistics based on both socialist and international concepts. For instance, it still used the concept of "Gross Social Product," which is the total "social" output of agriculture, manufacturing, construction, communications and transportation, and commerce. Unlike the internationally accepted national income concept (which is based on value-added approach), gross social product counts all outputs at all levels of production, and hence it contains a lot of "double counting" in its gross aggregation process, e.g., the output of one industry is used by another industry as input.

Accordingly, the gross social product had exaggerated growth. If 1978 was used as a base year of 100, China's gross social product increased to 306 in 1989 while national income increased to only 250. Later in the 1990s, as the National Bureau of Statistics continued with its reform and modernization of China's domestic statistical system by moving closer to the international standards, it dropped gross social product approach. Subsequently, it had also done a few rounds of revising national income statistics upwards, particularly after it had undertaken a proper valuation of its service sector activities that were all along underestimated because of the socialist legacies.

Secondly, looking back, China in 1990 was still a messy half-reformed economy, particularly for its industrial sector in urban areas. Most of the key commodities were still under price controls while the state sector (state-owned enterprises) heavily dominated the economy. As a result, price distortion occurred everywhere. This made it hard to have a proper valuation of economic activities that would make national income a better reflection of the performance of the economy.

Worse still, the situation made it difficult to evaluate China's national income or per-capita GDP/GNP from the international perspective, as all international comparison of GNP had to start with converting domestic national income into US dollar terms; and this would involve he exchange rate problem. China's exchange rate was artificially fixed, and it was grossly overvalued until the exchange rate reform in 1994.

The World Bank first started to monitor China's economic growth in 1976 and put down China's per-capita GNP for 1976 (the year Mao Zedong and Zhou Enlai died) as US$410. Subsequently, per-capita GNP was adjusted downwards, partly to reflect the exchange rate movements, to US$230 for 1978 when Deng Xiaoping introduced economic reform, and US$290 for 1980. By 1989, it went up to US$350, giving an average annual growth of 9.7% for the period of 1980–1989.

In other words, most of China's domestic economic activities in the initial phases of economic reform were grossly under-priced (a serious downward bias). This was further complicated by the overvaluation of the

Renminbi exchange rate, which works in the opposite direction by exaggerating China's GDP in international perspective. This problem was not specific to China, but was in fact common to all developing countries. But the problem was more serious for China as a transitional economy moving from central planning to the market system.

To remove the distortion caused by domestic price and exchange rate biases, economists led by Irving Kravis used the concept of "international price" to re-calculate a country's domestic GNP for international comparison. This is conceptually similar to what is now commonly known as the purchasing power parity (PPP), which is essentially a kind of price index to compare prices of similar commodity in different countries.

This chapter goes into the PPP concept of China's per-capita GNP in the 1980s, which was largely unfamiliar to economists and officials in China at that time. Thus, China's "real" per-capita GDP at "1985 international prices" for 1988 was US$2,308, as compared to $786 for India, $10,417 for Singapore, $12,209 for Japan and $18,339 for the US. But China's nominal per-capita GNP for 1988 was only US$330, i.e., it was almost seven times lower. The US–China difference in PPP per-capita GNP was about eight times. Twenty-five years later, in 2012, China's per-capita GDP in PPP terms, as estimated by International Monetary Fund (IMF), was $8,400 while that for the US was $48,000. The US–China gap is still more than six times.

China has achieved spectacular economic growth performance for over three decades with its GDP increasing at 9.9% a year. By 2012, China had already overtaken Japan as the world's second largest economy, with its total GDP slightly over 50% of the US level. In term of per-capita GDP (which can better reflect the average living standard), China's nominal level at the start of 2013 is about US$6,000 or $9,000 in PPP terms. China is still a long way from becoming an affluent society.

This chapter, apart from explaining China's GDP/GNP at the starting point of its economic reform and its various ramifications, also provides a simple, easy-to-understand explanation of various methods of national income accounting. This should be a useful update for non-specialists of the needed basic concepts to understand and interpret China's economic progress.

Conventional Indicator Tends to Mislead

For lack of a better measuring rod, governments and international organizations have been consistently using increases in GNP (gross national product) — defined as the total volume of goods and services produced in a country — as an indicator of economic growth, and also using per-capita GNP (GNP divided by population) as a yardstick to judge a country's living standards and its level of productivity. But the problem comes to a head when a large, poor country like China, which has experienced record economic growth in the 1980s in both total GNP and per-capita GNP terms and yet its per-capita GNP expressed in US dollar shows little increase over the past decade. Clearly, such conventional measure has failed, in this circumstance, to reflect the actual level of material progress China has achieved during the last 10 years.

In 1978, the World Bank published the first issue of *World Development Report* which gave China's per-capita GNP for 1976 as US$410 (compared to US$150 for India and US$2,700 for Singapore for the same year). In the subsequent yearly reports of the World Bank, China's per-capita GNP, as shown in Fig. 1a, plummeted to US$230 for 1978 and then fluctuated around US$300 until it reached US$350 for 1989 (compared to US$340 for India and US$10,450 for Singapore). A layman would certainly be baffled as to why China's per-capita GNP in the 1980s had become stagnant while the other less fast-growing Asian economies had registered a steep rise in their per-capita GNP levels, as evident in Table 1.

Economists could explain away the problem by arguing that the World Bank had probably overestimated China's GNP in the late 1970s to begin

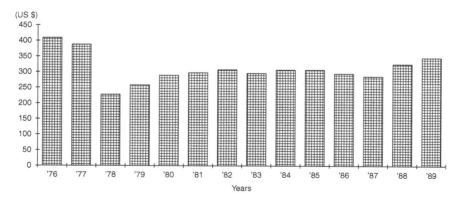

Figure 1a.   China's Nominal Per-capita GNP in US Dollars, 1976–1989.

Source: World Bank. *World Development Report*. (From 1978 to 1991.)

Table 1.   China's Nominal Per-capita GNP in Regional Perspective (US Dollars).

Years	1976	1977	1978	1979	1980	1981	1982	1983	1984	1985	1986	1987	1988	1989	Average Annual Growth Rate (%)	
															Per Capita GNP, 1965–1989	Total GDP, 1980–1989
China	**410**	**390**	**230**	**260**	**290**	**300**	**310**	**300**	**310**	**310**	**300**	**290**	**330**	**350**	**5.70**	**9.70**
Japan	4,910	5,670	7,280	8,810	9,890	10,080	10,080	10,120	10,630	11,300	12,840	15,760	21,020	23,810	4.30	4.00
ASEAN																
Indonesia	240	300	360	370	430	530	580	560	540	530	490	450	440	500	4.40	5.30
Malaysia	860	930	1,090	1,370	1,620	1,840	1,860	1,860	1,980	2,000	1,830	1,810	1,940	2,160	4.00	4.90
Philippines	410	300	510	600	690	790	820	760	660	580	560	590	630	710	1.60	0.70
Thailand	380	514	490	590	670	770	790	820	860	800	810	850	1,000	1,220	4.20	7.00
NIEs																
Hong Kong	2,110	2,590	3,040	3,760	4,240	5,100	5,340	6,000	6,330	6,230	6,910	8,070	9,220	10,350	6.30	7.10
Singapore	2,700	2,880	3,290	3,830	4,430	5,240	5,910	6,620	7,260	7,420	7,410	7,940	9,070	10,450	7.00	6.10
S. Korea	670	820	1,160	1,480	1,520	1,700	1,910	2,010	2,110	2,150	2,370	2,690	3,600	4,400	7.00	9.70
Taiwan	1,041	1,193	1,443	1,758	2,155	2,443	2,419	2,573	2,890	2,992	3,646	4,825	5,798	6,889	—	7.99
For comparison																
India	150	150	180	190	240	260	260	260	260	270	290	300	340	340	1.80	5.30
USA	7,890	8,520	9,590	10,630	11,360	12,820	13,160	14,110	15,390	16,690	17,480	18,530	19,840	20,910	1.60	3.30

Source: World Bank: *World Development Report* (from 1978 to 1991); for Taiwan, *Statistical Yearbook of Republic of China, 1990* (Taipei, Executive Yuan, 1991).

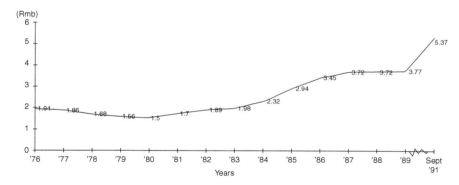

Figure 1b.   Fluctuation in China's Exchange Rate, 1976–1991 (Rmb Per US Dollar).

Source: Economic & Development Resource Center. Asian Development Bank. *Key Indicators of Developing Asian & Pacific Countries*. 1989–1990.

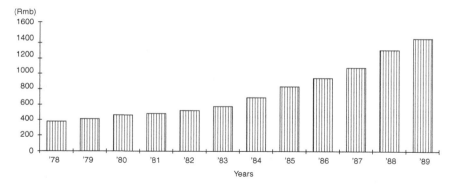

Figure 1c.   China's Nominal Per-capita GNP in Renminbi, 1978–1989.

Sources: World Bank. *China: Macroeconomic Stability & Industrial Growth Under Decentralized Socialism, 1990*. And, *Statistical Yearbook of China, 1990*.

with, because China was then following the socialist GNP accounting system (to be explained later); and that China's per-capita GNP through the 1980s was "brought down" by several rounds of depreciation of the Chinese *Renminbi*, i.e., due to distortion from the exchange rate conversion (Fig. 1b). This can be seen from the fact that China's per-capita GNP as *expressed in Renminbi* clearly shows steady increase (Fig. 1c). Nonetheless, the upshot serves to highlight one of the basic deficiencies of this important economic indicator.

Worse still, when the per-capita GNP figures of countries are all listed in terms of the US dollar, one inevitably tends to use them to compare if a certain country is rich or poor, "developed" or "developing". A Singaporean, for example, will be tempted to pass the judgment that Singapore's per-capita GNP being 30 times higher than that of China, the average Singaporean should be economically or materially 30 times better off than the average Chinese. This is simply not the case. A typical Singaporean worker may take home a pay-packet which is many times, perhaps 10 times but certainly not 30 times, more than his counterpart in China can take home. Furthermore, the pay of our Singaporean worker certainly does not enable him to purchase the amount of goods and services in Singapore which is 30 times more than the Chinese worker can buy in China out of his own pay — we all know that most daily necessities and essential services are so much cheaper in China than in Singapore.

To correct such a bias in international comparison, economists have separated the concept of *nominal* per-capita GNP from that of *real* per-capita GNP. The former refers to the conventional measure, which is widely used by governments and international media. It is obtained simply by converting a country's GNP in its national currency into US dollars at the prevailing exchange rate. More sophisticated, the latter is purported to provide an adequate inter-country comparison by taking into account the purchasing power of the national currencies over the GNP of the countries involved, i.e., GNP for different countries is all expressed in the same set of "international prices" or in the common "international dollars", so that the problem of price differences such as a bottle of Tsingtao beer for S$4.20 in Singapore vis-a-vis Rmb 1.20 (equivalent to S$0.40) for the same bottle in China is duly taken care of.

Recently, Professor Angus Maddison, Chief Economist at the OECD Development Centre, has calculated the *real* GDP of China for 1987 at 1980 "international" prices and arrived at the estimate of *US$1,748*, which is six times higher than China's *nominal* level of US$290 from the conventional estimate by the World Bank.[1] In a separate study by Professors Robert Summers and Alan Heston, the *real* per-capita GDP of China for 1988 at current "international prices" was worked out to be

---

[1] Angus Maddison (1989). *The World Economy in the 20th Century*. Paris: OECD Development Centre Studies.

US$2,472, which is more than seven times higher than China's *nominal* level of US$330 from the World Bank.[2] The new figures would rank China with the world's "lower-middle-income" countries, with China's real GDP per capita being higher than that of Indonesia and the Philippines but lower than that of Thailand. Also, Singapore's *real* per-capita GDP was only 4.2 times of China's, not 30 times as indicated by the nominal measure. Viewed in this context, China is not really that poor.

"Nominal GDP" vs "Real GDP"

National income (NI), gross domestic product (GDP), and GNP are closely related concepts, which are often used interchangeably, with only minor differences. Broadly speaking, the three terms refer to the total monetary value of all goods and services produced in an economy over a period of time. "National income" is more like a generic concept. "Gross domestic product" measures the total final outputs of goods and services produced by the economy within the country's territory by both residents and non-residents. "Gross national product" measures the total domestic and foreign output claimed by residents of a country. Thus it should comprise gross domestic product plus factor incomes accruing to residents from abroad. Except for economies with large external activities, the GDP and GNP for most countries are quite close. For China, the two in Renminbi are almost identical.

GNP accounting has been standardized by the United Nations into the System of National Accounts or *SNA* for all market-based economies. Generally speaking, NI can be computed by three methods: (i) income approach: this adds up all incomes from wages, rent, interest, and profits (both dividends and undistributed profits) together with indirect business taxes to form net national income at market prices; (ii) Value-added approach: this adds up the *final* output of all firms or sums up the

---

[2] Robert Summers and Alan Heston (1991). The Penn World Table (Mark 5): An Expanded Set of International Comparison, 1950–1988. *Quartely Journal of Economics* 106(2). Both Summers and Heston have been long-time associates of the pioneer in this field, Irving B Kravis, who started the International Comparison Project (ICP) in the late 1950s.

value-added at each stage of production (i.e., sales minus costs to leave out intermediate products so as not to "double count") to arrive at GDP at factor cost; and (iii) expenditure approach: this adds up total private consumption expenditure, government expenditure, total domestic fixed investment, and changes in stocks, and then adjust for exports and imports, to arrive at GDP at factor cost. Finally, when foreign incomes are adjusted for local residents, GDP will become GNP. The formidable problems that generally face developing countries in computing an accurate SNA are well-known, e.g., the data availability and problems of definition. Since large segments of productive activities in developing countries are in agriculture and services, it is difficult enough for them to measure all the outputs, not to mention valuing them properly. Furthermore, the GNP of a poor country is more likely to be under-estimated because many economic activities do not go through the market system, and hence they are exclusion from the GNP account.

Socialist countries, following Marx's prejudice against services by considering them "unproductive", have generally used a narrower concept of net material product or *NMP*, which is roughly equivalent to the conventional GNP minus some but not all service activities. In the socialist approach to NI, the key step is to make a distinction between "material" and "non-material" production. Thus, all activities and services directly contributing to the production of goods are material; and all other services including all personal and most public services are non-material and are to be excluded from NMP. This gives rise to some rather absurd situations: e.g., a freight train carrying goods is productive service, but a passenger train is not. China used to follow the NMP approach but it shifted to SNA in the early 1980s, after joining the World Bank and IMF. In any case, it is possible to convert NMP into SNA by simply including non-material services produced. The main question is whether the extension of the market-based SNA to cover an economy which is not fully exposed to market forces will inevitably bring about biases in the accounting, e.g., services are known to be seriously under-priced in socialist economies.

Despite the many conceptual and empirical difficulties, SNA has been, from the outset, used by all marker-oriented economies or for that matter,

NMP by all socialist economies, to measure their respective economic growth, mainly because there is no better alternative tool. Comparing yearly GDP changes within the same domestic price system does not normally pose serious problems. Comparing GNP change over time is technically called "inter-temporal comparison of GNP". But long-term comparison can throw up serious problems due to the structural change of the economy. However, any inter-country comparison of GNP would immediately bring to the fore the inherent flaw of the conventional SNA approach, particularly for countries which are of different economic and social structures or at different stages of development. The conventional way is to convert GNP of all countries into US dollars, normally in accordance with their respective official exchange rate vis-a-vis the US dollar, as practised by virtually all international organizations. Such a measure yields only *nominal* GNP or GDP.

It is so obvious, especially in these days of flexible exchange rate regime marked by highly volatile fluctuation, that a country's exchange rate is unlikely to reflect closely the actual purchasing power of its currency. While many less developed countries (LDCs) with foreign exchange control have their official exchange rates over-valued, many industrial countries also find their exchange rates artificially too high or too low as a result of speculative capital movements. This brings us to the concepts of "nominal" and "effective" exchange rate. In simple terms, the former refers to the prevailing market rate caused by such monetary changes as movements in capital flow or interest rate while the latter is weighed by a country's trade with its major trading partners. Thus, a few years back, the Hong Kong dollar, being pegged to the US dollar, was found to be "undervalued" in terms of effective exchange rate. Even if a country's exchange rate was found to be clearly a free-market equilibrium price, i.e., the rate of currency conversion approaches purchasing power parity (PPP) for the two currencies concerned, such a rate reflects *only* the relative purchasing power of those goods and services that enter international trade — the so-called *tradable goods*. There are many goods (e.g., local fruits) and most of the service activities (from construction to civil servants, school teachers, and barbers etc.), called *non-tradables*, which are never traded internationally or cannot enter world trade because of trade restriction or protection. Since the existing exchange rate does not cover these activities, there will be invariably downward biases against low-income countries (which contain many non-tradables) in any attempt of inter-country comparison of *nominal* GNP.[3]

Not surprisingly, the *nominal* per-capita GDP concept based on the exchange rate conversion of GDP of different countries into the US dollar does not provide a reliable basis for true international comparison. In nominal terms, Japan's per-capita GNP in US dollars in 1989 was 68 times of China's. But 100 yen (which can hardly buy anything in Japan) when converted into Renminbi will buy so much more in China. The main aim of a true inter-country comparison is to compare their actual volumes of goods and services free from the distortion of prices — both exchange rate distortion (which is the price of two currencies) and the price deviation caused by non-tradable activities. This gives rise to the celebrated concept of *real* GNP or GDP.

Irving Kravis was a pioneer in the field of international comparison of real GDP. For three decades, he and his colleagues laboriously collected data from 150 countries and painstakingly computed them into real GDP for the purpose of "unbiased" multilateral comparison.[4] The basic

---

[3] In simple terms, this means, for example: initially, Japan has successfully exported many manufactured goods such as cars and cameras and this led to a higher yen as well as higher wages for Japanese workers. Later, Japanese restaurant workers (non-tradables) also enjoyed higher wages, even though their services were not traded internationally, because of internal factor mobility. Eventually the Japanese nominal GDP expressed in US dollars went up due to the higher external value of the yen. In contrast, many low-income countries are not successful in their manufactured exports, i.e., having too many non-tradables, so the external value of their currencies (or their exchange rates) will remain low, apart from the fact that the wages for their workers in *both* tradable and non-tradable sectors will also remain low. Eventually, their total goods and services converted into US dollars (or their nominal GDP) will be low. For a more detailed but technical discussion of these ideas, see Irving B Kravis *et al.* (1978). Real GDP per capita for more than one hundred countries. *Economic Journal* 88(350), pp. 215–242.

[4] Kravis first started to work on the project, ICP (International Comparison Programme) for the United Nations in the late 1950s, and later continued to work, with the collaboration of Robert Summers and Alan Heston and the backing of many international organizations including the World Bank. The major findings were published in 1978. See Irving B Kravis, Alan W. Heston and Robert Summer (1978). *International Comparisons of Real Product and Purchasing Power.* Baltimore: World Bank. Subsequently, they continued to work on the *Penn World Table* of which "Mark 1" was published in 1980, "Mark 2," in 1982, "Mark 3" in 1984, "Mark 4" in 1988, and "Mark 5" in 1991.

methodology is relatively simple. First, prices of hundreds of identically specified goods and services of the participating countries are collected and their national expenditures broken down, and then a weighted average "international price" is worked out for each commodity and each service activity — the idea is to overcome such enormous price differential as the price of a haircut in New York versus that in New Delhi. Second, a PPP-based foreign exchange rate is computed on the basis of the average international price so as to arrive at an "international dollar", which equalizes the purchasing power of all currencies. In essence, for the *real* GDP approach, all goods and services of all the participating countries are valued by a single set of prices.[5]

What Does it Mean for China?

According to Maddison's calculation, as shown in Table 2, China's *real* (PPP) GDP per capita in 1987 was US$1,748 or *six* times the nominal per-capita GNP level as provided by the World Bank. The latest findings by Kravis' associates, Summers and Heston, are shown in Table 3, which puts China's *real* GDP per capita for 1988 at US$2,308 at 1985 prices or US$2,472 at current prices, which is over *seven* times the nominal level given by the World Bank. This means that in terms of world average

---

[5] PPPs are essentially price indices, which are used not just to compare the prices of the same commodities in different countries but also to express the rate at which one currency may be converted into another. Viewed from a different angle, a PPP is also a rate of exchange which equalizes the prices in both countries. For instance, if the current exchange rate between Singapore dollar and Malaysian Ringgit at S$1.00 = M$1.50 were to reflect the true PPP of these two currencies, a Singaporean with S$100 should get the same basket of goods in a supermarket in Singapore as a Malaysian with M$150 would get in a supermarket in Kuala Lumpur. Should this be the case, the prevailing exchange rate of S$1.00 = M$1.50 would also be the PPP exchange rate, and domestic prices in both countries are considered to be at the "international price" for these two countries. Further, the "international dollar" for them would also be such that one international dollar equals one Singapore dollar, and one and a half Malaysian ringgit.

Of course, the real world is not at the simple equilibrium situation as depicted above. In practice, it is quite complicated to compute the PPPs for so many countries. There are also technical problems of aggregation. For more details, see *Purchasing Power Parities and Real Expenditures*. Paris: OECD, Dept. of Economics and Statistics. 1985.

Table 2. International Comparison of Real GDP and Nominal GNP, 1987.

	A	B	C	D	
	Real GDP Per Capita in "International Dollars" and at 1980 Prices (US $)	Nominal GNP Per Capita in US Dollar, as used by the World Bank (US $)	Ratio of "Real" to "Nominal", B/A	Average Annual Growth of Real GDP (%)	
				1950–1973	1973–1987
China	1,748	290	6.02	5.80	7.50
India	662	300	2.20	3.70	4.10
Indonesia	1,200	450	2.66	4.50	5.40
Philippines	1,519	590	2.57	5.00	3.20
Thailand	2,294	850	2.70	6.40	6.20
Taiwan	4,744	4,825	1.02	9.30	7.80
South Korea	4,143	2,690	1.54	7.50	7.90
Japan	9,756	15,760	−1.62	9.30	3.70
USA	13,550	18,530	−1.37	3.70	2.50

Note: "A" reflects the PPPs of GDP at the 1980 price level.

"B" is the conventional measure by converting national GNP into US dollars, at the prevailing exchange rates.

Sources: For A, Angus Maddison (1989). *The World Economy in the 20th Century*. Paris: OECD, Development Centre, p. 19.

For B, World Bank, World Development Report 1989; for Taiwan, *Statistical Yearbook of Republic of China*, (Taipei, Executive Yuan, 1990).

prices, China's *real* per-capita GNP should command the actual purchasing power six or seven times more than as implied it he conventional nominal measure. Viewed from a different angle, the average level of domestic prices in China in 1987–1988 is about one-sixth or one-seventh of the average world price. Inflation started to build up in China in the middle of 1988, reaching 29% in December, 1988. Although the inflation was brought under control in 1990, the average price level in China has certainly gone up a lot since 1987. This seems to conform to the general impression of many visitors who have travelled widely in China. (Figure 2 compares the real per-capita GDP of China and Some Asian countries.)

Table 3.   International Comparison of Real GDP and Nominal GNP, 1988.

	(A) Real GDP Per Capita at 1985 International Prices (US $)		(B) Real GDP Per Capita at Current International Prices (US $)		(C) Nominal GNP Per Capita, 1988 (US $)		(D) Ratio of "Real" to "Nominal" B/C
China	2,308	100*	2,472	100*	330	100*	7.50
India	786	34	870	35	340	103	2.60
ASEAN							
Indonesia	1,714	74	1,822	74	440	133	4.10
Malaysia	4,727	205	5,070	205	1,940	588	2.60
Philippines	1,947	84	2,168	88	630	191	3.40
Thailand	2,879	125	3,282	133	1,000	303	3.30
NIEs							
South Korea	5,156	223	5,682	230	3,600	1,090	1.60
Taiwan	4,708	247	6,528	264	5,798	1,757	1.10
Hong Kong	13,281	575	14,014	567	9,220	2,794	1.50
Singapore	10,417	451	10,417	421	9,070	2,748	1.10
Japan	12,209	529	13,645	552	21,020	6,369	−1.50
USA	18,339	795	19,851	803	19,840	6,012	1.01

*Indices using China as a base.

Note: "A" and "B" are GDP based on a common set of international prices, which reflect the PPPs. "C" is the conventional approach by converting GNP of countries into US dollars at the prevailing exchange rates.

Source: Robert Summers and Alan Heston (1991). The Penn World Table (Mark 5): An expanded set of international comparison, 1950–1988, *Quarterly Jouranl of Economics*, *op cit.*

Table 3 also supports the general theoretical argument that the poorer the country, the more its nominal GDP is undervalued by the standard of PPP. Thus, the nominal GDP of the ASEAN countries has been undervalued by two to three times the average world price level while the real per-capita GDP of the NIEs is generally quite close to their nominal per-capita GNP, particularly for Singapore and Taiwan, implying that the domestic prices in Singapore and Taiwan in 1988 approached the average world price level. But why has China's nominal GDP deviated so widely

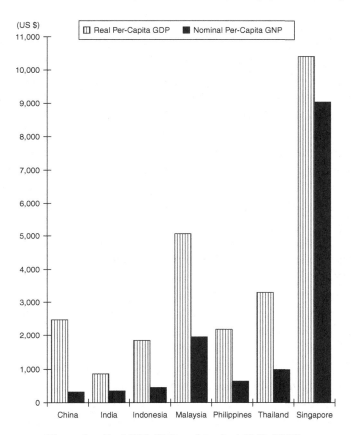

Figure 2. Real PPP-GDP vs. Nominal GNP (1988).

Source: Table 3, Columns B and C.

from its real GDP, or why was China's GDP so much undervalued — more so than in India?

As a part of its socialist legacies, China's price system must have been grossly distorted. Its non-tradable sector, particularly its personal and public services, has certainly been seriously undervalued in the original nominal GDP accounting, and hence a large correction was required in the subsequent real GDP calculation. For instance, China's medical and education services and public transportation, under the collective system, were priced at only a small fraction of the world prices. On the other hand, both personal and public services in China are notoriously poor. But GNP, nominal or real, is not supposed to be concerned with the "quality" of goods and services produced. In a market economy, the quality of goods is taken care of by its price. Here, one might argue that in the case of China, there may be upward bias by pricing the services of numerous Communist bureaucrats by the average world standard!

Such a drastic upward revision of China's real per-capita GDP actually means very little for China. The volume of goods and services produced remains unchanged, and it is only their external valuation that has increased. China, along with many LDCs, is not keen to revise its per-capita GDP upward, perhaps for fear of losing some trade benefits. Deng Xiaoping and other Chinese leaders keep on stressing that China is "poor and blank". A higher per-capita GNP for a LDC may mean graduating it from a poor country to a middle-income country status. Apart from the possible loss of trade benefits like GSP, a country with higher per-capita income may stand to lose in terms of failing to get soft loans from the World Bank and so on. Also, it has to contribute more to international organizations like the UN. In the same way, Singapore used to resist "graduation" by putting up the indigenous GNP argument. For China, changing the price tag of its GDP or GNP does not change anything in substance. Certainly for a man in the street in Beijing, whether China's per-capita GDP in 1988 should be US$330 or US$2,472 does not materially make any difference to him. All an outsider can say is that China is economically much better off than it was made out to be from the conventional GNP figures. While China's low *nominal* per-capita GNP puts it in the "low-income group" in the World Bank classification, China's social indicators such as infant mortality rate, student enrolment ratio, life expectancy, and calorie-intake actually rank China with countries from the "middle-income group". Normally, a country's social development indicators closely follow its economic indicators. In this sense, a higher *real* GDP estimate for China is realistic.

Chapter 2

China's Entrepreneurial Approach to Economic Reform*

Introduction

Economic reform of China, as for other emerging economies, is actually an on-going process. After over three decades of breakneck economic growth, the present China's leadership is still talking about the need for "deepening and broadening" reform in order to accelerate macroeconomic rebalancing for the new growth pattern. Economic reform today for China basically involves fine-tuning, restructuring, and reorganizing, primarily within the existing institutional framework.

This chapter was written in late 1994 and circulated in early 1995. "Economic reform" in this context was really about "system transformation", a radical shift from central planning to the market system that was first introduced by Deng Xiaoping in 1978. This chapter is focusing on the most crucial phases of China's economic reform from the early 1980s to the early 1990s. The first shot of reform was fired in the rural areas, and agricultural reform had proved to be an instant success. But the second phase of reform involving industrial enterprises in urban areas had not been so smooth-going and it had in fact got bogged down by problems caused by the dual-tracked price system, giving to inflation and rent seeking that had eventually sparked out social protests, culminating in the Tiananmen event in 1989.

China was then formally called a "transitional economy", which was a new term applied to all the former socialist (or the so-called Soviet-typed) economies that were undergoing the market reform. In their process of

*The original version of the chapter was presented at the International Conference on "Systematic Transformation From State Command Society to Democracy", Kuala Lumpur, 19–21 October, 1994, organized by the Malaysian Strategic Research Centre and the German Goethe Institute.

making the transition from planning to the market, the former Soviet Union (and later Russia) and the other East European socialist economies had experienced enormous economic and social problems, marked by plunging economic growth and high inflation, which had eventually led to their political collapse of some regimes.

China's reform had also faced problems, but nothing remotely approaching the scale of the problems that were faced by its East European counterpart. During the period of 1978–1992, China's economy was growing rapidly at 9.5%, compared to zero or negative growth in Eastern Europe. China's average inflation during this period was only 6.5%, compared to the double-digit rates in Eastern Europe. Viewed from this angle, China's economic reform was considered an unequivocal success. To explain China's success, many Western scholars had made comparative study of the reform in China and that in Eastern Europe.

This chapter attributes Chinese reform success primarily to its unique reform strategy. In terms of policy and practice, it can be called "economic reform with Chinese characteristics". Furthermore, the main approach was not just endorsed by Deng Xiaoping, but its many characteristics were actually bearing the hallmarks of Deng's practical outlook and his pragmatism. It was entitled "entrepreneurial approach", because such drastic system transformation would inevitably involve a great deal of risk and uncertainty. The collapse of the former Soviet Union is the case in point.

When China under Mao started central planning, it had Soviet experts to come to help with the formulation its First Five-Year Plan (1952–1957). Now as China wanted to "unplan" its economy by introducing market reform, Deng had soon come to realize that this was an uncharted territory and he could find no textbook to teach Chinese reformers how to successfully go about it. So he had to take a gamble and grope his way around by falling back on to the traditional "Chinese way" of doing things, as best manifested in the famous dictum of "crossing the river by feeling the stones first". It therefore had to be gradual and piecemeal process, by "trial and error" and "learning by doing". It was opportunistic, as it would make two steps forwards and take back one step when in trouble. In short, this was a far-cry from the "technocratic" approach underlying the Big Bang strategy that was adopted by Russia and Eastern European countries. Chinese strategy based on gradualism is certainly the opposite of the "shock therapy" that was applied in the Soviet Union.

In any case, as China was then a huge underdeveloped economy with limited administrative resources and low technical capacity, it had no choice but to follow such a highly "unstructured" traditional approach. This also suited Deng very well. To him, what is best is what works, as reflected in his famous remark: "It does not matter if it would be a white cat or a black cat, so long as it could catch mice", To him, "economic reform cannot be absolutely fool-proof, nor must everything be 100% certain before it can be adopted".

China today is still grappling with the issue of reform in many areas. As China has developed, its institutional capacity has also grown. Its many new reform measures today are necessarily getting more sophisticated and more "structured", i.e., increasingly more technocratic. Some reform measures were first debated in the National People's Congress and then properly legislated before implementation. China has started to pay more attention to the issues of legality, and stress the importance of governance. Overall, however, the basic reform process to-date is still gradualist and experimental in nature. One basic rationale for this is that China is so vast and diverse, it will always be difficult to have a policy of "one size fits all". Any viable new policy has to be tried out first.

Entrepreneurial vs Bureaucratic

Compared to the dismal economic performance of the former Soviet Union and other East European countries, China's ability to achieve high economic growth along with its lower overall cost of transition to the market economy is *ipso facto* evidence that the Chinese approach to economic reform has been eminently more successful. Numerous books and articles have been written about the different reform experiences of China and East Europe.[1] Most discussions are focused on the gradual and incremental strategy adopted by China versus the "Big Bang" approach in East Europe.

---

[1]The latest debate on this subject can be found in the June 1994 issue of the *Journal of Comparative Economics,* Experiences in the Transition to a Market Economy, Guest Editors: Jeffrey Sachs and Wing Thye Woo. Sachs is a Harvard economics professor who a few years ago received wide international publicity for his economic advice given first to the government of Poland and later other East European countries. He can be considered a leading Western "guru" on the East European economic reform strategy.

This chapter argues that the Chinese past reform success also owes a great deal to its *entrepreneurial* style, as opposed to the mainly *bureaucratic* reform process which characterizes the East European approach. All public policy decisions involve a lot of risk and uncertainty, particularly so for those designed to restructure an economic system. Economic system transformation is apt to be full of surprises. The Chinese leadership from the outset recognized the uncertain nature of the reform process and adopted a strategy that was flexible, effective and well-suited to China's unique institutional conditions. In making certain hard decisions on reform, Deng Xiaoping was taking a political risk and in this, he was behaving essentially in ways not much different from a true entrepreneur making business decisions.

How does the entrepreneurial argument broaden our understanding of China's overall economic reform efforts? Since the entrepreneurial type of reform is by nature unplanned, unstructured, open-ended, and even *ad hoc*, it would be quite pointless to predict the course of China's future reform progress. True enough, the Chinese approach to reform has not been accompanied by any detailed guidelines or any sophisticated blueprints.

Can China's past strategy be still effective for the future? Chinese economic reform has passed its easy "honeymoon" stage, in which there were few losers, with policy changes mainly creating benefits to most people. The next phase of reform will be "technically, politically and socially more difficult to manage", as the World Bank chief in Beijing has recently put it.[2] In particular, the remaining key reform areas concerning money, banking, finance, taxation, state-owned industry, and social security are of macroeconomic nature, all closely interrelated; and they call for a comprehensive reform approach. In other words, the old strategy may not be effective in tackling the unfinished business of reform; and the post-Deng leadership will have to switch from the entrepreneurial to a bureaucratic type of reform based on more careful planning and concerted efforts.

---

[2]A German correspondent Peter Seidlitz interviewed Pieter P Bottelier, World Bank's country representative in China. "China: on track, but a tricky road ahead", *Business Times* (Singapore, 13 January, 1995).

Dynamic Growth after Reform

Chinese economy has experienced spectacular growth since it started economic reform and the open door policy in 1979. During 1978–1992, it achieved an average annual growth rate of 9.5%. It chalked up 13% real growth in 1992 and another stunning 13.4% in 1993, though its growth went down to 11.8% in 1994. Such outstanding growth performance was all the more remarkable as the former socialist economies in Eastern Europe were mostly in disarray, with their growth in recent years either in the negative or barely above the positive rates (Table 1).

China's external economic performance (which involves foreign partners) is equally impressive. In 1993, China exported US$110 billion worth of goods, as compared to US$25 billion for the Russian Federation — in 1978 China's exports were only 40% of the former Soviet Union's. Following the successful exchange system reform, (starting on 1 January 1994), the Chinese *Renminbi* has appreciated about 3% by the end of 1994, despite the high inflation rate of over 20%. The *Renminbi* is now on a managed float with limited convertibility on the current account. This in turn led to a sharp rise in China's foreign reserves which stood at the comfortable level of US$50 billion at the end of 1994. In short, China's strong external sector performance presents a sharp contrast to the sudden collapse of the Russian *Rouble* in October 1994.

Since the 8th National People's Congress in March 1993, China has officially become a "socialist market economy". What is "socialist market economy" essentially looks like a conventional mixed economy, with most economic activities becoming increasingly market driven. Thus, the prices of 90% of China's consumer goods and over 85% of intermediate goods are no longer fixed by the state, but are set by market forces. This, along with the rapid decline of the state sector, has actually rendered the Chinese economy increasingly more capitalistic in its operation and orientation.

Explaining China's Reform Success

Differences in the economic structures between the Chinese economy on the one hand and the former European socialist economies on the other, form the common starting point for scholars to explain the differences in

Table 1. Comparative Performance of Chinese and East European Economies.

	GNP per capita US$ 1992	Annual GDP Growth (%)				Annual Inflation Rates (%)				Exports			
		1980–1992 (Average)	1992	1993	1994	1980–1992 (Average)	1992	1993	1994	Annual growth (%) 1980–1992	Exports in US$ billion 1978	1992	1993
China	470	7.6	13.0	3.7	11.8	6.5	5	13	22	11.9	9.9	82.5	110.4
Russian Federation	2,510	2.4 (1986–1989)	–19.0	–18	–16	—	—	1,200 (Aug)	203 (Dec)	—	23.3	9.9	24.5
Bulgaria	1,330	1.2	–7.9	–5.0	–2.0	11.7	92	75	55	—	1.6	2.9	2.8
Czech Republic	2,450	0.6*	–5.0	0	2.0	3.5*	—	21	11	—	3.9	13.2	12.0
Hungary	2,970	0.0	–4.6	–2.0	0	11.7	25	24	25	1.6	7.2	10.9	12.6
Poland	1,910	1.1	1.5	4.0	4.0	67.9	43	39	28	3.0	7.4	17.6	20.4
Romania	1,130	–1.1	–10.2	0	–2.0	13.1	—	300	200	–10.4	8.0	5.8	6.5

*For 1980–1991.

Sources: World Bank, *World Development Report*, various years;

Transition (The Newsletter about Reforming Economies by World Bank's Policy Research Development); various issues; IMF, *Direction of Trade Statistics*, various years; and For China, State Statistical Bureau.

their reform progress. Thus, it is often argued that the initial conditions on the eve of their respective reforms were much more favorable for China than for Russia and other Eastern European countries. China was by far less industrialized, and its industrial sector constituted only 37% of its total Net Material Product (NMP) compared to 46% in Russia and 53% in Poland; and China's industrial sector employed only 15% of its total labor force compared to Russia's 32% and Poland's 28%.[3] China accordingly started off with what the eminent economic historian Alexander Gershchenkron called the "advantages of backwardness".

It is also common knowledge that reforming an agrarian-based socialist economy, as in the case of China, is comparatively easy as there were fewer relative prices to adjust, whilst reforming a developed and mature industrial economy is much more difficult because of its inherently complicated property rights and industrial relations problems. Furthermore, the Chinese economy even at its heyday of central planning under Mao was never so intricately planned as those in Eastern Europe. It was therefore easier for China to undo its planned economic system.

In a more concrete sense, the Chinese success was the product of its unique reform strategies based on gradualism, as opposed to the "Big Bang" approach generally followed by the East Europeans. China owed its smooth progress in reform to the right sequencing of reform policies to suit its economic structure and political and social conditions. Thus, China chose to start with agricultural reform first, and its impact was almost immediate: a rapid growth in agricultural production and a sharp rise in rural incomes for farmers. As agricultural productivity increased, more surplus labor was released for non-farm activities. This in turn led to the mushrooming of township and village enterprises (TVEs), which later became the driving force for China's economic growth.

Furthermore, it is also well known that in putting economic liberalization to precede political liberalization, China was better able to interface political changes with economic reform, especially in the initial phase.

---

[3]Wing Thye Woo (1994). The art of reforming centrally planned economies: Comparing China, Poland, and Russia. *Journal of Comparative Economics,* 18(3). For China and Hungary, see David M. Newbery, (1993). Transformation in mature versus emerging economies: Why has Hungary been less successful than China. *China Economic Review,* 4(2).

Basically China has followed closely the East Asian model of "economic development first and democracy later". Successful economic reform is used as a means of preserving the legitimacy of the political leadership, which is, in turn, under strong pressures to achieve better economic performance. In contrast, Russia put *glasnost* before *perestroika*. Consequently, vital reform measures were often delayed and bogged down by too much politics and polemics.

China's Entrepreneurial Approach

However, one significant fundamental difference in respect of their different styles of reform has rarely been discussed by scholars. It may be argued that the Chinese style of reform is basically *entrepreneurial* in nature, as opposed to the largely *bureaucratic* approach adopted by Russia and other East European countries. The Chinese way of reform bears the stamp of the pragmatic Chinese leadership style under Deng Xiaoping, whose thinking is best epitomized in his well-known adage: *It does not matter if the colour of the cat is black or white so long as she can catch mice.*

True enough, there was no textbook to teach Chinese reformers how to go about "unplanning" a socialist economy, and there were no blueprints to show them the right path to making a smooth transition toward the market system. Nor was it possible for China, on account of its size, backwardness, and lack of expertise, to design and implement a comprehensive reform program. Since reforming a socialist economy inevitably involves a great deal of risk and uncertainty, with outcomes often highly unpredictable, the best strategy for Chinese reformers was to take a gamble and grope their way around by following an incremental, trial, and error approach.[4]

This is also a process of "learning by doing" based on the old Chinese saying: *Taking two steps forward and (if in trouble) one step back.* It can

---

[4] Thus Deng Xiaoping said: "We are engaged in an experiment. For us, it (reform) is something new, and we have to grope around to find our way. ... Our method is to sum up experience from time to time and correct mistakes whenever they are discovered, so that small errors will not grow into big ones", Harry Harding, (1987). *China's Second Revolution: Reform After Mao.* Washington, DC: The Brookings Institution, p. 87.

best be illustrated by Deng Xiaoping's remark over the setting up of a stock market during his tour of South China in January 1992:

> Are such things as securities and stock markets good or not good? Do they exist exclusively in capitalism? Can they also be adopted by socialism? We cannot just say it is OK; but we must take firm steps to try it out. If our observation is correct and if the experimentation (of the stock market) proves correct after being carried out for one or two years, then the stock market experiment be generalized and extended; and if there is something wrong, it can be corrected or the market can simply be closed. It may be closed quickly or slowly if necessary; but a "tail can be left" if it is closed. There is nothing to be feared " —
> (Central Document No. 2 1992 of the Chinese Communist Party)

Accordingly, the Chinese overall reform strategy is not just experimental and piecemeal, but also unstructured and flexible, giving a lot of initiative to officials at the implementation level. In short, the Chinese approach is not merely entrepreneurial in nature; it also creates an environment for those with entrepreneurial talent to thrive. China is such a huge physical entity with so much local variation that Chinese laws and regulations pertaining to reform are necessarily simple and general so as to allow local officials sufficient leeway for flexible interpretation to suit their local conditions. Such loose institutional control virtually gives rise to what may be called the "reformer's invisible hand" at the local levels. This also explains why many TVEs and foreign joint ventures have been able to prosper.[5]

Typically, the Chinese reform would start partially from sector to sector, industry to industry, and area to area. Successful reforms in one sector serve as an experiment for others and create pressures for their matching reforms, and hence a self-reinforcing momentum. Most of China's successful reform schemes, including the setting up of Special Economic Zones and the foreign exchange adjustment centers (the "swap centers"), are the products of such an experimental approach. In fact, the very

---

[5]For a detailed account of how some TVEs have prospered and thrived by taking advantage of the loose institutional conditions in the rural areas, see John Wong, Rong Ma and Mu Yang (eds.) (1995). *China's Rural Entrepreneurs: Ten Case Studies*. Singapore: Times Academic Press.

conception of these schemes is itself a manifestation of the entrepreneurial flair and the risk-taking spirit of the Chinese reformers. To quote again from Deng's secret speech during his tour of South China:

> We must be bold in our reform and open-door policy. We should experi-
> ment bravely. We should not proceed too slowly like those old Chinese
> women with bound feet. Once we have seen clearly our objective, we must
> press forward boldly. The important lesson gained from our experience in
> opening up Shenzhen as a Special Economic Zone shows that it would not
> have succeeded if we did not have an adventurous spirit to blaze a new trail.
> Policies for economic reform cannot be absolutely fool-proof, nor must
> everything be 100 percent certain before it can be adopted — (Central
> Document No. 2 1992 of the Chinese Communist Party).

Not surprisingly, China's progressive transition toward a market system has proved far more effective than the "Big Bang" strategy undertaken by Russia and East Europe. Many reform programs in the latter were stifled by the reformers' rigid "visible hand" mired in the labyrinth of its domes-tic politics. Their bureaucratic approach has simply failed to foster the adventurous spirit of both their officials and people alike. In contrast, the Chinese reform schemes have been successful because they were able to ignite the latent entrepreneurial initiative of the people involved in the reform process. In short, China has made smoother transition to a market economy primarily because it has been more successful in promoting entrepreneurship, the very spirit of capitalism

The Downside of the Chinese Approach

There are obvious trade-offs in the Chinese approach. For one thing, the Chinese way of economic reform is apt to produce numerous rent-seeking activities and open corruption.[6] It is not known if the Chinese approach is

---

[6]For a more detailed discussion of this subject, see John Wong (1994). Power and market in Mainland China: The danger of increasing government involvement in business. *Issues & Studies*, 30(1). Also, Yan Huai (1994). *Corruption in China*, IEAPE Background Brief Nos. 73 and 74.

more prone to corruption, which is also rife in the former European socialist countries. What is certain is that the Chinese approach based on its characteristically weak institutional and legal framework is certainly conducive to a whole range of malpractice at all levels of government.

Another systemic drawback of the Chinese partial approach to reform is that it has given rise to a "half-reformed economy" most susceptible to macroeconomic fluctuations. Thus, whenever the Chinese economy was steaming in high growth, it also got overheated easily. On account of China's chaotic banking structure and weak public finance system, the government could not employ the usual indirect macroeconomic fine-tuning techniques to smooth out the periodic economic fluctuations. Because of chronic government deficits as well as the lack of a national taxation system, fiscal policy could not be used for macroeconomic stabilization.

Nor could monetary policy be any more effective, as China's central bank had little control over money supply, particularly in regard to credit expansion at the local levels. Furthermore, the banks were not free to set interest rates. In the end, the government had to rely on direct administrative intervention by slamming on a credit crunch, and the economy was brought to a screeching halt. Hence the frequent boom-bust cycle, which the Chinese economy has experienced since the start of economic reform.

The Chinese strategy so far has worked well in reforming the agricultural sector. But many critical macroeconomic reform measures like taxation, banking, finance, and foreign exchange do not effectively lend themselves to the gradualist approach by experimentation. All these reform measures are interrelated, and they have to be dealt with in one blow. This paved the way for the Third Party Plenum in November 1993 to adopt the 50-article "Decision" for a comprehensive reform of China's economic structure, which is, roughly speaking, the Chinese equivalent to a "Big Bang" approach to economic reform.

How much macroeconomic reform has been accomplished, one year after the Decision has been adopted? The reform of taxation and foreign exchange has been quite successful while the banking reform has been slow. But it is in the area of state-owned enterprises that the reform has made the least progress, because it critically hinges on the progress of social security reform. Without the provision of social safety nets, the government was unwilling to take the hard decision of retrenching redundant labor for fear of social unrest. And a viable social security system cannot be built up overnight.[7] Hence the Chinese failure in developing the necessary economic instruments for effective macroeconomic management, as clearly evidenced by the persistently high inflation.

The Challenge of the Unfinished Reform

It will clearly take China many more years to complete its transition to a full market economy. It is in the nature of the incremental style of reform that it starts with the easy areas where there were mainly winners and fewer losers. What is left in the unfinished reform agenda still constitutes a major challenge to the Chinese government, which eventually has to cope with the uneven distribution of cost and benefits arising from its reform activities. China's past entrepreneurial approach can no longer be effective in addressing its future reform efforts which are politically and socially more complicated.

However, it is doubtful if the present Chinese leadership, which is bracing itself for the difficult post-Deng transition, has the required political will to mount a carefully designed "bureaucratic type" of comprehensive reform program. But the least they can do is to maintain the present momentum of high economic growth, which offers them the best chance of "muddling through" with less disruptive adjustments. The next phase of the Chinese reform process is still full of uncertainty.

---

[7]For a more detailed assessment of the reform progress, see John Wong (1994). *What Has China Accomplished in Economic Reform in 1994?*, IEAPE Background Brief, No. 80.

Part II

The Politics and Economics of Deng's *Nanxun*

Chapter 3

The 7th Party Plenum 1990
and the Continuing Post-Tiananmen
Political Stalemate Over Reform

Introduction

The long-delayed meeting of the 7th Plenum of the 13th Central Committee (CC) of the Chinese Communist Party (CCP), which closed on 30 December 1990, was the most important Party meeting of the CCP in the immediate aftermath of the June 1989 Tiananmen crisis. According to the CCP's regulations, the Party must hold at least one plenum a year. The fact that this meeting was called in the last days of the year clearly reflected the continuing deep division of the top leadership after the Tiananmen. There had been four high-level meetings since June 1989, but the top leadership had apparently failed to reach a consensus over the key policy issues related to the Tiananmen and the direction of future political and economic development.

The first Party Plenum of the 13th CC of the CCP was convened in November 1987 when Deng Xiaoping was still actively involved in policy making and when Zhao Ziyang just took over from Hu Yaobang to be the General Secretary of the CCP. The reformist group under Zhao was riding high. In sharp contrast, the 4th Plenum, which was held on 23 June 1989 after the Tiananmen crackdown, marked the lowest ebb of the reformist group, with Zhao having been removed from all Party positions. Subsequently, two plenum meetings were held in quick succession, which were trying to cope with the exigent situation of the Tiananmen, namely, restoring political stability, Party unit, and the post-crisis economic retrenchment.

Political stability was soon regained after Zhao was sacked; but the issue of Party unity, as can be expected, remained a serious problem in the aftermath of the Tiananmen. On the economic front, by the middle of 1990, China's economy had started to recover from the effect of the Tiananmen, with basic economic policy orientation shifting from short-term "rectification and retrenchment" to the more positive aspects of resuming economic growth and returning to economic reform.

As the economy gradually returned back to normal, Beijing started to draw up the Eighth Five-Year Plan, due to start in 1991. Not just this regular Five-Year Plan, an additional longer plan called the 10-Year Program (1991–2000) was also put up for adoption at the 7th Plenum. In fact, the official communique of the 7th Plenum was basically about the "Ten-Year Programme and Eighth Five-Year Plan for National Economic and Social Development", which was also the original title of this chapter that was issued on 3 January 1991.

What was obvious at that point of time was that China's top leadership was still in a stalemate over the speed as well as the future path of reform. Initially, the conservatives dominated the policy debate on economic reform in the immediate aftermath of the Tiananmen, as most of them, led by the influential but conservative Party elder Chen Yun, were in favor of a cautious approach or even putting reform on hold for a while.

Toward the end of 1990, however, the more liberal views of the reformist group seemed to be rapidly gaining ground, along with increasing signs of economic recovery. The decisive policy move started from 7 October 1990 when Deng Xiaoping issued a directive for the coming Eighth Five-Year Plan to carry out economic reform and open-door policy "faster, better, and more effectively". This made it possible for the reformist group to put up a more reform-oriented platform in the 7th Plenum to counter-balance the cautious policies of the conservatives. It also serves to explain why the 7th Plenum had ended with a kind of "even-keel" communique with a policy line that was not dominated by policy prescriptions of either the reformists or the conservatives. This was the political climate of the time.

Looking back, the communique of this 7th Party Plenum is the single most important document in the aftermath of the Tiananmen. It was far from the case that the top leadership had at that time reached a consensus to resume economic reform and to proceed gradually and steadily within the existing institutional framework. It was only clear later that Deng

Xiaoping was not satisfied with the main policy mandate of the 7th Plenum. Obviously, Deng wanted the reform to proceed at a much faster speed and take a new direction. To him, resolving the fundamental problems of China's half-reformed economy in the aftermath of the Tiananmen was not just to complete the unfinished business of reform by moving faster, but also pushing the reform forward within an entirely new institutional framework.

Deng was unhappy with the kind of reform model that was advocated by Chen Yun, who wanted to carry out reform in a gradual and balanced manner, combining market and planning while keeping the reformed economy in balance, i.e., sticking to his theory of "proportionate development". Chen was at heart basically a central planner, whose version of economic reform is not about the free play of the market forces, but allowing the market to operate within the central-planning framework. This was hence dubbed "bird cage economics", i.e., the bird as the market is only "free" inside the cage.

In contrast, Deng after the Tiananmen was increasingly convinced that the only way out for China's economy at that time was to complete the march to the market economy. Deng wanted a full marketization based on socialist objectives, i.e., the socialist market economy. Apparently, such a radical reform strategy did not go down well with most top leaders in Beijing. As Beijing (which was the center of the Tiananmen unrest) was so besieged by conservatives, Deng went out to Shanghai and Guangdong to appeal to the more liberal reform supporters there.

That was the origin of Deng's celebrated Nanxun in early 1991. That started a new reform breakthrough, opening up a new chapter of reform and development for China's economy and sparking off over two decades of dynamic growth. Looking back, the historical significance of the 7th Plenum was the way it catalyzed China's reform breakthrough toward the establishment of the "socialist market economy".

The 7th Plenum

The long-delayed 7th Plenum of the 13th Central Committee of the Chinese Communist Party (CCP) closed on 30 December 1990 in Beijing and adopted the proposals for the drawing-up of the 10-Year Program

(1991–2000) and the Eighth Five-Year Plan (1991–1995) for China's economic and social development. The proposals were supposed to set forth the basic principles and policies for China's long-term economic and social developments for the 1990s.

According to the Party's regulations, the CCP needs to hold one plenum meeting a year. But there have been four meetings since the Tiananmen incident, reflecting both the exigent situation after the incident and the failure to reach a consensus over the key policy issues.

The 1st Plenum of the present 13th Party Congress was convened in November 1987 when Deng Xiaoping was still very active in policy making and when Zhao Ziyang and his reformist group were riding high in power.

In contrast, the 4th Plenum, which was held on 23 June 1989, marked the lowest ebb of the reformist group, with Zhao being removed from all Party positions. The subsequent two plenum meetings, held in quick succession, were mainly concerned with the dominant issues of the time, namely, political stability, Party unity, and economic retrenchment.

By mid-1990, as the Chinese economy started its recovery, the focus of economic policy shifted from rectification and retrenchment to the more positive side of how to carry on with the unfinished business of economic reform. In the meanwhile, Beijing started to draft the Eighth Five-Year Plan, due to begin in 1991. Hence, economic reform was back on the national agenda as a top policy issue in the second half of 1990 and it eventually formed an important part of the main theme of the 7th Plenum.

Initially, the conservatives dominated the policy debate on economic reform and were in favor of a cautious approach. But the more liberal views of the reformist group rapidly gained ground toward the end of 1990, along with the resurgence of the economy. The decisive policy swing seemed to start from 7 October 1990 when Deng Xiaoping gave a directive for the coming Eighth Five-Year Plan to carry out economic reform and open door policy "faster, better, and more effectively". This made it possible for the reformist group to put up a reform-oriented platform in the 7th Plenum to counter-balance the policies of the conservatives. It also served to explain why the 7th Plenum had ended with an "even-keel" communique with no clear-cut policy prescription for either group.

The Outline of the Communique

The 7th Plenum concluded its meeting with an official communique, which contained broad guidelines to be hammered out later as detailed economic development blueprint for Premier Li Peng present at the National People's Congress (China's Parliament) in March 1991.

The communique had seven sections:

- The main objective to strive for and the basic policy guidelines.
- The strategic industries for economic development and their overall national implications.
- The tasks and policies for promoting developments in science and technology, education, and culture.
- The improvement in people's livelihood and the strengthening of the social security system.
- The direction, tasks, and measures for deepening the economic system reforms.
- To further expand the open-door policy.
- To unite the Party and the nation in the struggle to realize the objectives of the 10-Year Program and the Eighth Five-Year Plan.

Specifically for the Eighth Five-Year Plan, a number of key guidelines were laid down for it "to firmly adhere to":

- the road of building socialism with Chinese characteristics;
- the policy of economic reform and open-door;
- the policy measures that would sustain continuing economic growth in a stable and co-ordinated manner;
- the principle of national development based on self-reliance, hard work, and diligence;
- the principle of promoting both material culture and socialist morals.

The Significance of the Communique

The fact that the 7th Plenum was finally convened after so many months of delay carried considerable political and economic significance at that juncture. It implied that the central leadership in Beijing had been able to strike out a compromise however discordant it was, over the many key policy issues. More importantly, it marked and end to the Tiananmen incident aftermath, characterized by policy confusion and uncertainty, by giving out a clearer signal that the leadership had regained sufficient stability and confidence for it to look ahead more positively to the challenge of the 1990s.

The 7th Plenum also came at a good timing. In the wake of the Tiananmen Square incident on 4 June 1989, China was plunged into political and economic disarray. But over a year later, China had staged a dramatic turnaround in its overall political and economic situation. To break out from diplomatic isolation imposed by the West (which was outraged by Beijing's violent crackdown on the pro-democracy movement), China undertook new diplomatic initiative toward the Asia-Pacific countries, culminating in the normalization of diplomatic relations with Indonesia and Singapore. China's responsible behavior in the 1990 Gulf crisis and her positive stand toward the solution of the Cambodian conflict had also facilitated Beijing's efforts to mend diplomatic fences with the Western countries. To cap all these, the successful holding of the 11th Asian Games had further enabled Beijing to regain much of its lost international standing.

On the economic front, Beijing was equally successful in putting its economic house in order. As a result of implementing the stringent austerity program, rampant inflation was put under control (though initially at the cost of higher unemployment), from the high of 29% in December 1988 to about 1% in the first quarter of 1990. This enabled the government to ease some of its belt-tightening measures in order to reflate the economy. Consequently, real economic growth for the first three quarters of 1990 was 2.7%, with a good promise of ending 1990 with around 5% growth — China's economic growth in 1989 nosedived to 3.9%, from 11.2% in 1988.

Meanwhile, other leading economic indicators had also reversed their declining trends of the late 1989. Thus, both domestic and foreign investments in the same period had picked up; tourism had recovered; and exports had grown (by 14%). Above all, the agricultural sector continued to enjoy another good year of bumper harvest with the estimated total output of food-grain reaching 420 million tons for 1990.

Such rapid rebound of the economy, together with the favorable shift of the international political climate, must have contributed to the renewed confidence of the Chinese leadership, leading to a more relaxed political environment conducive to the formation of more liberal economic policies. The voice of the reformist group in the leadership, whose credibility had suffered gravely in the immediate aftermath of the Tiananmen event, had accordingly been strengthened as a result.

In the circumstances, the published communique of the 7th Plenum had all the indications of a product of political compromise, reflecting the delicate balance of the two contending groups, the conservatives and the delicate balance of the two contending groups, the conservatives and the reformists, in the power configuration. It was essentially a mixture of political and ideological rhetoric, which appealed to the conservatives on the one hand, and the reaffirmation of continuing economic reform and the open-door policy, which was clearly aimed at the reformists on the other. From the operational point of view, it was no concrete blueprint for charting the economic and social development of China through the 1990s. Neither were there surprises, as most proposals were already known to the outside and had in fact been widely discussed by China specialists in Hong Kong and Taiwan. Viewed from a different angle, it was a highly "elastic" document, *deliberately vague*. So it was open to interpretation by both the conservatives and the reformists to their respective satisfaction.

From the standpoint of the conservatives (labeled "hard-liners" by the Western media and were supposed to include Chen Yun, Wang Zhen, and Li Peng), they gained considerable political ground by emphasizing the socialist mode of economic development with "firm adherence" to the Four Cardinal Principles (i.e., keeping to the socialist road, and upholding the people's democratic dictatorship, the leadership by the Communist Party, and Marxism-Leninism and Mao Zedong's thought). They have also succeeded in giving prominence to the need for promoting socialist morals and spirit in the pursuit of material progress. Above all, they have brought in a clause to warn against the "tendency to become impatient for success", which was an explicit indictment of what was considered to be reckless reform policies carried out in the last days of the Zhao Ziyang regime. Such a call for caution was unmistakably the very idea of the arch-conservative Chen Yun.

Indeed, the 7th Plenum had the basic ideological framework to implement in full Chen Yun's so-called "bird-cage" theory of socialist economic development, with the market-based segments developing within the overall confines of the planned economy. In stressing the continuing importance of the state sector in the economy and the need to maintain the key "structural ratios" for the purpose of achieving "balanced" economic growth, the report of the 7th Plenum had actually contained elements of Chen's development strategy. As an ardent Marxist, Chen, while recognizing the dynamic nature of the capitalist system, had strong prejudice against the market economy for its being liable to unbalanced and chaotic development (Marx's idea of the "anarchy of the market").

The reformers, on the other hand, can also take comfort in the fact that the 7th Plenum did not pass policy or measure which was conspicuously anti-reform in nature. Although it did not endorse any large-scale macroeconomic reform, it gave a clear green light to continue, in a co-ordinated manner, with the "structural reform in the fields of enterprises, circulation (of goods), prices, finance, taxation, banking, planning, investment, and labor and wages". After all, there was *no retreat* form economic reform, which would certainly have been the case if the Eighth Five-Year Plan was to be put forward a year ago. For all practical purposes, the reformers could take it as the log-awaited official blessing for them to "continue business as usual". In the medium term, it was also possible, within the political and ideological confines of the decisions of the 7th Plenum, for economic reform to be extended further.

All in all, the official communique of the 7th Plenum, lacking clear-cut operational details as to the speed and scope of economic reform, was obviously not the document to guide the long-term economic and social development to China through the 1990s. On the contrary, it was simply a mirror image of the policy stalemate over the exact direction of the Chinese economy between the contending groups in the central leadership. In the short run, it nonetheless provided sufficient political and ideological flexibility for economic reform to fumble along.

The Economic Implications

Economic reform for any socialist country was fraught with serious problems and obstacles. It was essentially a process of great political and social transformation. There was actually no blueprint or theory for reformers to go by. Regardless of how the reform process was planned, there would still be an enormous amount of externalities in the implementation. The 7th Plenum hailed the "tremendous success" of the first round of reform and opening up to the outside world. How would the second round fare under the auspices of the 7th Plenum?

As already pointed out in the above analysis, the 7th Plenum did not actually provide any clear direction to the future reform process beyond calling for the "deepening of reform". Strictly speaking, the communique of the 7th Plenum was not a document for "further reform" but was rather one for "reform consolidation", which nevertheless fitted quite well with the state of the Chinese economy at that time.

However, even though the 7th Plenum had not embraced any innovative measures for a large-scale macroeconomic reform, a great deal of significant changes at the micro level could still be brought about, e.g., measures taken to strengthen enterprise management, to stimulate greater market competition, to increase labor mobility to improve export competitiveness, and the like. The reform of the last decade had indeed developed on a wide front. The time had come for its consolidation. There were still many areas where modification and changes could be usefully undertaken within the broad political and ideological confines sanctioned by the 7th Plenum. And these activities could still add up to real reform progress, apart from paving way for more major reforms later. Thus, the main problem of the 7th Plenum at that juncture did not lie in its lack of concrete measures for more thorough-going reforms.

Rather, the 7th Plenum failed to address a number critical issues which had continued to plague the Chinese economy. Both the conservatives and reformists were aware of those issues. But they only argued their importance instead of coming up with real solutions. The case in point is how the planner can get the key "structural ratios" right in the absence of a completely free market. Central to Chen Yun's theory was the need to stick to the "correct" ratios in order to keep the economy in balance in its process of growth (the so-called "proportionate development"); but there were no practical means of working out those optimal ratios correctly — e.g., What is the right mix of the state sector and the market sector? How to integrate them in order to achieve "proportionate development"? Failing to do that, the Chinese economy would continue to experience macroeconomic instability, swinging from one extreme to another, once strong growth starts building up momentum.

Another critical issue which was crying out for more effective solution concerns the economic relations between the central and local authorities. The 7th Plenum had only stressed the need to "handle properly" such relationship, but without providing concrete measures. Historically, Chinese imperial rulers had to expend a lot of energy in trying to strike out a delicate balance in the set of power relations acceptable to both the center and provinces. But economic reform had now complicated such a historical problem. In fact, the reform process of the last decade had been a constant tug-of-war between the central and local authorities over the control of the investible surplus. The decentralization, in particular, had not been altogether a happy experience for the central government. While localities tended, to over-invest and over-spend to suit local interests, the central authorities had to subsidize losses and make up for deficits out of its declining revenue share. Worse still, local authorities even openly introduced measures to block inter-provincial resource flow, much like the "regional protectionism" practiced by the feudal lords in medieval Europe. Hence, the question of a viable central–local in relationship was a real issue, which was also highly political in nature. It was argued that if the present leadership could not confront this problem, how would it be possible for the younger leaders in future without the same political clout of the present old guards to deal with such economically powerful provinces as Sichuan, Guangdong, and Fujian?

Finally, it should be noted that the Chinese leadership, ever since its first brush with its Soviet-designed First Five-Year Plan, 1953–1957, was not known to have followed any of the subsequent plans rigidly. Furthermore, the whole reform program had been essentially a "learning by doing" exercise, with the Chinese leadership resorting to the old Chinese pragmatism of "taking three steps forward and retreating two steps (when in trouble)" as the working strategy. It is well-nigh impossible for the Chinese government to take another "three steps forward" at any time in future, political conditions permitting, regardless of the structure and orientation of the 10-Year Program and the Eighth Five-Year Plan adopted at the 7th Plenum.

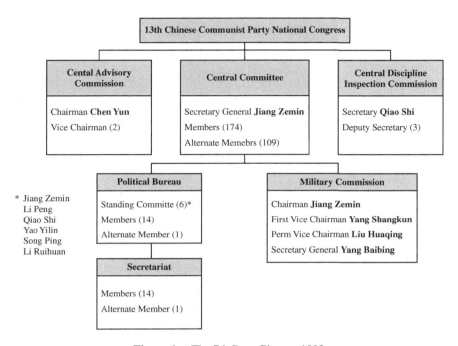

Figure 1.   The 7th Party Plenum 1990

Chapter 4

What is the Surname, She or Zi: The Post-Tiananmen Ideological Discord

Introduction

This chapter was originally drafted in Chinese by Zou Ziying, a research fellow at the IEAPE. EU Chooi-Yip translated it into English. In the process of editing this chapter, I held many rounds of discussion with both Zou and Eu. Initially, we thought the topic of this chapter merely reflected the special interest of the Shanghai group who were arguing for the development of Pudong. "She" stands for socialism while "Zi", for capitalism. The Shanghai people and officials, pragmatic and entrepreneurial, would naturally take the side of Mr Capitalism in the debate so as to create a favorable public opinion for their gigantic Pudong project to take off.

The outside world at that time knew very well that China's top leadership was still divided between the conservative reformers and the liberal reformers, with Deng Xiaoping clearly on the side of the latter. Both sides wanted reform, but disagreed on the speed of reform and even on the nature of the reform, i.e., how far should the market reform be allowed to go relative to the underlying socialist institutional framework.

At first, we thought that the successful convening of the 7th Party Plenum on 30 December 1990 had broken the stalemate, signaling that both sides seemed to have come to a compromise so that the reform would soon be resumed. After all, the Chinese style of reform was inherently very flexible and pragmatic, as it was supposed to be based on trial and error, like "crossing the river by feeling the stones". The exact manner in which how the reform should be conducted was a matter of technicality that would not be politically so crucial.

However, what appeared to be originally a technical difference over the reform had soon escalated into a heated ideological debate between two groups of advocacy if the reform should be fundamentally socialist (she) or capitalist (zi) in nature. We all knew that once things had become ideological in the Communist regime, they would politically get very complicated. The past political struggles of the Chinese Communist Party were much like a political "shadow boxing", full of all sorts of insinuations and innuendoes. What appeared to be a perfectly innocuous article in the *People's Daily* could subsequently turn out to be the first salvo of a big political camgaign. We were at that time actually thinking how Mao's Culture Revolution was sparked off by Yao Wenyuan's newspaper article "Hai Rui Ba Guan" (Hai Rui Dismissed from Office) in Shanghai in November 1965.

We were therefore wondering if Huang Huping's newspaper articles in Shangai would similarly lead to something politically very big? Was Mr She or Mr Zi the allegory for someone very high up in the leadership? Was this debate a prelude to some nasty political struggle like the Cultural Revolution?

All we knew was that the Shanghai group was liberal and pro-reform. Zhu Rongji was at that time the Party Secretary of Shanghai. Zhu was obviously in favor of reform as he had the long-term ambition of developing Pudong to be a "Future Hong Kong". Furthermore, as Deng Xiaoping and Yang Shangkun used to spend the Chinese New Year in Shanghai, the Shanghai leadership must also have been very close to Deng.

At the same time, we also knew that Beijing was then the stronghold of the conservatives as Huang's articles from Shanghai actually suppressed in Beijing. His articles were not reprinted or republished in the media in Beijing. Furthermore, Beijing side published a strong critique by Qiu Si of Huang's article in the Guangming Ribao. Since Huang's articles quoted a lot of pro-reform messages from Deng Xiaoping, the "counter-attack" from Beijing was quite audacious, implying that the conservatives and the leftist ideologues might have already got an upper hand in the debate. Who was the "Leftist King" in Beijing? People thought it was Chen Yun.

Little did we know that the top leadership at that time was really so seriously split over the issue of reform. Deng had already stepped down from all formal positions in the Party. We did not know that the conservative and the leftist factions had succeeded in using the excuse of preventing the "peaceful evolution" of China — i.e., to prevent China from going down like the former Soviet Union, to block Deng's policy of resuming the reform. Even Deng's appainted successor Jiang Zemin was not enthusiastic about Deng's route to reform. Deng must be very frustrated. A few months later, he started the Nanxun.

Twenty years later on the 20th anniversary of the Nanxun, the full story of Huang's article and its historical significance came into full light. Huang wrote his pro-reform articles actually in the full knowledge of Deng Xiaoping's aides or Deng himself. Huang provided the first voice for Deng's Nanxun talks. In this sense, the first shot of Deng's Nanxun was actually fired in Shanghai, not in Shenzhen.

It had also turned out that "Huang Huping" was the pen-name of Zhou Ruijin, who was then the editor-in-chief of Shanghai's *Jiefang Ribao* and deputy-editor-in-chief of Beijing's *Renmin Ribao*. The series of pro-reform articles were written by Zhou and his colleagues. "Huang Huping" sounds close to the Shanghai's Huangpu River while "Huping" also indirectly suggests "supporting Deng Xiaoping". Even without these interesting anecdotes, this chapter is truly of high historical significance in the context of China's economic reform.

Origin of the Debate

Jiefang Ribao, the Party organ in Shanghai, published three articles by Huang Fuping, entitled "There must be New Thinking for Reform and Opening Up", "There must be a Stronger Consciousness of Opening Up Further", and "Reform and Opening Up require a lot of Cadres with Talent and Moral Integrity" on 2 February, 22 March, and 12 April 1991 successively. All these articles emphasized the need for further "emancipating the mind and discarding all conservative, ossified and isolationist ideas" and "avoiding intellectual ossification" in order to achieve "deepening of reform and further opening-up". In the second article, special mention was made of "developing Pudong, establishing a bonded area, implementing a special free port policy of free entry and exit and exemption from export duties". It was pointed out further in the article that "if we hobble ourselves by raising the question of whether it bears the surname of "She" (Socialism) or that of "Zi" (Capitalism) in regard to the attempts to create a socialist Hong Kong out of Pudong, that would only mean losing a golden opportunity".

Such viewpoints and language, when compared with the public opinion created at the beginning of the reforms 10 years ago, sound much more cautious and do not contain anything surprisingly new. But their appearance in the news media, at a time when there is a tight control on public opinion, cannot fail to attract widespread attention. The clampdown on ideological matters has been more severe and effective than that on economic matters since 4 June 1989. Never since the later part of the Cultural Revolution has any campaign against bourgeois liberalization shown such severity. The major newspapers and journals have repeatedly and tirelessly conducted propaganda against bourgeois liberalization and an educational campaign to preach socialism, class struggle, and prevention of peaceful evolution. To talk about "emancipating the mind" had not been heard for a long time. As soon as the articles containing such views appeared, people sat up and took note. In view of the fact that when the first article was published, Deng Xiaoping and Yang Shangkun were spending their Spring Festival (Chinese New Year) in Shanghai, and extracts from Deng's internal talks were quoted in the article,[1] observers in Hong Kong jumped to the conclusion that it was a declaration of war by Deng who wanted to start a "northern expedition" (the war launched by the KMT (then based in South China) against the war-lords in North China in 1925–1927) against the conservatives in Beijing. After this, there was a talk about Huang Fuping being "silenced". It was predicted that the "Leftist King" in Beijing would counter-attack.

As a matter of fact, no rebuttals appeared between April and July. This probably was due to the fact that 1 July was the 70th anniversary of the founding of the Chinese Communist Party, and the floods had diverted public attention during this period. On 7 August 1991, the *Guangming Ribao* reprinted an article by Qiu Si entitled "Let's Ask Whether the Surname is "She" or "Zi" which appeared in the journal, *The Theoretical*

---

[1] The exact words are: "Planning and market are two methods and forms of deploying resources and are not marks of either socialism or capitalism. There is planning in capitalism and there are markets in socialism".

Front of the Higher Educational Institutions (No. 3, 1991).[2] This is precisely the expected rebuttal to Huang Fuping's article. Right from the beginning, the article bluntly asserts that "whether or not to ask if the surname of the reform and opening up is "She" or "Zi" is an important question of right and wrong that has been confused by the ideological trend of bourgeois liberalization. Even now there are people who favor ignoring the question on the grounds that it reflects a "conservative" and "isolationist" attitude. In fact, whether or not to ask for the surname of reform and opening up to see if it is "She" or "Zi" is a realistic question which is worth discussing". Setting this sentence by the side of Huang Fuping's relevant passage, it becomes clear at once who the target of Qin Si's article is.

Without going into the background and deeper implications of the articles of Huang Fuping "Review of the Huangpu River") and Qin Si ("Think diligently"), one can say with some certainty at this point that serious differences exist within the Communist Party leadership regarding the question of reform and opening up of Pudong.

Deng Contradicting Himself

Qin Si severely criticizes Huang Fuping's article. But there is something in common between them: they both quote liberally from Deng's writings to buttress their own positions. The only difference is that Huang Fuping quotes Deng's views on emancipating one's mind and speeding up reform and opening up, while Qin Si cites Deng on the importance of upholding the Four Cardinal Principles and opposing bourgeois[3] liberalization.

This fact throws into sharp relief the self-contradictory nature of Deng's views. Deng will be hard put to it to reconcile his views on reform and opening up with those on the Four Cardinal Principles.

---

[2] A journal controlled jointly by the Propaganda Department of the Party's Central Committee, and the State Commission of Education.

[3] The Four Cardinal Principles: (i) the socialist road, (ii) the people's democratic dictatorship, (iii) the leadership of the Communist Party, (iv) and Marxism–Leninism.

The decision of the Shanghai authorities to speed up the development of Pudong after the 4 June incident was taken at the wrong time and under unfavorable circumstances. The momentum of China's reform and opening up had slackened; Shanghai is far away from Hong Kong, Macao, and Taiwan; funds from overseas have dwindled; what is even worse, it will be very difficult for Pudong to attract the thousands or hundreds of thousands of pioneers in reform like Shenzhen did in its early days. It was these pioneers who brought to Shenzhen the initial capital, technical skills, and entrepreneurship which have proved of inestimable value.

What Huang Fuping wanted to do at the most was to create public opinion favorable to the development of Pudong. Without a call for emancipating the mind and without creating a climate of opinion in favor of reform and opening up, how does one persuade anyone to bear some responsibility for the reform and opening up, to open up stock markets, or to form joint enterprises with foreigners? Huang Fuping's article could not possibly be a challenge to leading Party officials in charge of ideology. The purpose was clearly limited: to create a conducive atmosphere for the development of Pudong.

And yet, even such efforts were not tolerated by the defenders of the faith in charge of ideology. They accused Huang Fuping of betraying the Four Cardinal Principles and going against the spirit of the 7th plenary session of the 13th CC of CPC. To these people, the most vital concern for China today is not economic reconstruction, much less intellectual emancipation, but to oppose bourgeois liberalization and to conduct class struggle to prevent peaceful evolution. They are politically and theoretically very fragile and sensitive. So they look upon the slightest sign of dissidence as a serious challenge.

Resurrecting Mao's Doctrines on the Quiet

It is not difficult to discover after reading Qin Si's article that they do not really believe they can successfully rebut Huang Fuping's arguments with Deng's theories. They are just exploiting Deng's immense prestige. The more indefensible Deng's theories are, the easier it will be for them to have final recourse to the most thorough-going Marxist theoretical weapon — the Maoist doctrine of conducting class struggle for the prevention of peaceful evolution, in other words, the doctrine of continuing the revolution under the proletarian dictatorship. They understand fully that they cannot refute Deng's theory about reform and opening up by using Deng's own theories. They can succeed only by seeking help from the theories of Mao and resorting to Marxist logic.

Of course, Qin Si and his ilk know that Mao's doctrine of continuing the revolution under the proletarian dictatorship is totally discredited and has become highly unpopular in China. That is why they have been resurrecting it bit by bit in an experimental manner. After 4 June 1989, Mao's theory on class struggle and prevention of peaceful evolution has been quietly reaffirmed. Qin Si referred to an off-quoted dictum of Mao's: "There exists the contradiction between the socialist system and the capitalist system in the world. Inside the country, there is a struggle between the two roads of socialism and capitalism". This is obviously another attempt to revive one of the basic Maoist doctrines. If they continue to do this, it is not too farfetched to predict that something more saddening than 4 June could happen. Such a possibility really exists!

Signs are Ominous

The fact that Huang Fuping's article was criticized and that he was subsequently silenced is itself not an important political event. The backroom bosses who orchestrated the incidents on both sides have remained in the background. No drastic change is likely to appear in the political scene and nobody is going to lose his job. Even so, there are potential undesirable consequences which will affect the political and economic situation of China.

First of all, with the shadow of unfavorable "public opinion" hanging overhead, those in charge of the development of Pudong will have to pick their steps extremely carefully and will act only when they have the prior approval of the octogenarians. Even measures about opening up further, which have been decided upon, may be subjected to reconsideration.

Secondly, cadres in Shanghai and elsewhere will adopt a wait-and-see attitude. Everybody is concerned about his own security, less the big stick of class struggle rains blows on one's own torso. For these reasons, nobody is keen to run any risk for the sake of the reform and opening up.

It appears that the conservative ideologues may have got the upper hand for the time being. It is too early to judge its impact on the development of Pudong. Undoubtedly, they will, in keeping with their theoretical logic, pursue their struggle against bourgeois liberalization further. While it is not clear who their next target will be, it is not unlikely that he will be a central leader engaged in economic work.

Chapter 5

Economic Upsurge in 1992:
An Immediate Nanxun Effect

Introduction

In February 1992, Deng Xiaoping launched his tour of South China or
Nanxun, boldly calling for a more thoroughgoing market reform and a
wider opening up of China to the global economy. Local officials and
local governments were at once confused, as the existing basic policy line
from the central government in Beijing toward reform progress was still
one that was based on a cautious approach.

In had since become clear that General Secretary Jiang Zemin, a great
survivor himself, had quickly changed tack and joined Deng's new reform
bandwagon. In a short span of a few weeks, the central leadership in
Beijing, which was originally under the swing of the conservative
Chen Yun, shifted its basic policy stand by embracing Deng's reform tac-
tics. In April 1992, the speeches that Deng had made during his trip to
Shenzhen and other places were edited to become the Central Document
No. 2 that was circulated to all senior officials in local governments to
study and use as a reference for introducing their new reform policies.

Deng's speeches, often informal and impromptu, contained many radical
and iconoclastic remarks that clearly challenged the prevailing ideological
orthodoxy of the time. Basically, Deng was saying that any good policy or
scheme that works well in the capitalist economy can be adopted and tried
out in China. If a capitalist economy has a stock market, why cannot the
socialist China also have one? China should try it out first. If it does not
work, then close it down, but always leaving "a tail behind" for the future.

Business moved even faster. Within weeks of Deng's first appearance in Shenzhen — contents of Deng's speeches in Shenzhen and
Zhuhai were quickly leaked into the Hong Kong media — Hong Kong
businessmen had quickly grasped the new political climate in China

and soon followed up by looking for new investment opportunities in South China. Thus, hectic trade and investment activities cropped up in a matter of few months. Deng's Nanxun and sparked off an immediate economic boom.

By the end of 1992, all these economic bustling and hustling associated with the influx of foreign direct investment (FDI) and the export boom had translated into higher gross domestic product (GDP) growth and higher inflation. When this chapter was circulated on 29 December 1992, preliminary figures showed that economic growth for that year was 12%, compared to 7% in 1991. But the actual growth rate of 1992 from today's adjusted statistical series was 14%, truly a great economic boom that was created by Deng's Nanxun in a short span of 10 months. The strong spurt of growth was basically fueled by sharp increases in consumption, rising fixed investment and an export boom (exports up 16% in 1992). Underlying the strong performance in all these three components was the unprecedented foreign investment boom, as FDI alone rose 250% in 1992!

In the meanwhile, the economic boom had also created inflationary pressures and shortages of key raw materials and energy. It was clear that the 1992 boom lasted until 1995, with duble-digit rates of growth for three consecutive years. In the process, it led to serious economic overheating and high inflation that subsequently Premier Zhu Rongji had to spend a lot of efforts to overcome.

China's economic performance in 1992 was of great historic significance in China's modern economic growth because it operated as a clear watershed. The year marked the beginning of near double-digit rates of dynamic growth for the next three decades. The growth process can further be divided into two periods. High growth during 1992–2001 can be attributed to the "Nanxun effect", i.e., high growth was the result of increased efficiency and higher productivity due to market reform. In November 2001, China was formally admitted into the World Trade Organization (WTO) which marked another new departure in China's open-door policy. Thus, China's economy experienced double-digit rates of growth for the period of 2002–2011 due to the working of the "WTO effect", i.e., increased efficiency and higher productivity arising from greater integration with the global economy.

Chinese Economy in High Gear

The Chinese economy, from preliminary statistics, ended the year 1992 with a 12% growth in real gross domestic product (GDP). This was China's first double-digit rate of growth since 1988, and also the highest growth rate since 1985. At that time, China was a bright spot in the global economy hit by general recession. It made history in 1992 as the best-performing economy in the world.

The economic upsurge in 1992 was buoyed by strong external demand as a result of the continuing export boom, and also strong domestic demand in terms of rising consumption expenditure and a sharp growth in fixed capital investment. Foreign trade for the first 11 months had already surpassed the total of last year. Total exports for 1992 was expected to come close to US$80 billion. For the first time, China's exports caught up with the levels of Taiwan and South Korea, putting China in the rank of the world's top 10 exporting economies.

Domestic demand was boosted by increases in consumption and investment: from January to October, retail sales went up by 15% while domestic investment by a hefty 37%. The surge in domestic investment was induced by strong economic growth and progress in economic reform; but it was also fueled by the unprecedented influx of foreign capital. In the first nine months of 1992, foreign investors were reported to have pledged an incredibly large sum of investment commitments worth US$31 billion, or equivalent to 60% of the previous 13-year total.

Since the economic boom in China at that time started to accelerate only in the first half of 1992 and since many of the investment projects on account of their time-lag effect produced their impact only many months later, the high growth momentum was expected to sustain through the first half of 1993. Consequently, the Chinese economy in 1993 was projected by both Chinese and foreign sources to continue with its double-digit rate of high growth.

At the same time, the cycle likely peaked in the second half of 1993. There were already many signs of increasing infrastructural bottleneck and supply constraint for energy and key raw materials. The thrust of growth was also blunted by an external shock. A more restrictive trade policy adopted by President-elect Bill Clinton or a further escalation of

Sino-British conflict over the democracy issue in Hong Kong had set back the economic boom in South China, with adverse repercussion on the rest of the Chinese economy.

A far more likely scenario was for the Chinese government to slow down what increasingly appeared to be a runaway growth with policy intervention. The spurt of growth had already stroked up serious symptoms of inflation. In November 1992, consumer prices for China's 35 major cities increased by 12.8%. The inflationary pressures clearly mounted in 1993 as the economy continued with its rapid expansion. China would possibly gain the dubious reputation of having the highest inflation rate in 1993. Haunted by the bad experience of the 1988 hyperinflation (which led to the Tianamen turmoil), the authorities were likely to come down hard on the economy with a credit crunch should it get further "overheated".

All in all, barring a serious domestic political instability such as an unexpectedly rough leadership transition following the departure of Deng Xiaoping, China was likely to remain the epicenter of surging economic activities in the Asia-Pacific for 1993. It was predicted that at worst, should the present growth conditions be moderated as a result of the above-mentioned unfavorable circumstances, China would still be able to chalk up a near-double digit rate of high growth.

Riding on Deng's Whirlwind

In a fundamental sense, Deng Xiaoping was the real architect of the economic boom in China at that time. In 1991, China had fully recovered from the shock of the Tiananmen turmoil, with a 7% economic growth. But China's top policy makers were left divided over the issue of "growth vs stability". Most bureaucrats together with the conservative Premier Li Peng himself were in favor of a slower economic growth as a trade-off for greater economic stability. In launching China's Eighth Five-Year Plan in March 1991, Li Peng specifically called for only 6% annual growth for the Plan period 1991–1995. More significantly, the Chinese economy at the beginning of 1992 was officially targeted to grow at 6% for the year.

Against the "pro-stability" was the "pro-growth" group which included reform-minded liberals as well as provincial leaders from the more prosperous South. It had since been known that Deng Xiaoping was in fact a leading advocate for faster economic growth. In late January 1992, Deng made the historic tour of South China, calling for faster economic growth and deeper economic reform — Deng's speech was later circulated as Internal Document No.2 for senior cadres in China to "study". "Deng's whirlwind", as it was called, sparked off an unprecedented trade and investment boom in South China, which soon spread to other cities. At the annual National People's Congress meeting in March, some members openly criticized Li Peng for sticking to the slower economic growth target. But in the first halfof 1992, the Chinese economy registered 10.6% real growth in GNP, far above the original official target of 6%. The pro-growth school had won the day.

In fact, by the middle of 1992, Deng was contemplating far more significant basic changes in the Chinese economic system. In July, China started to call itself "socialist market economy", replacing the old concept of "planned commodity economy". Formally adopted by the 14th Party Congress in October, the new concept can spare the leadership from being trapped into endless but often futile debate between those who argue for more market solution and those who want to retain the basic central planning framework in resource allocation. In any case, such a new "ideological line" was needed to endrose the many significant reform measures that have been introduced on a wide front. This includes a more liberalized import regime, opening up of more industries and more sectors to foreign investment, an official sanction of the securities exchange, and greater efforts towards reforming the price system and the state industry. In retrospect, all these market-oriented policies have provided the basic institutional framework to underpin the current economic boom.

Thus, China's gross industrial output (GIO) from January to October 1992 increased by 19.7%, compared to 12.9% for the whole of 1991 (Fig. 1). "Gross Industrial Output" or GIO is the most important piece of monthly economic statistics on China from the State Statistical Bureau. GIO is defined as the sum total of output value of all industrial enterprises, including those producing output for use by others as input (i.e., intermediate goods). Because of double-counting, the value of GIO is usually, though not necessarily, larger than that of GNP, which is based on the value-added concept. Further, GNP is more complete than GIO in coverage, as GNP

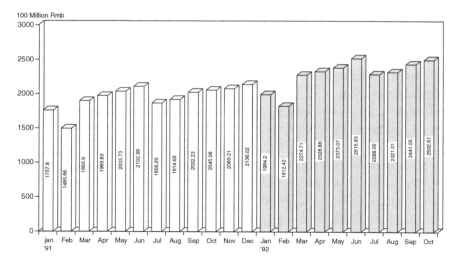

Figure 1.   China: Gross Industrial Output, 1991–1992.

Source: China's Statistics Information Consultancy Service Centre: *China's Latest Economic Statistics*. (Feb. 1991–Nov. 1992.)

also includes economic activities from the non-industrial sector such as agriculture and services. For 1992, such GIO growth translated into 12% growth in gross national product (GNP), the highest rate for China since 1985. But the growth had been uneven for different localities. As can be expected, Jiangsu (which included the industrial belt outside Shanghai) and Guangdong (which included the Special Economic Zones of Shenzhen, Zhuhai, and Shantou) registered over 30% growth in GIO, while Hainan Island, Zhejiang, Guangxi (which bordered Guangdong and Vietnam), and Shangdong (which was close to South Korea) had more than 20% growth. The interior provinces in Southwest (which included the most populous Sichuan) and Northwest experienced below national-average performance.

The external source of China's economic growth had been its dynamic exports. Foreign trade in 1992 hit a new record high. Its total turnover (exports plus imports) increased by 21% during the first 11 months to US$141 billion (the total for 1992 was expected to swell to US$160 billion), which already surpassed the whole of 1991.[1] With

---

[1] "Foreign trade hits new high", *China Daily* (Beijing, 10 December, 1992).

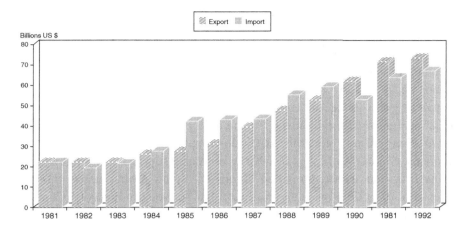

Figure 2.   China's Foreign Trade, 1981–1992.

Source: China Statistical Yearbook, 1992.

imports of US$67 billion and exports of US$74 billion, China yielded a smaller trade surplus of US$7 billion as compared to the US$8 billion of 1991, because China's imports in 1992 grew faster than its exports on account of strong domestic demand. As a result of sustained trade surplus for the past few years, as shown in Fig. 2, China built up a comfortable foreign reserves amounting to US$45 billion. However, this strong external economic position did not avert the gradual devaluation of the *Renminbi*, which had gone down by 10% during the past four months from US$1.00–Rmb5.42 to US$1.00–Rmb5.83, according to the official exchange rate. The black market rate in some places was 1 for 7.4. The devaluation was in part due to the sharp demand for foreign exchange in China as the Chinese economy became more open to foreign investment and foreign trade. But there was also a strong speculative demand for foreign exchange in China in anticipation of the eventual free convertibility of the *Renminbi*, which can only come after further downward adjustment of the official exchange rate.

However, China's persistent trade surplus vis-à-vis the United States proved to be more a bane than a boon for China. More than a source of trade friction between the two countries, the United States ever since the 1989 Tiananmen event made use of its trade gap with China to put political pressures on Beijing to improve its human rights record by threatening to withdraw China's Most Favoured Nation (MFN) status. Despite the efforts by China to step up imports from the United States, China's trade surplus with the United States for 1992 was expected to shoot up to US$18–20 billion, from US$15 billion of 1991.[2] The trade surplus figures looked much smaller if viewed from China's own customs clearance statistics, which did not include re-exports of Chinese goods from Hong Kong. Nonetheless, trade imbalance remained a dominant issue for Sino-US relations in 1993 as well as a source of external uncertainty for the export-propelled boom in South China, even though President-elect Clinton lately indicated that he would not revoke China's MFN status.[3]

The internal source of China's GIO growth came from increases in domestic demand. Consumption demand, as measured by retail sales of consumer goods from January to October rose by 15.5% over the same period of the previous year. More important than the consumer boon, so visible in Chinese cities at that time had been the hefty increase in fixed assets investment, at 37%. In particular, housing construction for the first time went up by 83% as a result of the relaxation of control in the real estate sector.[4]

The surge in domestic investment in 1992 went hand in hand with the unprecedented foreign investment boom. The official Xinhua News Agency reported that China in the first three quarters of 1992 had approved 27,000 new foreign investment projects amounting to

---

[2] See "Deficit may threaten MFN status" and "Sino-US trade gap narrows in October", *South China Morning Post* (Hong Kong, 18 December, 1992).

[3] In his first post-election policy statement on China, Clinton stated: "I don't think we'll have to revoke the MFN status"; but at the same time he said that the United States had an obligation "to be insistent about the things in which we believe". What he means in policy terms is for the United States to continue with the MFN treatment for China subject to some (vaguely defined) form of human rights improvement on the part of China. This constituted a major policy shift from Clinton. See "Clinton spells out human rights link to MFN status", *South China Morning Post* (16 December, 1992).

[4] *China's latest Economic Statistics*, November 1992 (Part 1), published by China's Statistics Information Service Centre and CITIC Research International (Hong Kong).

"US$30.6 billion, more than 6% of the total of the previous 13 years".[5] Though the actual amount of foreign investment for the period was only US$6.6 billion, this represented a significant jump over the actual volume of US$4.2 billion in 1991. As China opened up to foreign economic interests, new localities in the interior provinces, new sectors like service industries, and a greater share of the domestic market, such a huge influx of foreign capital was indeed not surprising.[6]

Suffice it to say that as China's export engine was going strong, and its consumer boom and investment fervor were showing no signs of weakening, any growth forecast based on the *ceteris paribus* assumption was inevitably one of bullishness. Consequently, the Chinese economy was projected by many Chinese and foreign economists to continue with its high performance in 1993.

The Risk of Overheating

It was a truism that any economy in such dynamic growth was apt to carry with it a downside risk. This was particularly the case for the Chinese economy plagued by structural weaknesses. Twice or thrice during the past 13 years when growth built itself into a double-digit rate, the economy would invariably run into severe supply constraints in terms of infrastructural bottleneck, energy, and raw material shortages. Such supply strains were already in evidence: the transportation system was severely overburdened; energy production was lagging behind; and prices of steel and cement have shot up.

The structural shortcomings of the Chinese economy were further aggravated by its "economic-system weaknesses", party caused by macroeconomic mismanagement and partly due to the "half-reformed" nature of the economy. Thus, whenever the economy was growing full steam ahead, it easily got "overheated" in terms of fast-rising inflation. For lack

---

[5] "Foreign investment in China", *Asian Wall Street Journal* (24 November, 1992).

[6] It may be noted that the statistics on the contractual value of foreign investment has grossly exaggerated the real worth of actual investment commitments, as many investment pledges on land deals may never materialize. For further discussion on this subject, see "Chinese Data Show Prosperity and Posturning", *Asian Wall Street Journal* (25 November, 1992).

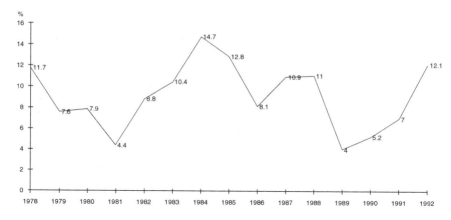

Figure 3.   China's Economic Growth 1978–1992.

Source: State Statistical Bureau, *China Statistical Yearbook*, 1992.

of effective macroeconomics instruments for fine-tuning, the Chinese
government would often heavy-handedly apply a credit squeeze through
administrative means. This would then force the economy on a down-
swing, and hence the familiar boom-and-bust cycle so characteristic of
China's pattern of economic growth over the past 13 years, as shown in
Fig. 3. Despite its impressive progress in economic reform, the Chinese
economy had to develop effective built-in stabilizers. Neither had it developed any effective macroeconomic control mechanism for moderating the
boom-bust cycle.

Still haunted by the damaging inflation of 1988, the Chinese leadership
had reportedly watched any warning sign of inflation very closely. In the
past few months, China's media was full of reports and commentaries on
the issue of "economic overheating". Many Chinese economists took the
view that China would not repeat the panic buying and hoarding of 1988,
as the economy at that time had an over-supply of goods while it had also
extensively "marketized" as a result of progress in economic reform. But
the real situation looked more menacing.

As it happened, in the first 11 months of 1992, the retail sales price
index increased by 5.2%, compared to the 2.9% for 1991. A more accurate
measure of price inflation in China was the consumer price index for

35 major Chinese cities, which soared to 12.8% in November.[7] It was expected that inflationary pressures would further increase in the next two months because of traditional festive spending around the Chinese New Year. Another bout of inflation was clearly looming.

Apparently alarmed by the spectre of inflation, Party General-Secretary Jiang Zemin, in a recent high-level national economic planning meeting, warned that China "should take measures to prevent the economy from becoming overheated".[8] Also attending the same meeting was Zhu Rongji as well as the "pro-stability" Li Peng and Yao Yilin. Evidently, the government was on the brink of intervening in the economy in order to reduce the inflationary pressures.

It remained to be seen how much government intervention would be needed this time to bring inflation under control and how much slowdown in growth would result. In any case, the main concern for China in 1993 was not whether the economy would continue with its upsurge but whether it would continue to get "overheated". Some trade-off from high growth seemed inevitable.

---

[7] "Economy expands — at a cost", *China Daily*, (12 December, 1992).
[8] "Take steps to stop overheating of Chinese economy: Party chief", *Straits Times* (Singapore, 21 December, 1992).

Chapter 6

What has China Accomplished in Economic Reform in 1994?

Introduction

Once Deng Xiaoping's economic reform policy started to take hold following his Nanxun in early 1992, the economy responded positively and promptly, sparking off an economic upsurge. As economic growth continued to build up momentum through 1993, policy makers started to map up a more comprehensive economic reform program so that the reform could proceed in a more systematic and orderly manner.

Looking back, it was a well-designed integrated reform package, which was formally adopted by the Third Party Plenum in November 1993. By this time, there was no more political and ideological polemic over the path and destination of economic reform: China's economy was slated to move toward a "socialist market economy" as fast as practically possible. No more debate over the relative share of the planning and market. To achieve the marketization of the economy, the reform programme was aimed at tackling all the interrelated macroeconomic issues of money, banking, finance, taxation, foreign exchange, and the state-owned enterprises (SOEs) in one blow. These reform measures were to start immediately after the Third Plenum, but most reform measures were implemented in 1994.

This puts 1994 as the single most important landmark year for economic reform next to the rural and agricultural reform in the early 1980s. This chapter was, circulated in December 1994 which summarized what had been achieved in terms of reform. It has since become clear that some reform measures like taxation reform and exchange rate reform had produced almost immediate effects; but others like the SOE reform were going to be a long-drawn process — but that was not so obvious at that time.

To begin with, the tax reform was an unequivocal success. Apart from unifying the tax code and simplifying the taxation system, China had taken steps to overhaul its antiquated tax administration and collection system. Beijing had finally started to tackle the crucial age-old taxation issue of revenue-sharing between the Central and local governments, i.e. which tax should go to the Central, which should be shared between the Central and locals and so on. Clearly this would alter the pattern of implicit power relationship between the Central government and localities, which is historically the single most important political issue for China, which as a vast continental-sized country has continued to insist on operating as a unitary state.

When China started economic reform in 1978, the Central's share of the state's total revenue was only 15%, indicating that China was then economically highly decentralized. On the eve of implementing the tax reform in 1993, the Central share went up to 22%. In 1994, as the tax reform was implemented, the Central's share jumped to 56%, and its share had since stayed around 50% for the subsequent two decades. But then, on the expenditure side, the locals had to carry an increasing burden of development spending such as infrastructure building as well as undertaking the provision of most of the social services like health and education.

Most local governments were therefore financially in a straitened position, which was made worse because local governments were in principal not allowed to raise revenue by issuing bonds. In the circumstances, many local governments had to resort to irregular means of raising revenue such as selling land or going into property development. This had resulted in the increases of local government debt across the country. Two decades later, many experts in China were again calling for a new round of tax reform.

The foreign exchange reform based on the abolition of the dual-exchange system was another success story. From 1986 to 1993, China operated a dual exchange system with a periodically adjusted official rate existing side by side with a broadly market-based rate set by "swap centers". However, this dual system not only hampered the conduct of foreign exchange but also distorted the exchange rate market. The system would also not be able to cope with a potential foreign exchange crisis arising from the sudden loss of confidence in the local currency.

The government therefore decided to unify the exchange rates on January 1, 1994. With this reform, the Renminbi was initially put on a managed float with limited convertibility on the current account along with strict capital control. The official exchange rate before the exchange reform was 5.8 *yuan* for 1 US dollar and then sharply dropped to 8.7 *yuan* per US dollar after the exchange unification, representing an immediate depreciation of 40% for the Renminbi. This had proved most conducive to China's export growth.

Then during the 1997 Asian financial crisis, China decided to maintain a more stable exchange rate by closely pegging it to the US dollar. This lasted until 3 July 2005 when the Renminbi went off the US dollar peg for more than 10% appreciation. By early 2013, the Renminbi has appreciated almost 30% against the US dollar, and it is on course toward greater internationalization and also gradual capital account liberalization. It has gone a long way from the 1994 exchange reform.

Banking reform was another reform breakthrough. The main thrust of banking reform in 1994 was to make the People's Bank of China (PBC) as a real central bank of the nation, capable of carrying out independent monetary policy through open market operation and the use of reserve requirements and discount rates. This was formalized by the passing of the Central Banking Act by the National People's Congress in March 1994.

At the same time, the four specialized state banks, namely, the Bank of China, the Industrial and Commercial Bank of China, the Construction Bank of China, and the Agricultural Bank of China, were to be commercialized by operating on purely commercial basis, leaving "policy lending" to the three newly created policy banks: the State Development Bank, the Export and Import Bank, and the Agricultural Development Bank. However, the commercial banking reform was not an immediate success, as many banks had continued to lend to the SOEs, thereby running into serious non-performing loan problem.

This led to the last but the most important aspect of economic reform that involved the SOEs. Initially, efforts were made to modernize the management system of the SOEs and also to corporatize them through the shareholding system. But the corporatization itself had proved to be a rather prolonged process. Furthermore, neither management reform nor corporatization could ensure the operational efficiency or the profitability of the SOEs. Ultimately, all SOEs would need to operate under a real "hard budget constraint", i.e. closing down the unprofitable SOEs. But the government still did not have enough political will to carry out such drastic measures for fear of social instability. In short, the SOE reform had to wait for Premier Zhu Rongji to muster enough political will tackle it many years later.

All in all, 1994 was still a bumper year of economic reform. By September 1994, the Fourth Plenum was convened, with the focus shifting to Party building and other urgent political matters crucial for the smooth post-Deng leadership transition.

The Politics of Reform

The Chinese Communist Party's Fourth Plenum in September 1994 set its focus on Party building and other political arrangements aimed at bolstering the "core leadership" centring on General-Secretary Jiang Zemin. This was in sharp contrast to the 3rd Plenum of November 1993, which adopted a package of measures for the sweeping reform of the economy. What had happened to all those economic reform measures, which were supposed to be implemented in 1994, dubbed the "Year of Reform"? How much economic reform had actually been accomplished since the Third Plenum? Why was there this shift of focus back to politics when China was still dogged by many burning economic issues like high inflation and ailing state-owned enterprises (SOEs).

The top Chinese leadership clearly saw an urgent need to strengthen and rejuvenate the Party, particularly its grass-roots organizations, which experienced a serious decay as a result of the erosion of the Marxist ideology due to the growth of materialism and widespread corruption. The rural Party organizations suffered the most, with 75% of the rural Party branches reportedly having lost their "combat-readiness". For China as a Communist state, the decline of the Communist Party inevitably spelled the loss of legitimacy and effectiveness of its governance. This also undermined the Party's efforts toward a more stable leadership transition. This was the rationale for the 4th Plenum to adopt a political blueprint to "save the Communist Party from crumbling in the post-Deng Xiaoping era".[1]

---

[1] "Blueprint devised to save Party after Deng" by Willy Wo-Lap Lam, *South China Morning Post* (Hong Kong, 26 September 1994).

The issue of the Party's survival apart, there was also the practical necessity for Beijing to return to political concerns. The leadership was aware that some of the economic reform measures adopted by the Third Plenum in November 1993 got bogged down or ran into political constraints, i.e., their implementation was dependent on further political and institutional changes. In other words, economic reform in China at that time looked more to be a matter of politics than economics. It was predicted that the future course of economic reform will increasingly depend on strong political will as well as the effectiveness of the central leadership. Viewed in this light, the move by the Fourth Plenum to strengthen the Party leadership was a logical sequence to the economic reform focus of the Third Plenum.

Much had already been written by both the Chinese and foreign media about the reform package adopted by the Third Plenum in November 1993. Suffice it to say that the main thrust of the package was to seek and establish: (1) a modern enterprise system; (2) a macroeconomic management system based on indirect economic instruments; (3) a national social security system; and (4) a series of laws and legislations to facilitate the implementation of the above. The long-term objective of these measures was to lay down the necessary institutional conditions for the efficient functioning of the "socialist market economy". The immediate goal was for the government to develop a market-based macroeconomic management mechanism, so that the government could rely on economic levers rather than the previously crude administrative order to deal with macroeconomic instability. Specifically, the key macroeconomic problems such as money, banking, financial sector developments, taxation, exchange, and state enterprises are all interrelated, and they need to be tackled in one blow. Hence, the rationale for the Third Plenum to adopt a comprehensive reform approach.

Where Is the Progress or Lack of It?

How much economic reform progress had actually been accomplished, one year after its promulgation? Many of the reform measures were supposed to start from the beginning of 1994, which was hailed by Chinese officials as the "Year of Reform".

Tax Reform

The tax reform aimed at unifying the tax code and simplifying the tax system and administration came into effect on 1 January 1994. Thus, the old product tax (Consolidated Industrial and Commercial Tax) was replaced by a new value-added tax (VAT) at the 17% standard rate, to be supplemented by a consumption tax (mainly for luxury goods) and a business tax (mainly for the service sector). A single personal income tax for both foreigners and Chinese nationals was also introduced.

Of greater importance was the reform of the tax administration and collection systems. It was rather strange that for such a big country as China, the central government all along did not have a nationwide tax administration, with the bulk of its tax collection delegated to local governments. Thus, reforming the tax administration by separating the tax authority between central and local governments marked a truly significant move. Further, a new revenue-sharing arrangement between the central and local governments replaced the complex contract-based intergovernmental revenue system, historically called "tax farming".[2]

How successful was the tax reform? In the words of the former Chinese Finance Minister Liu Zhongli, the new tax system was working "beyond our expectations", with the national revenue for the first half of 1994 having grown by 22.6%.[3] Except for Tibet, separate state and local tax administrations were already in operation in China's 29 provinces and autonomous regions. In March 1994, the National People's Congress also

---

[2] In general, custom duties and consumption tax, taxes on the large SOEs and the communication network like railway and airlines belong to the central government, and taxes on financial activities will go to the central government. Business tax, personal income tax, real estate tax as well as tax on local enterprises will go to local governments while the VAT is to be shared between central and local governments on the ratio of 3 to 1, and stamp duties on stock transactions on the 1 to 1 ratio. For a good discussion of the tax reform, see Tsang Shu-ki and Cheng Yuk-shing (1994). China's tax reforms of 1994. *Asian Survey*, XXXI, (9) September. Also, Ma Junlei and Luo Liqin (1994). Important reforms in China's tax system. *JETRO China Newsletter*, (110) May–June.

[3] "New Tax System Smoothly on Track", *Beijing Review* (15–21, August 1994), p. 5. Also, "New Tax System Operates Smoothly", *Beijing Review* (19–25, September 1994).

The government is obviously a bit too optimistic, because inflation in the first half of 1994 was also over 20%. This means that tax revenue in real terms was not increasing.

passed the Budget Law, which required local governments to run balanced budgets and the central government to finance deficits with bond issues rather than to borrow directly from the central bank.

It was suggested that success in tax reform would certainly strengthen the role of fiscal policy in macroeconomic management in the long run. But China was still quite a long way from using fiscal instruments for effective macroeconomic stabilization partly because of its chronic fiscal deficit and partly because of the loss of its tax bases to local governments.[4] For more effective fiscal operation, the central government must be able to command an adequate share of the country's economic resources.

Since the reform in 1978, the size of the state budget shrunk from about one-third of grass national product (GNP) to one-sixth at that time. On top of this, most of the retained earnings and depreciation provisions of SOEs were considered "extra-budgetary funds", lying outside the budget domain. The growing business interests controlled by the armed forces (People's Liberation Army (PLA)) were also outside the purview of the Ministry of Finance to form "off-budgetary" activities. Despite China being a socialist country, Beijing actually commanded no more resources than governments of other East Asian market economies, whose budgets were slightly more than a quarter of their GNP.[5]

Exchange Reform

From 1986 to 1993, China operated a dual exchange system with a peri-odically adjusted official rate existing side by side with a generally mar-ket-based but depreciated rate set by various Foreign Exchange Adjustment

---

[4] The new revenue-sharing system would be phased in gradually over a number of years. In exchange for support from local governments for this fiscal reform program, the central government had to guarantee that tax revenue for local governments would not fall below a "basic amount", i.e., what they were supposed to be getting in 1993. As a result of this and other technical problems surrounding, the new tax collection, the central government would not see a substantial rise in the revenue yields in the short term. See Zhou Xiaochuan and Yang Zhigang, "China's 1994 Taxation Reform: Achievements and Remaining Problems", (in Chinese). Paper presented at Zhou's Seminar given at the Institute of East Asian Political Economy, Singapore, on 13 October 1994.

[5] World Bank, *China; Budgetary Policy and Intergovernmental Fiscal Relations.* (Vol. 1, Main Report, 28 July 1993).

Centers or "Swap Centers". Under this dual system, domestic enterprises and foreign trade corporations had to surrender their export earnings as foreign exchange retention rights (which entitled their owners to purchase foreign exchange at the official rate), which could be traded at various swap centers. For a while, this rather ingenious way of operating a dual exchange rate with the support of swap markets worked reasonably well. When the *Rmb* was seriously overvalued, the swap market could ease the black market activity while the foreign exchange retention rights system could also operate as incentives for the export enterprises.

However, any dual-exchange system necessarily distorts the market and cannot be counted on to deal with a serious foreign exchange crisis, e.g., a sudden loss of confidence by the public in the domestic currency. This actually happened in June 1993 when the *Rmb* was under strong devaluation pressures. Hence, the government's resolve to unify the exchange rates on 1 January 1994.

With the unification of the exchange markets, the foreign exchange retention system was abolished and the use of foreign exchange certificates (FECs) was discontinued. Enterprises had to surrender their export proceeds to the designated banks, and this made it possible for the central bank to intervene in the interbank market to moderate any short-term volatility of the exchange rate through purchases and sales of foreign exchange.[6] In other words, China had entered into a managed float system with partial convertibility of the *Rmb*, broadly on the account at that time. China targeted full convertibility in the year 2000.

The exchange system reform was carried out hand in hand with the liberalization of the trade system. To strengthen its case for the re-entry into the General Agreement on Tariffs and Trade (GATT), China removed a large number of commodities from import licensing and controls, and lowered the average tariff rate from 40% in January 1992 to 36% in December 1993.[7] As a result of all these reforms and trade liberalization

---

[6] It should be noted that the reform has in effect centralized all foreign exchange supply in the interbank market, which facilitates the government's control over the foreign exchange flow and makes it possible for the government to carry out direct administrative intervention by limiting access to the foreign exchange market.

[7] On 1 September 1994, China's GATT negotiation team undertook to further cut the average tariff rate to 19% as a for condition for entering the GATT, and within five years to

measures, along with the continuing strong performance of exports and foreign investment inflow, the exchange rate of the *Rmb* remained quite stable, even showing a slight appreciation of 2% against the US dollar despite the persistent inflation.[8]

Banking Reform

From the standpoint of macroeconomic management, banking reform constituted the most vital component of the whole economic reform package. For the proper operation of the "socialist market economy", China needed a proper financial framework for the operation of monetary policy. China had to develop such key monetary instruments as money supply and interest rate for macroeconomic stabilization.

Before economic reform, China operated a monobank system, which in 1984 evolved into a two-tier banking system, with the PBC operating as the country's central bank while policy and commercial lending were assigned to the four specialized state banks — the Bank of China, the Industrial and Commercial Bank of China, the People's Construction Bank of China, and the Agricultural Bank of China. Prior to 1988, the annual credit plan was the mainstay of China's "monetary policy".

---

reduce to the non-tariff items from 1,200 to 200. "China ready to carry out demands of Gatt", *China Daily* (Beijing, 2 December 1994).

[8]The *Rmb* exchange rate per US dollar rose from 8.53 on 1 January 1994 to 8.7 in early October 1994, and the official reserves at the People's Bank of China (PBC) rose from US$21 billion at the end of 1991 to US$32 billion in September 1994. While the continued robust export growth and the continued influx of foreign investment in the first half of 1994 has no doubt strengthened China's foreign reserves (and hence also the *Rmb*), the new exchange system, which requires all domestic enterprises engaged in foreign trade to submit receipts to the designated banks and hence reduces capital flight by under-invoicing or over-invoicing, has also contributed to the increased supply of foreign exchange to the interbank market. (Zhou Xiaochuan (1994). Reform on China's Exchange Rate Regime. Lecture given at the East Asian Consultancy, Singapore, October 12).

Ironically, the influx of foreign investment, which has led to the slight appreciation of the *Rmb*, was also inflationary. The PBC, in buying up foreign exchange (which increased China's overall foreign reserves), also created more money supply in the domestic market and hence increased the inflationary pressure.

As economic reform took hold, the shortcomings of such a credit plan, for both its formulation and implementation, became increasingly apparent. Apart from the basic contradiction of operating a credit rationing system in an increasingly market-driven economy, the central bank had simply lost control of money supply growth. In-fact, the use of the administratively-controlled annual credit plan (which is often arbitrarily implemented at the local level), as the primary monetary policy tool had been the root cause of China's recurrent macroeconomic instability. Vice-Premier Zhu Rongji knew only too well all these problems when he took over the PBC as its governor in the summer of 1993.

The main thrust of the banking reform as approved by the Third Plenum includes (1) setting up a strong and independent central bank, with the primary responsibility of maintaining monetary and exchange rate stability; and (2) commercializing the banking system in which the state-owned specialized banks would operate on purely commercial basis, leaving "policy-lending" to the three newly created "policy banks": the State Development Bank (SDB), the Export and Import Bank, and the Agricultural Development Bank (ADB). (1) The SDB, responsible for financing key infrastructure projects, is to be financed with capital from the Ministry of Finance and by taking over a number of existing construction funds. (2) The Ex-Im Bank, for providing long-term credit for the import of large-scale machinery and technology, and for exports, is also to be financed with capital from the Ministry of Finance. (3) The ADB, for promoting agricultural development, is to be financed by bond issues to the financial institutions.

In this regard, the Central Banking Act was drafted and submitted to the National People's Congress in March 1994 for approval. Apart from providing a legal basis for the PBC to carry out its central banking functions, the new law gave the PBC operational autonomy by making it directly responsible to the National People's Congress instead of under the State Council.[9] The PBC concentrated on conducting monetary policy through

---

[9] Apart from the Central Banking Act, the government has completed the drafting of a number of important financial legislations such as the Banking Act, the Bills of Exchange Act, the Insurance Act, the Exchange Control Regulations, the Securities Regulations and so on. See The People's Bank of China, *China Financial Outlook 1994* (Beijing, 1994).

open market operation (which was recently tried out in Shanghai) and the use of reserve requirements and discount rates.

At the same time, the PBC would no longer act as the cashier of the government by directly providing funds to the Ministry of Finance. It had also made it more difficult for local governments to force the 2,500 or so local branches of PBC to extend unauthorized credit. In time to come, the PBC would be reorganized along regional lines, much like the US Federal Reserves system, so as to further reduce unwarranted administrative intervention from individual provinces. To better monitor the operation of its numerous branches, the PBC was reported to have started modernizing the inter-bank payments system with the introduction of a huge computer network linking all its branches.[10]

For the commercialization of the banking system, the first step taken was to remove from the specialized state banks the burdens of financing the less profitable long-term loans for large infrastructural projects, the so-called "policy lending". Thus, in April 1994, the SDB officially came into being by merging the six investment corporations set up by the State Planning Commission in 1988.[11] The other two "policy banks", namely, the Export and Import Bank and the ADB were also launched in the later part of 1994.[12]

As the policy banks came into existence, the specialized state banks rejected applications for high-risk loans. At the same time, the specialized banks were required to sever links with their non-bank financial institutions, which would have to operate on a commercial basis. The government was also planning to reorganize the country's more than 5,000 credit

---

[10] "China Bank to Upgrade", *South China Morning Post* (Hong Kong, 3 February 1994).

[11] The SDB would take over the funding of 345 major capital projects including the mammoth Three Gorges Dam project, and was planning to issue 65 billion *yuan* bonds later this year. See "New China development bank aims to curb investment frenzy", *Straits Times* (Singapore, 15 April 1994).

[12] The ADB was the last policy bank to be launched in 1994. Capitalized at 20 billion *yuan*, the ADB's working capital would come mainly from the issue of financial bonds to domestic and foreign banks, and from the PBC. "China sets up new rural bank", *Straits Times* (Singapore, 21 November 1994).

cooperatives into local commercial banks.[13] In short, the Chinese authorities had no doubt grasped what was needed for the effective functioning of the banking system in a market economy.

However, this does not mean that China's banking reform had achieved its objectives. Has the PBC started to operate like a true central bank? The fact that inflation in October 1994 ran at 27.7% was a telling evidence that the PBC failed to put its independent monetary policy in operation. The PBC could not even set the interest rate close to the market level, with the lending rate at that time being negative by more than 10 percentage points.[14] The PBC reportedly refrained from applying a strong anti-inflationary credit crunch at that stage for fear of hitting too many ailing SOEs. In other words, the PBC simply did not muster sufficient political autonomy to overcome the demand from certain established interest groups for the continuation of an easy monetary regime.

Nor were the specialized banks anywhere near to operating like true commercial banks. The four specialized banks and their numerous branches spawned huge bureaucratic organizations, which in 1992 were staffed with 1.6 million employees. Long used to operating as administrators and bureaucrats, obviously very few of these bank employees were trained professional bank officers, accountants and financial analysts, with such banking experience as assessing commercial loans.

Beyond the problems of overstaffing and bad management, these state banks were all saddled with a large amount of unsecured, non-performing loans, called "triangular debt". From the balance sheet of China's specialized banks in 1993, of their total assets of 3,439 billion *yuan*, 2,587 billion *yuan* or 75% were loans, compared to about 45% for Singapore's commercial banks.[15] Because of the lack of financial instruments (other than

---

[13]Zhu Xiaohua. Deputy Governor of the People's Bank of China. "Toward the 21st Century: Financial Reform in China" (October, 1994). Paper presented at a public lecture organized by East Asian Consultancy Pte Ltd on 10 November 1994 in Singapore.

[14]Yet despite high inflation and the negative interest rate, which is even higher for savings, household savings deposits with the banks were still rising and reported to be 477 billion *yuan* for September 1994, or 95% higher than January. See "China's foreign reserves and bank savings up". *Straits Times* (Singapore, 14 November 1994).

[15]The People's Bank of China, *China Financial Outlook 1994*. p. 89. For Singapore, *Monetary Authority of Singapore Annual Report, 1992/93*.

government bonds) and the general backwardness of China's financial market, Chinese commercial banks were generally highly geared to loans. Worse still, as a socialist legacy, most loans had not been commercially assessed. In 1993, these specialized banks committed 710 billion *yuan* to industry, mainly to SOEs. Since many SOEs were also trapped in the "triangular debt", the specialized banks were therefore heavily weighed down by non-performing loans, estimated to be at 600 billion *yuan*. In the final analysis, it was the unreformed SOEs which had proved to be the major stumbling block to China's banking reform efforts.

Reform of State-Owned Enterprises (SOEs)

In 1978, SOEs accounted for 78% of China's total industrial output. By 1993, the figure sharply declined to 43%. In 1978, SOEs employed 71% of the total industrial labor force; and the proportion also dropped to 65% in 1993.[16] This relative decline of the SOE sector over the years merely reflected the dynamic expansion of the non-state sector, which included township and village enterprises (TVEs) and various forms of individual enterprises and foreign ventures.

Viewed from a different angle, the SOE sector held the key to China's industrial growth. Despite its relative shrinkage, the SOE sector remained large in absolute size as well as in total employment (68 million workers in 1992). In the first five months of 1994, SOEs delivered, in the form of taxes and profits, 60% of China's total state revenue. Most SOEs were engaged in raw materials production and heavy industry, including a wide range of capital-intensive basic industries which had to operate on the economies of scale and were shunned by TVEs and foreign ventures. In fact, some 80% of China basic industrial raw materials and intermediate products were produced by SOEs.[17] China had published its "500" largest enterprises, most of which were essentially SOEs, including the best performing "Top Three" (namely, the three top iron and steel corporations of Baoshan, Shougan, and Anshan).[18] So were those enterprises which have

---

[16] State Statistical Bureau (1994). *1994 Statistical Yearbook of China*. Beijing.

[17] "State firms still play major role in economy", *China Daily* (Beijing, 25 August 1994).

[18] "Top 3 Chinese firms are state-owned", *Straits Times* (Singapore, 2 September 1994).

been listed as "H" shares on the Hong Kong Stock Exchange. After all, SOEs were not necessarily inefficient. Does this mean that the reform of SOEs was progressing well?

The above picture can be misleading. Notwithstanding many successful individual SOEs, the overall performance of the SOEs remained weak, because many SOEs operated under the "soft budget constraints". In 1993, about one-third of SOEs were reported to have made losses, with another third just breaking even. It may be pointed out that it was sometimes rather meaningless to speak of "profit" and "loss" of any enterprise operating under China's half-reformed economy, because prices of many inputs and outputs were not determined by the free market forces of supply and demand.

The case in point were the coal and oil industries, which accounted for the largest share of the industrial SOE losses mainly because the government kept the coal and oil prices well below market prices. Furthermore, the old socialist accounting practice of putting some cost items before profit and making inadequate provision for bad debt and depreciation, also obscured the correct definition of "profit".[19] Finally, the economic reform process itself such as price adjustment and the foreign exchange and taxation reforms had also caused losses to many SOEs.

Regardless of the real extent of the SOE losses and their real causes, the SOE sector without doubt had continued to cause serious problems for the Chinese economy. First, this was the sector which had achieved the least progress in economic reform. In fact, the SOE sector had actually become an obstacle for the reform efforts in other sectors, particularly the financial sector reform, as discussed above. Secondly, the government's subsidy of the SOE losses had been a significant cause of the chronic state fiscal deficit.[20] For these reasons, the Third Party Plenum had rightly recognized that

---

[19] This, in part, explains why the proportion of loss-making SOEs in the first half of 1994 had risen sharply to 46%. "Economy steady, with 11 percent rise in GDP", *China Daily* (Beijing, 19 October 1994).

[20] The government direct subsidy to SOEs has in fact declined in recent years. But in 1993, it still amounted to 41 billion *yuan* equivalent to 8% of the state revenue or 1.3% of China's GNP. *Renmin Ribao* (*People's Daily*), 25 March 1994, p. 2.

the establishment of a modern enterprise system by reforming SOEs constituted an important component of its overall economic reform package.

There was no lack of debate among Chinese scholars on how best to reform the SOE sector. Except for the outright privatization (currently still an ideological taboo), the Chinese government had actually been quite flexible in experimenting with various strategies of reforming SOEs. Prior to 1993, the reform of SOEs put its emphasis on the progressive increase in managerial autonomy and accountability of SOEs. More recently, greater emphasis had been placed on "corporatization" by converting SOEs into "shareholding companies", especially for the large and medium ones. "Corporatization" was merely the Chinese version of gradual privatization.

Thus, efforts have been made to restructure the enterprise governance, including measures to define the enterprise rights as legal entities, to manage the state-owned assets, and to separate government supervision from enterprise management. This culminated in the promulgation of the new Company Law on 1 July 1994, which was supposed to provide the much-needed legal framework for the formation of shareholding companies. It was recently projected that by the end of this century, 70% of China's SOEs would be corporatized.[21]

However, the corporatization progress so far had been very slow. By 1992, only some 3,700 shareholding companies had been formed, of which 70 were listed. In 1993, 100 more SOEs were corporatized. In general, those more efficient SOEs were more easily corporatized. It was well known that many SOEs, heavily debt-ridden, had very weak capital structures with high debt–equity ratios. These SOEs would need to go through drastic financial restructuring and re-capitalization beforehand, i.e., some means of securitizing their debt into equity. But financial restructuring of SOEs could not be carried out before the banking sector had completed its commercialization. More precisely, the specialized banks would have to decide on how to deal with their 600 billion *yuan* or so non-performing debt with SOEs.

---

[21] This was estimate made by the Vice-President of China Conference for Reforming SOEs, Mr Sun Xiao-liang. *Hong Kong Economic Journal* (18 May 1994).

It should be stressed that mere corporatization by itself, with its main focus on ownership reform, cannot ensure the efficiency or profitability of SOEs, which eventually would have to go through a management reform to learn how to behave like true private enterprises in the market place. Many government departments, especially those below the provincial level, would have to sever administrative links with the SOEs under their patronage.[22] The SOEs on their part would ultimately have to operate under a real "hard budget constraint". Thus, those hopelessly unprofitable SOEs would have to be shut down instead of being artificially pushed through corporatization. China passed the bankruptcy law in 1986; but the government had been extremely reluctant to allow ailing SOEs to fold up for fear of social instability. So far, fewer than 500 SOEs have been officially declared bankrupt.[23] Recently, the government decided to allow 156 loss-making SOEs to go under by the end of 1994.[24]

The slow progress of corporatization coupled with the mounting losses of the SOEs had accordingly prompted the government to renew its efforts to crack "the hardest nut of the country's economic reform", with 1995 slated to be the year of reforming SOEs.[25] About 100 SOEs were selected as guinea pigs for experimenting a modern management system.[26] No further details were available as to how such a program would work. Presumably, it would combine both ownership and operational reforms in

---

[22] For a detailed discussion of the Chinese government's link with business, see John Wong (1994). Power and market in Mainland China: The danger of increasing government involvement in business. *Issues & Studies,* 30(1) January.

[23] "State workers protest at cuts", *South China Morning Post* (Hong Kong, 29 October 1994).

[24] "36 Chinese state firms to go bust by year's end", *Straits Times* (Singapore 7 November 1994). The old bankruptcy law has been outdated by new developments. It was recently reported that China was preparing for the amendment of the old bankruptcy law in order to facilitate the liquidation of the bankrupt SOEs. (*Lianhe Zaobao,* Singapore, Sunday, 20 November 1994.)

[25] "In a special meeting held early (November 1994) Vice-Premier Zou Jianhua has revealed that the government finally decided to deal with hardest nut of the country's economic reform, the reform and modernization of the State-owned enterprises (SOEs), as an overriding task for the country's economic restructuring next year", *China Economic News.* XV(44), 14 November 1994.

[26] "100 state-run Chinese firms to experiment with market system", *Business Times* (Singapore, 23 November 1994).

the selected SOEs. But it remained doubtful if such a gingerly, piecemeal approach to SOE reform is going to significantly transform the ailing SOE sector comprising over 13,000 large firms.

The problem of reforming the SOE sector was enormously complicated, involving larger political and social issues. In particular, many large SOEs exist like "mini-welfare states", whose objective was not limited to maximizing profits but their operations included taking care of such social responsibilities as housing, education, healthcare, and other welfare services for their workers on behalf of their local governments.[27] Though previous reform measures have brought flexibility to the remuneration system, the basic wage and welfare package of the SOE workers were protected by state policies. The trouble is that workers of SOEs were considered state employees, who have long been indoctrinated by the Party ideology as China's industrial proletariat and masters of society. Hence also their resistance to market reforms.

Any radical reform of SOEs must therefore start with decoupling production from their non-production social functions. This would entail the retrenchment of numerous redundant workers (i.e., breaking their "iron rice bowls"), which was politically infeasible to carry out on a massive scale, certainly not before the government had introduced an effective social safety net. In other words, the reform of SOEs was tied up with the crucial social security reform. It was reported that the government in 1995 would introduce a "unified social security system" covering unemployment insurance, old age pensions, and medical care.[28] But its implementation was expected to be a slow process, simply because the cash-strapped government, faced with so many competing demands for funds, was

---

[27] For example, the Anshan Iron find Steel, which is among the best run SOEs in China today, has to struggle hard to cope with its welfare burden. This is a huge steel complex with 103 subsidiaries and over 400,000 employees. In 1993, it turned out 8.3 million tons of steel with a total sales of 17.6 billion *yuan*. It has to take care of 130,000 retired workers, whose pensions amounted to 440 million *yuan*. During the past 15 years, it has spent 2.2 billion *yuan* on building apartments for its employees. It provides free social services to its employees and their families through its 16 hospitals, 13 colleges and vocational schools, 33 schools and 21 kindergartens. "Cot to coffin duty cripples firms", *China Daily* (20 August 1994).

[28] "Social security shake-up plan", *South China Morning Post* (19 October 1994).

financially not in a position to take on such a huge burden of social security obligations. Thus, both the social security and SOE reforms were destined to be a long drawn-out process.

More Difficult for Remaining Efforts

At the Third Party Plenum in November 1993, the Chinese leadership embarked on a broad-front economic reform package in order to establish a market-based macroeconomic management system. The government had obviously not achieved such an objective, as manifested in its failure to bring the high inflation under control. Of the main reform measures in the package, only the exchange rate and fiscal reforms made satisfactory progress as planned while the critical banking and SOE reforms (which are actually interdependent) made no important breakthrough: they, in fact, ran into political and social constraints.

It was sufficiently clear that the Chinese government could not apply any "shock therapy" to the reform of both the banking and SOE sectors, which was expected to go through a painful gradual process. The Chinese leadership that was under Jiang Zemin, in the face of the imminent post-Deng transition, was in any case loath to take hard decisions by introducing more radical reform measures. The government's reform efforts were also hampered by inadequate financial resources and lack of trained manpower.

Macroeconomic policy making in China, as in other market economies, was increasingly complicated by conflicting demands, e.g., the trade-off between inflation and unemployment, between balancing economic overheating in coastal cities and slower growth in the interior, and so on. Gone are the days when China could just apply simple and straightforward reform measures and reap immediate results, as Deng Xiaoping did in the early 1980s with the agricultural reform. It was expected that future reform measures, in addressing the question of economic efficiency, would satisfy the larger political and social needs. Thus, the overall political environment for China's further economic reform efforts would become more difficult. The best reform strategy for the unfinished agenda is still the one that would build reform into economic development. It was predicted that with successful economic growth, the Chinese leadership could perhaps "muddle through".

Chapter 7

Soft-Landing of the Economy in 1995: The Nanxun's Climax

Introduction

The economic effects of the Nanxun were almost immediate. Once the central leadership in Beijing started to embrace Deng's bold reform concepts of establishing a "socialist market economy", the reform program was soon reignited. At the same time, the economic growth engine was also rapidly recharged. The first waves of new reform and development initiatives understandably came from Guangdong and Shanghai, which had served as the political platform for Deng to propagate his radical reform ideas to his conservative colleagues in Beijing.

What was most surprising was that businessmen in Hong Kong and Taiwan and foreign investors elsewhere seemed to have grasped the fundamental importance of Deng's Nanxun policy faster than those conservative leaders in Beijing. Within a few months after the Nanxun, foreign capital and foreign direct investment (FDI) poured into the Pearl River Delta and Shanghai. The total influx of FDI in the immediate post-Nanxun years of 1992–1995 surged to US$110 billion, compared to only US$25 billion for the whole period of 1979–1991.

Accordingly, the Chinese economy, fueled by rising FDI and rising foreign, trade, experienced three years of breakneck hypergrowth at 13% in a row for the period of 1992–1995. Such heady growth had also plunged the economy into serious overheating, with consumer price index (CPI) rising to 14.7% in 1993 and further to the record level of 24.1% in 1994—this has proved to be the highest level since the economic reform in 1978.

Zhu Rongji, then Vice-Premier, was in charge of economic affairs. His first economic task was to speed up economic reform in 1994 in several crucial areas such as the tax reform and the foreign exchange reform. As the booming economy was getting out of hand, his next task was trying to rein in the economic overheating with tough "macroeconomic control" or hong-guan tiaokong measures. The macroeconomic management tools that were employed by Zhu in those days were basically administrative measures, as the Chinese economy at that time was not sufficiently marketized for Zhu to use the more indirect lever of fine-tuning in an effective manner.

Thus, the Chinese economy in 2005 grew at 9.3%, down from 13.1% of 1994. But inflation in 1995 was also brought down to 17.1% from the 24.1% of 1994. In other words, the 1995 economy had achieved a success-ful "soft landing", i.e., still with very high growth but with a declining inflation.

The year 2005 was a turning point. The kind of "Wild West" pattern of hectic and chaotic growth that was sparked off by the Nanxun, had finally come to an end. In the following few years, Zhu would continue with his austerity policy with further macroeconomic control measures so as to consolidate both the reform and economic growth.

A Soft Landing

The Chinese economy, which has been steaming ahead in double-digit rates of growth for three consecutive years from 1992, had come to a soft landing in 1995. Economic growth for 1995 was around 9.5% in real terms, down from 11.6% of 1994 (Fig. 1). Inflation, which at one time in 1994 raged to the high of 27%, was finally brought down to the targeted level of 15% by the end 1995, thanks to government's draconian macro-economic control measures.

The Chinese leadership with Jiang Zemin "at the core" heaved a sigh of relief. Jiang stared off in 1995, the first year of the post-Deg leadership transition, with great trepidation. He offered his "Eight Points" to Taiwan as a condition for its long-term reunification with the Mainland, only to be met by a defiant Taiwan leadership under Lee Teng-hui, who was deter-mined to break out of the diplomatic isolation imposed by the Mainland. In June, Lee made a trip to the United States in the teeth of very strong opposition from Beijing, thereby sparking off a sharp escalation of tension over the Taiwan Straits and bringing Sino-American relations to a new low. Domestically, Jiang was also besieged by the corruption scandal of Chen Xitong, a Politburo member.

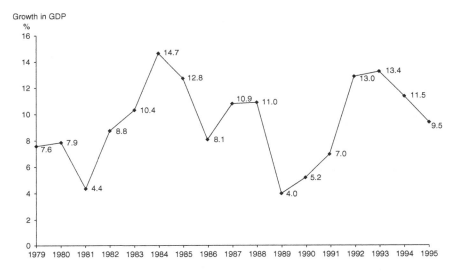

Figure 1.   China's Economic Growth and Fluctuation.

Source: State Statistical Bureau, Beijing.

Though development across the Taiwan Straits remained potentially explosive, China's relations with the United States stabilized and the political spillover of the Chen Xitong affair was contained. Jiang's leadership thus ended 1995 manifestly more secure, and it looked forward to 1996 with greater confidence.

Zhu Rongji, the Vice Premier in charge of the overall management of the economy during 1998–2003, declared that the government would not loosen its tight macroeconomic control.[1] This meant that China's economic growth for 1996 would slow further to around 8–9%, with the inflation rate squeezed down a few more percentage points. It was expected that such a moderate and yet still robust growth would be a blessing in disguise for China. After three straight years of heady growth, the Chinese economy needed to settle down to greater stability, allowing infrastructure

---

[1] Zhu said on 9 December 1995 that China at present could not give up its control over bank loans or it would risk reigniting inflation. ("State not ready to give up economic control: Zhu", *Straits Times* Singapore, 10 December 1995).

to catch up and the government more time to address critical long-term structural and institutional problems.

In any case, with the economies of Hong Kong, Taiwan, and Japan all set to a slower growth, and with the "China euphoria" among foreign investors subsiding, China was unlikely to see a repeat of "hyper growth" in the next few years. The year 1996 may have well marked the beginning of a new phase of lower growth for the Chinese economy.

Squeezing the Hyper Growth

The dominant concern of the Chinese government at the start of 1995 was how to bring down the rampant inflation to the targeted 15%. Fueled by a strong domestic investment boom, high export growth, and sharply rising food prices, the Chinese economic became seriously overheated from the second half of 1994, with inflation threatening to get out of hand. Thus, the main economic preoccupation of the government throughout 1995 was to reduce overheating. This had to be done in China, in the absence of effective market-based macroeconomic stabilization instruments, by relying heavily on direct administrative intervention, i.e., mainly by tightening industrial credit. And a vigorous credit squeeze inevitably carries with it trade-off for lower growth and higher urban unemployment, albeit in a disguised form.

China's industrial value-added for the first 11 months of 1995 grew by 13.2% over the same period of 1994 (Fig. 2). This formed the basis for the preliminary estimate of about 9.5% guess domestic product (GDP) growth for the whole of 1995. As in other market economies, China's economic growth in 1995 was buoyed by rising domestic and external demands. Thus, fixed capital investment for the first 10 months of 1995 increased by 18% from the same period of 1994, while retail sales of consumer goods went up by 29%. For external demand, export growth had also been strong, rising to US$132 billion fort the first 11 months of 1995, or up 28.3% from the same period in 1994.

However, China's overall GDP growth for 1995 had come down by tow percentage points from 1994, and signs of slower growth were already in evidence. First, fixed capital investment in 1995 had fallen sharply, by 11 percentage points over 1994 as a result of the government's tight credit

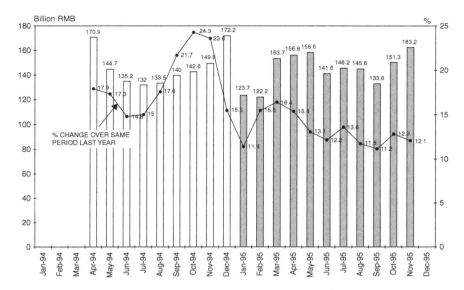

Figure 2. China's Monthly Industrial Value-Added 1994 and 1995.

Source: State Statistical Bureau of China. (Before April 1994, China publish its value of industrial output only in gross term.)

policy. Secondly, exports were losing their growth momentum as the year-on-year rate of export growth had been declining rapidly from 88% for January to 35% for the third quarter, and further to a negative 3.8% for November. Accordingly, the trade surplus in 1995 was expected to be smaller than in 1994, even though China's trade surplus with the United States had remained large.[2] It was anticipated that export slow-down was likely to continue in 1996 on account of a further cut in tax rebates to exporters from January 1996. Still, in an overall sense, China's external

---

[2] China's total trade surplus for the first 11 months of 1995 amounted to US$18 billion. But it was expected to shrink in 1996 because of the expected lower export growth (in part due to reduction in VAT rebates to exporters) along with potentially higher imports. At the APEC meeting in Osaka in November 1995, Jiang Zemin, in a bid to join WTO, announced an unprecedented trade liberalization package based on slashing tariffs on 4,000 import items by 30%, effective from 1 January 1996. This stimulated China's import growth in 1996. ("Beijing unveils trade reforms", *South China Morning Post International Weekly*, 25 Novermber 1995).

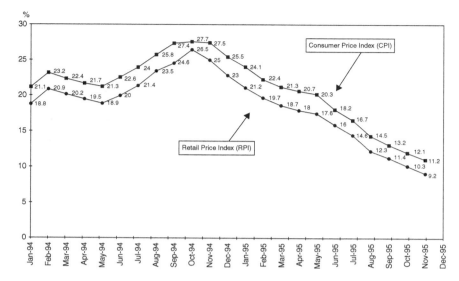

Figure 3.   China's Inflation 1994 and 1995 (Year-on-Year Changes of CPI and RPI).
Source: State Statistics Bureau of China.

sector in 1995 currently looked pretty robust, with its total foreign reserves reaching US$70 billion and the *Renminbi* basically stable.

Viewed from a different angle, Zhu Rongji's macroeconomic control program apparently worked well. The inflation rate in terms of RPI (retail price index) had been declining steadily from 21.2% for January to 9.2% for November so that the official target of reducing the annual rate of inflation for 1995 to 15% was within reach (Fig. 3). The growth of money supply, as expressed in the narrow definition of M1, also came down, from the average of 30% in the first quarter of 1995 to 18% during August–October.

The costs of macroeconomic adjustment have been uneven. High-growth coastal provinces like Zhejiang, Jiangsu, Guangdong, Fujian, and Hainan as well as some low-growth provinces in the interior were beginning to feel the pinch of the credit crunch. So were certain sectors and industries (e.g., housing and real estate development). In particular, macroeconomic adjustment had sharpened the pain of microeconomic inefficiencies in the economy. The case in point were the growing woes of state-owned enterprises (SOEs), many of which ran into deeper debt and were operating at half capacity. In all, 40% of SOEs were reported to be in the red in 1955, with their losses having increased by 20% Consequently, the government was under increasing pressure to relax its macroeconomic control.

Entering the Era of "Normal" Growth

The outlook for 1996 much depended on when the government would start loosening its macroeconomic control. But the government had already made it clear that its tight credit policy would last through 1996 for fear of reigniting the inflation.[3] Indeed, the latent inflationary pressures in Chinese economy remained strong: (i) despite the tightening of credit (which had slowed down industrial investment and production), consumer spending had remained high; (ii) personal and household savings continued to grow, posing a potential inflation threat; and (iii) despite better agricultural harvest in 1995, food prices continued to increase. And rising food prices were one of the basic causes for the high inflation in 1994.

With the macroeconomic austerity program set to continue, coupled with the anticipated weaker growth in exports and foreign investment, economic growth for 1996 was therefore likely to slow down to 8–9%, with inflation possibly down further to 10–12%. Such a lower but nonetheless respectable growth rate was actually close to what the Chinese economy could sustain over the longer run. In fact, the Ninth Five-Year Plan (started 1996) called for "stable and healthy growth" to realize China's long-term economic and social objectives.[4]

---

[3] At the "Central Economic Work Conference" held in Beijing on 5–7 December 1995, the emphasis was to "continue efforts to strengthen and improve macroeconomic control", so as to lay a stable economic environment for the long-term growth of the Chinese economy. ("The conclusion of the economic work conference, with restraining inflation to remain the priority task", *Ming Bao*, (Hong Kong, 8 December 1995).

[4] China's Ninth Five-Year Plan, 1996–2000, which was endorsed by the Fifth Party Plenum on 28 September 1995, has envisioned that China's real per-capita GDP by 2000 will quadruple from 1980 level, having generally eliminated basic poverty and being able to provide the people with basic needs. From 2000 to 2010, China will again double its per-capita income so as to become a moderately affluent middle-income (or *xiao kang*) country. See John Wong (1995). China's Ninth Five-Year Plan: Economic Agenda of the Fifth Party Plenum, *IEAPE Commentaries* No. 17.

With slower growth, 1996 marked the downward swing of China's fourth cycle since the start of economic reform in 1978. At that time, it was difficult to predict if the Chinese economy in a few years time would swing back to another economic upsurge. It is the slower and steady growth (not the heady, double-digit rate of growth), which is more approximate to the "normal" long-term growth of the Chinese economy. In any case, a stable growth in 1996 provided the government with the much needed breathing space to address the many structural shortcomings of the Chinese economy.

The Chinese government recognized that its most important (and also the toughest) unfinished reform agendas, such as the reform of SOEs and the financial sector reform, defied the "big bang" approach. Instead, they had to be tackled gradually as a long-term challenge. Certainly, the reform of SOEs could not be hastened; nor could it be effectively implemented prior to the social security reform. It was expected that a "normal" process of steady economic growth would thus allow the government to tackle the SOE reform problem at its own pace.[5]

Furthermore, the government also came to grips with the institutional problems of the Chinese economy. In 1995, China enacted a number of important economic legislations, including the central banking law, the commercial bank law, and the insurance law. In 1996, the securities law, the state assets law, the new bankruptcy law, the trust law, and others were tabled before the next session of the People's Congress.

With problems of inflation and economic overheating under control, the Chinese government was able to concentrate on improving the institutional conditions of China's economic growth. It was predicted that in this way, the overall business environment in China would also improve.

---

[5] For the reform of SOEs, the government emphasized the new strategy of *Zhua-da fang-xiao*, or to concentrate on the big SOEs by tacking their problems carefully while boldly let go on smaller SOEs.

Chapter 8

China's Ninth Five-Year Plan, 1996–2000

Introduction

China's Eighth Five-Year Plan, 1991–1995, that was presented along with the 10-Year Program by Premier Li Peng in the immediate aftermath of the Tiananmen at the 7th Party Plenum, had never been seriously followed up. Its major historical significance was the signal the leadership wanted to convey to the public that it was time for the top leadership to stop the endless debate over the path and direction of economic reform by returning to reform and development. Unfortunately, as already discussed in Chapter 3, the Eighth Five-Year Plan embodied reform strategies and policy orientation of the Conservative faction of the Party led by Chen Yun. Right from the beginning, Deng Xiaoping had a lot of misgivings with this approach. Consequently, this Plan was soon to become irrelevant once Deng forcefully put up his new reform strategies during his Nanxun.

Toward the end of 1995, it was time for China to plan for the Ninth Five-Year Plan, 1996–2000 and to make it the main agenda of the 5th Party Plenum. By this time, Deng's reform strategies were firmly in place, and the country was moving rapidly toward the "socialist market economy" that was endorsed by Deng. The economy was clearly booming, ending 1994 with an average growth rate of 12%, along with 12% inflation.

Instead of laying down a detailed plan, the 5th Plenum endorsed the broad economic and social objectives of China's "socialist modernization" under the Ninth Five-Year Plan and its Long-Term Vision for 2010. China would march into the 21st Century with a new "Vision". In concrete terms, China's real per-capital gross domestic product (GDP) by 2000 would quadruple from the 1980s level, or double and double again — fan-liang-fan. Furthermore, from 2000 to 2010, China would again double its per-capita GDP, so that China would develop into a xiao-kang (or moderately affluent) society in 15 years, having resolved the problem of basic needs for the common people. Deng had referred to the idea of xiao-kang many times before.

Looking back from today, what can we see from the score-board? China's per-capita GDP in 1980 was 463 yuan, and it rose to 7,858 yuan in 2000 or 17 times more, i.e., it had doubled again the "quadruple" (another fan-yi-fan). By 2010, China's per-capita GDP rose to 30,015 yuan, and that is four times from the 2000 level or 65 times from 1980, i.e., doubling the base year of 1980 five times.

Economic growth as increases in GDP works on compound interest principle. As China's economy grew at an average annual rate of 10% during these three decades of 1980–2010, the total GDP had doubled, doubled, and doubled again — in fact, about 90 times more. In the same period, as China had added 350 million populations, its per-capita GDP growth was smaller than total GDP growth. Viewed from any angle, China had over-achieved its long-term vision as first visualized in 1995.

This chapter was circulated on 2 October 1995. Apart from looking at the potential problems that Jiang Zemin would be facing in the run-up to the 21st century, it also provided a brief review of the previous Eighth Five-Year Plans. At that time, it was already clear that a Five-Year Plan provided only a rough indication of the leadership's long-term vision. It would have little useful operational relevance to the real economy. This is because as China's economy was increasingly marketized, it would also become increasingly "unplannable".

New Development Programs for 21st Century

The Fifth Plenum of the Fourteenth Central Committee of the Chinese Communist Party ended in Beijing on 28 September 1995 with a six-part "Decision" endorsing China's proposed new economic and social development program under the Ninth Five-Year Plan (FYP), 1996–2000, and the long-term vision for 2010. This marked the second phase of China's "socialist modernization" based on a new development strategy, and prepared China in its march into the 21st century.

According to the new "Vision", it was expected that China's *real* per-capita gross domestic product (GDP) by 2000 would quadruple from the

1980 level, despite the addition of over 300 million more population. China by then would have basically eliminated poverty, being able to provide for the basic needs of its people, or *xiao kang*. From 2000 to 2010, China would again double its per-capita income so that China in 15 years would develop into a moderately affluent middle-income country.

Economic Agenda to Predominate

In recent years, the Party Plenum had become an occasion for the Party to endorse a particular policy direction and then mobilize the whole Party to follow. Thus, the First Plenum was convened on 19 October 1992, immediately after the conclusion of the 14th National Party Congress, to formalize key Party appointments and high-level personnel changes. The Second Plenum on 5 March 1993 adopted the concept of "socialist market economy" for China. The Third Plenum on 11 November 1993 approved a comprehensive package of economic reform measures. The Fourth Plenum on 25 September 1994, however, focused on the politics of Party building and the urgent need to stem the decline of the Party.

Admittedly, the Fifth plenary session that marked the beginning of the post-Deng leadership transition had to tackle a myriad of internal and external problems. But still the Fifth Plenum set its focus on one dominant set of problems, i.e., the new pattern of economic and social development under the Ninth FYP. Once again, the thrust was on the economic agenda.

Most of the economic issues endorsed by the Fifth Plenum were actually known and openly discussed by China's economists before the session. The Chinese economy, having undergone reforms and changes for 16 years, had left behind a number of problematic areas that needed to be tidied up, especially in regard to the continuing need to reform state enterprises. At the same time, a new development strategy with greater emphasis on economic efficiency and reducing the economic disparity between the coastal region and the inland provinces had to be mapped out in order to lead China into the 21st century.

In coming to grips with many tough domestic problems at the Fifth Plenum like the expulsion of the Beijing Party chief Chen Xitong from the Politburo, General Secretary Jiang Zemin had apparently seized the opportunity to further consolidate his hold on power. His economic agenda was aimed to further project his image as a leader with a long vision, being concerned about China's *kua-shi-ji* (cross-century) development problems.

The Perils of China's Planning

Traditionally, a Five-year plan was regarded as a necessary accompaniment of a command-type socialist economy. For China, however, the merging of the main economic agenda of the Fifth Plenum into the blueprint of the Ninth FYP should not be construed as the Party's renewed blessing for the anachronistic central planning. Rather, it was obviously done as a matter of convenience because the Eighth FYP (1990–1995) came to an end and the Ninth FYP began in the following year.

Since the economic reform, particularly following the adoption of "socialist market economy" in 1993, China got rid of most of the elements of a centrally planned economy. With the prices of over 90% of the consumer goods and 85% of intermediate goods no longer fixed by the state but by market forces, the Chinese economy was substantially market driven. Indeed, 16 years of economic reform have grossly reduced the economic role of the government, so that by 1994, the share of government expenditure declined to 13% of GDP from 32% in 1979, and the proportion of industrial output from the state sector dropped to 38% from 73%. This alone would render any central planning ineffective and irrelevant for China.

As a matter of fact, China had never seriously of effectively taken to the Soviet-type central planning except for the short episode of its First FYP (1953–1957), which was imposed on China by Soviet experts together with Soviet economic aid. Though the First FYP was a great economic success, Mao had a strong dislike for the rigid Soviet-type of economic planning because of its implied over-centralization and growth of bureaucratism. In the event, Mao soon launched the Great Leap Forward movement, which superseded the Second FYP, 1958–1962.

As shown in Table 1, the subsequent three FYPs had never stood a chance because of continued political upheavals caused by the Cultural Revolution and its aftermath. The political and social conditions of China throughout the 1960s and the 1970s were really a nightmare for a central

Table 1. A chronology of China's past five-year plans and major events before 1980.

Plan Periods	Year	Major Events
Economic rehabilitation period	1949	Formation of the People's Republic
	1950	—
	1951	The Korean War
	1952	Land Reform
First Five-Year Plan Average growth: 8.9%	1953	—
	1954	Cooperativization
	1955	—
	1956	Collectivization
	1957	"Let Hundred Flowers Bloom"
Second Five-Year Plan (short-lived)	1958	Formation of People's Communes
	1959	Great Leap Forward
	1960	Sino-Soviet Ideological Disputes
	1961	Natural calamities (1959–1961)
	1962	Serious economic setback
Economic adjustment period	1963	—
	1964	—
	1965	—
Third Five-Year Plan (unpublished)	1966	The Cultural Revolution
	1967	—
	1968	Downfall of Liu Shaoqi and Deng Xiaoping
	1969	—
	1970	The Lin Biao Incident
Fourth Five-Year Plan (unpublished)	1971	China's admission into UN
	1972	Nixon's visit to Beijing
	1973	Large complete-plant imports
	1974	—
	1975	The Four Modernisations
Fifth Five-Year Plan — as part of the 10-Year Plan	1976	Downfall of the "Gang of Four"
	1977	Economic readjustment
	1978	Open-door policy adopted
	1979	Economic reform started
	1980	Emerging of new pragmatic leadership under Deng Xiaoping

planner. Even the State Statistical Bureau, the basic apparatus of central planning, was disbanded during the Cultural Revolution. Cynics can now argue that it was precisely because the Chinese economy under Mao even at its heyday of socialism was never so intricately planned (as in Eastern Europe), that it was therefore much easier for Deng Xiaoping' subsequently to undo its planned economic system.[1]

As it happened, China's orderly economic development returned only after 1979 when Deng Xiaoping resumed power and started economic reform and the open-door policy. The Sixth FYP, 1981–1985, (probably the brainchild of Chen Yun), was launched when the reform was concentrated on agriculture, yielding good results. The Seventh FYP, 1986–1990, was unleashed when the economic reform focus shifted to the much more complicated industrial sector in the urban areas, which eventually sparked off China's first runaway inflation since 1949. The Eighth FYP, 1991–1995, which was launched under a much subdued political atmosphere of the Tiananmen-aftermath, ended paradoxically in a spurt of double-digit hyper economic growth.

Figure 1 brings out the pattern of China's economic growth during 1981–1995, which covers the last three FYPs. It is clear that the Chinese economy since 1980 grew and fluctuated in several "reform cycles", responding to reform initiatives or other exogenous policy shocks which had nothing to do with a particular FYP. In other words, the pattern of economic growth since 1980 bore no relationship whatsoever to the planned objectives of the three FYPs spanning this period.

The superfluity or futility of the three FYPs was easily apparent by examining the Eighth FYP document as presented by Premier Li Peng in March 1991, against what had actually happened in China in 1995. Li Peng was then gingerly targeting the average economic growth for the Eighth FYP at 6% whereas it actually turned out to be 11.7%. Li Peng called for steel production to increase to 71 million tons in 1995 and automobile to 900,000 units; but by 1994, steel output was already 92 million tons and automobile, 1.4 million units. Of course, Li Peng at that time never did anticipate Deng Xiaoping's celebrated tour of South China in

---

[1]For a more detailed discussion of this subject, see John Wong, (1995). *China's Entrepreneurial Approach to Economic Reform,* IEAPE Internal Study Paper No. 8.

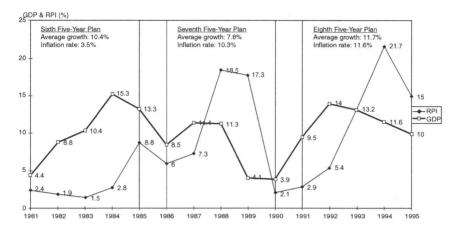

Figure 1.   Growth and Inflation in China (1981–1995).

Note: RPI, Retail Price Index; GDP : Gross Domestic Product.

the following year, which touched off a tremendous export and foreign investment boom for the past three years. And, of course, the very term of "socialist market economy" was then politically unmentionable.

It was therefore argued that the Ninth FYP would be equally superfluous and futile. The problem of uncertainty apart, the Chinese economy had grown increasingly "unplannable". At best, the Ninth FYP could serve only as a kind of "perspective plan" or as a rough indicator of government intention. It would not be useful to predict the year-to-year performance of the Chinese economy. It was predicted that the Ninth FYP may well be China's last FYP, as the future leadership from 2000 may not even wish to continue with such a ritual.

Problems Well Known, Solutions Uncertain

At that time, it was not possible to go into a detailed analysis of the Ninth FYP, as Beijing normally released the whole blueprint after it had been formally approved by the National People's Congress in 1996. However, as pointed out earlier, the main problems and issues covered by the Ninth FYP were already sufficiently well known. So were the key problems that plagued the Chinese economy in the short and medium run.

What is significant is that Chinese planners and technocrats, amidst their usual rhetoric, were realistic enough to recognize the crucial problems faced by the Chinese economy. Thus, the Ninth FYP called for the Chinese economy to sustain "rapid but *healthy*" growth. The Chinese economy, having experienced a long period of breakneck growth at the cost of high inflation, wide instability, low efficiency, and high wastage, was expected to trade off for a little lower growth with greater efficiency (or more productivity gains) and more stability. The Ninth FYP emphasize that in future it is not just the *rate* of economic growth, but also the *nature* or *pattern* of growth that has to be taken into account. This new development strategy is understandable.

Just how would China realize such new pattern of economic growth? China must strive to complete its unfinished business of economic reform. Here, Chinese planners have rightly emphasized the urgent need to accomplish the reform of state-owned enterprises (SOEs) — "taking the reform of SOEs as the central link in restructuring the economy". This was the most significant point in the action agenda of the Ninth FYP.

True enough, most of China's economic ills in 1995, from inflation and macroeconomic instability to its chronic fiscal deficits and fragile financial structure, were directly or indirectly traced to the lack of progress in the SOE reform. But the SOE problem goes beyond economic considerations. In 1995, it was politically infeasible for the government to carry out a radical reform of SOEs (which risked throwing out millions of redundant workers to the street) before an effective social security safety net was firmly in place.[2]

At that time, it was far from certain if the then leadership under Jiang Zemin had sufficient political will and the required political capacity to tackle head-on China's major economic problems, particularly the reform of SOEs. Some of the problems brought up by the Fifth Plenum were truly of *kua-shi-ji* nature, i.e., they might well drag on to the next century.

---

[2]For more detailed discussion of the SOE and other reform problems, see John Wong (1994). *What Has China Accomplished in Economic Reform in 1994?* IEAPE Background Brief No. 80.

Part III
Agricultural and Rural Development

Chapter 9

The Quiet Industrial Revolution in the Chinese Countryside: Township and Village Enterprises (TVEs)

Introduction

In the wake of the successful agricultural reform, 1979–1982, numerous small to medium collectively owned rural industries called *xiangzhen qiye* or township and village enterprises (TVEs) sprang up in rural China, providing non-farm employment to millions of surplus agricultural rural labor. The TVE phenomenon had no parallel in the former Soviet Union and Eastern European socialist countries: it actually represents a unique Chinese experience of bringing industrialization to the countryside during China's transition from central planning to market economy.

Nominally, most TVEs belonged to township and villages as "collectively owned enterprises", but they basically operated outside the state economic plan. Behaving much like conventional privately owned enterprises, TVEs had to bid for their raw materials from the non-state free markets; sell their products through competition; and pay their workers competitive wages, usually on piece-rates. Unlike the large state-owned enterprises (SOEs), most TVEs had to stay competitive to survive, i.e., they had to operate under "hard budget constraints". This is because if they were not efficient and ran into a financial trouble, their township governments would be too weak to bail them out. This explains why many TVEs were "dynamic" business enterprises in those days.

Although TVEs had their historical roots in Mao's development strategy of "walking on two legs" — i.e., the existence of both small and medium enterprises in the rural areas like numerous fertilizer plants run by the people's communes, along with the large SOEs in urban areas they started to thrive only in the 1980s, when economic reform and the open-door policy took hold. The market reform opened up a big demand for all kinds of consumer's and producer's goods that could not be sufficiently produced by SOEs while the nascent private sector was still very weak to take up the slack.

Thus, during 1978–1989, TVEs increased from 1.5 million units to 18.7 million, with their employment rising from 28.2 million to 93.7 million workers. In 1989, the total value output of TVEs exceeded that of agriculture. Furthermore, their rapid growth had posed a menace to the state sector, as they had continued to outgrow and outperform the SOEs.

Not surprisingly, some conservative leaders had come to fear TVEs as becoming ultimately a capitalist Trojan Horse in the countryside. But then, there was precious little that Beijing could do to stem the growth of TVEs at the time, which had already developed a viable symbiotic existence with local governments — TVEs were their main source of revenue as well as local employment.

Different TVEs from different localities had come up by successfully utilizing their local advantages and local characteristics. For instance, TVEs in southern Jiangsu (the so-called Sunan prototype) had successfully capitalized on their locational advantages by capturing the positive development spillovers from their nearby industrialized Shanghai and Wuxi. Similarly, the TVEs around Wenzhou city on the southeast coast of Zhejiang had developed with great entrepreneurial skills associated with this trading city. Many TVEs around Guangzhou had also developed by utilizing their overseas connections from Hong Kong and Macau.

This chapter was circulated in January 1992, shortly before Deng Xiaoping's Nanxun. At that time, TVEs were still growing, showing no signs of losing their dynamism. However, the growth of TVEs would soon peak in the early 1990s and then started to decline once the post-Nanxun marketization process took roots. With the Chinese economy becoming extensively marketized, there would be less room for the "collective sector" to grow and the TVEs had to evolve and transform accordingly. Many TVEs had grown up to become export-oriented and then incorporated or privatized. Some were dissolved or absorbed by SOEs.

Thus, by 2011, the number of collectively owned enterprises accounted for only 1.3% of all enterprise units in China, compared to 41% for the privately owned, 44% as share-holding companies, and 13.7% foreign owned. Though TVEs were rural industries, they were from the outset put under the administration of the Ministry of Agriculture. As industrialization and urbanization continued to grow had in hand, the rural sector itself had rapidly shrunk.

In 1990, 74% of the total population were still classified as "rural". By 2011, rural population had declined to 49%. In China as in the rest of the world, continuing urbanization is the future trend. Hence also the inevitable demise of the TVEs. But they had played an important role at the transitional stage of China's reform and development.

Rural Industry as a Star in Reform

China's successful rural reform has brought unprecedented economic benefits to millions of its peasants. Even more significantly, it had sparked off what amounts to a quiet Industrial Revolution in the Chinese countryside, with the mushrooming of numerous small- to medium-sized rural industries, officially known as Township and Village Enterprises (TVEs). Indeed, the surge of TVEs in recent years had rapidly transformed the economic and social life of Rural China and sowed the seed of incipient capitalism.

TVEs have been the main beneficiaries of China's economic reform. In 1978, on the eve of launching the reform, China had only 1.5 million TVEs with a total employment of 28.3 million workers and a total output value of Rmb 49.3 billion. By 1989, there were 18.7 million TVEs, providing employment to 93.4 million workers or about 17% of the national labor force; and producing Rmb 840 billion worth of output, or 38% of China's total gross industrial output. In fact, in 1989, the total value output of TVEs exceeded that of agriculture by a significant margin of 22%.[1]

TVEs have become the most vibrant sector of the Chinese economy. Between 1978 and 1989, the output of TVEs had grown at the average

---

[1] *Zhongguo nongye nianjian 1990* (The Agricultural Yearbook of China 1990), Beijing, 1991. According to a report, the total value output of TVEs for 1991 was expected to exceed Rmb 1,000 billion, which would be 20 times over the level of 1978. *Renmin Ribao* (People's Daily), 11 November 1991.

annual rate of 29.4%, as against the 16.2% for China's total gross indus-trial output.[2] In other words, it was the TVE sector which had actually constituted the major source of China's phenomenal economic growth over the last decade when the reform program was introduced.

Though the reform had also improved the average performance of the state sector, a great many of the state industries have remained in a bad shape or heavily strapped in debt.[3] So the real economic heroes of the reform decade have been the myriad of non-state TVEs across the Chinese countryside, particularly those in the coastal region, which have success-fully responded to new economic opportunities created by the reform and the open-door policy.

The reasons for the economic dynamism of TVEs are simple. As eco-nomic units existed below the *xian* (county) level, TVEs are basically non-state entities [though technically many TVEs are supposed to be col-lectively owned by the people in their respective village or *zhen* (sub-county or township)], which operated outside the state economic plan. This practically means that most TVEs have to function like a truly busi-ness enterprise. TVEs have to bid for their raw materials from the open market; they have to sell their products through market competition; and they have to mind the problem of work incentives by paying their workers on piece-rates. In simple economic parlance, most TVEs have to operate under "hard budget constraints" in accordance with the harsh rules of the market-place, including the rule of economic survival.

Not surprisingly, TVEs have been able to establish for themselves a niche in the half-reformed Chinese economy. The success in the agricul-tural reform had created widespread rural prosperity and hence a ready-made market for a wide variety of consumer goods, which the slow-moving state enterprises could not satisfy. Hence, many TVEs sprang up to fill the vacuum. In Guangdong, Fujian, and other coastal regions, TVEs took advantage of the open-door policy by joining up with foreign economic

---

[2] *ibid.* In 1990, the total output of TVEs still expanded by 16.2% over 1989 (as opposed to only 8.6% for the total gross industrial output) despite the severe retrenchment policy.

[3] For a good analysis of the problems of China's state enterprises and their remedies, see Goh Keng Swee (1991). Li Peng on China's State Enterprises, *IEAP Discussion Paper No. 14.*

interests for export processing — one-third of the larger TVEs were producing for exports and their foreign exchange earnings accounted for one-fourth of the national total.[4]

The rapid expansion of the TVE sector was understandably seen by the state sector as an encroachment on its own interests, if not a threat to its long-term existence. In 1978, the state sector accounted for 78% of China's total gross industrial output; but its share had since declined to 65% in 1985 and 55% in 1990. In the retail markets, the state sector in 1978 took up 55% of total retail sales; but its share declined to 40% in 1990.[5] The state sector was becoming economically irrelevant to the great rural masses. The conservatives in Beijing were particularly disturbed by such a sharp relative decline of the state sector.

There was, however, precious little that the central government could to stem the growth of TVEs. Beijing had learned the high economic and social costs of suppressing the growth of this sector in 1989.[6] Administratively, TVEs were within the purview of the Ministry of Agriculture while sate enterprises were directly under the jurisdiction of the State Economic Commission. Apart from the bureaucratic complications, there was also a conflict of interest between the central and local governments over TVE policies. Just as the state sector was the economic base of the central government, TVEs provided the main source of revenue for local governments. Not surprisingly, township governments were loath to carry out whole-heartedly any central government policy which may be detrimental to their own TVEs.

Analytically speaking, the growth of TVEs was but a natural consequence of China's overall economic development process. As productivity in agriculture grew, more farm labor was rendered redundant and had to be transferred for non-agricultural pursuits. Since the Chinese government had all along (quite rightly) restricted the movement of labor into its

---

[4] Township enterprises will keep their kick, *China Economic News* (Hong Kong, Vol. xii, No. 44, 18 November 1991).

[5] *Statistical Yearbook of China*, 1991, Beijing, p. 26.

[6] In 1989, as to be discussed later, Beijing applied a credit squeeze to deal with the rampant inflation nation-wide, and this led to the collapse of many TVEs, causing the rural unemployed to flock to the cities. Eventually, Beijing had to relent for the sake of maintaining rural stability.

already over-crowded urban centers, rural enterprises had to be set up to absorb the surplus agricultural labor. The development of TVEs can also be seen in the context of the unique Chinese experiment of bringing industrialization of the countryside.

Growth and Development

Rural industry is found in every developing country. But the Chinese TVEs bore the stamp of the three-level organization of the past people's commune era. "Township and Village Enterprise" (*Xiangzhen qiye*) is actually a generic term covering four types of rural industry in a township: they are the collectively owned enterprises belonging to the township (*zhen* or sometimes *xiang*, but formerly the commune) and to the village (*cun*, formerly the production brigade), the jointly owned partnerships formed by a few households (equivalent to the former production team), and privately owned individual enterprises (*geti-hu*). Most discussion of TVEs refers to the larger and more established township-run and village-run structures, even though these two categories constituted only 8.2% of the total number of TVEs in 1989.[7] (Table 1).

The history of TVEs in China can be traced back to the Great Leap Forward (1958–1960) when millions of peasants, after having been organized into communes, were mobilized to make steel in their backyard furnaces and to produce goods from small village workshops, in order to carry out Mao's development strategy of "walking on two legs", i.e., pursuing both modern industry in urban areas and the labor-intensive industry in rural areas. Though the Great Leap had turned out to be a disaster, the commune system continued, leaving behind a convenient organizational framework for the subsequent setting up of TVEs.[8] In fact, throughout the 1960s and the early 1970s, rural industry continued to grow. Mao, in particular, pushed for the development of the "five small industries" (cement, chemical fertilizer,

---

[7]The term *Xiangzhen qiye* came into being for frequent official use only after 1984. Previously, TVEs were referred to as *Shedui qiye* or "commune and brigade enterprises".
[8]The communes took over the townships. With about 20,000 population each, a commune is ideal for setting up a primitive from of self-reliant economy: it comprises agricultural, manufacturing and service activities.

Table 1. China's township and village enterprises, 1989.

	Total	%	Township	%	Village	%	Partnership	%	Private	%
No. of TVEs	18,686,282	100	405,677	2.2	1,129,988	6.0	1,069,411	5.7	16,081,206	86.1
Employment	93,667,793	100	23,835,675	25.4	23,365,691	25.0	8,837,475	9.4	37,628,952	40.2
Size: Average no. of workers for enterprise	5.0	—	58.8	—	20.7	—	8.3	—	2.3	—

Source: Zhongguo Nongye Nienjian 1990 (Agricultural Yearbook of China 1990), Beijing.

machinery, power, and iron and steel) in the rural areas as a key component of his overall self-reliant development strategy. There are two basic reasons as to why rural industry could expand in the 1960s: (i) in fear of the possible spread of the Vietnam War to China, Beijing took measures to decentralize its industrial bases and urged various localities to develop industry with their own resources in an effort to attain a higher level of local self-sufficiency; and (ii) in the late 1960s as urban industrial production was disrupted by the Cultural Revolution, the rural areas had to set up industries to produce for their own demand. By 1971, the rural industry produced 60% of the national nitrogen fertilizer and one-fifth of the national output of pig iron.[9]

But rural industry did not *thrive* in the Mao period, in part due to the unfavorable political and ideological climate of the time and in part because many rural enterprises were primarily formed on unsound economic rationale. There were numerous examples of localities pushing the self-reliant model to the extreme by setting up production without due regard to costs and prices or availability of raw materials.[10] Thus, many rural enterprises were later scrapped once the basic ideological premises of self-reliance was removed under economic reform.[11]

The 3rd Plenum of the 11th Central Committee of the Chinese Communist Party in December 1978, which formalized Deng Xiaoping's rural reform program, marked the watershed for the development of the "new generation" rural enterprises. First, the introduction of household production responsibility system (*baochan daohu*) led to a substantial increase in agricultural productivity, which in turn released more surplus farm labor for non-agricultural activities. Second, higher agricultural output was eventually translated into higher disposable income and higher

---

[9] See Carl Riskin, (1978). China's rural industry: Self-reliant systems or independent Kingdom, *China Quarterly*, (73) London.

[10] See Christine Pui Wah Wong, (1982). Rural industrialization in the People's Republic of China: Lessons from the Cultural Revolution decade, In *US Congress Joint Economic Committee*, China Under the Four Modernizations, Part 1. Washington: US Govt. Printing Office.

[11] It was reported that 20,000 communes and 85,000 brigade enterprises were closed in 1981, with the loss of 500,000 jobs. See Christine P. W. Wong (1988). Interpreting rural industrial growth in the Post-Mao period, *Modern China*, 14 (1).

purchasing power for peasants. Hence a greater demand for a wide range of consumer products to be manufactured by TVEs.

More specifically, the government had also introduced a number of measures to promote TVEs: (i) The government dismantled the communes and removed the Maoist restrictions on non-agricultural activities. This led to the growth of rural markets for agricultural sidelines and other business ventures. (ii) To boost its rural reform results, the government raised the procurement prices of agricultural products during 1980–1984. Technically, this means turning the terms of trade in favor of agriculture, which amounted to the transfer of industrial surplus for rural industrial capital formation. (iii) Starting in 1981, the government granted a three-year tax holiday as an incentive to all new TVEs.

Of equal importance is the fact that once the economic reform and open-door policy took hold, township governments were no longer ideologically inhibited from mounting profit-oriented industrial and business activities. Thus, new types of market-oriented TVEs were set up or old TVEs restructured and reorganized. In 1984, the State Council Document No. 4 regularized or formalized the political status of TVEs, making it easier for them to get bank loans for their expansion.[12] In 1985, the State Science and Technology Commission launched the "Spark Programme" to facilitate technological diffusion to TVEs.[13] Spurred by easy bank credit and the generally favorable political and economic environment, TVEs thus experienced rapid growth from 1985 onward.

---

[12]The loans extended to TVEs amounted to Rmb 35.3 billion for 1985, 55.4 billion for 1986, 70.8 billion for 1987, 86.7 billion for 1988, and 99.6 billion for 1989. See *1990 Zhongguo jinrong nianjian* (Almanac of China's Finance and Banking, 1990), Beijing, 1990, p. 47.

[13]The main objective of the Spark Programme was to promote the transfer of more advanced technological and managerial knowledge from China's "modern" sector, which included the research institutes and the large state-owned enterprises. The first objectives of the Programme were to train one million young peasants, to establish 500 model TVEs, and to develop 100 sets of equipment suitable for TVEs by 1990. The plan was fulfilled in two years. (*China Today*, No. 12, December, 1991). According to the World Bank, the Programme has made some impact on TVEs but its total effectiveness in real terms is difficult to ascertain. Admittedly any diffusion of technology on such a large scale is not easy: it depends also on adequate finance, training, and organization support.

Table 2.   Growth of township and village enterprises 1978–1990.

	1978	1980	1985	1988	1989	1990
No. of TVEs (1,000)	1,524	1,425	12,225	18,882	18,686	18,850
Employment (1,000)	28,266	29,997	69,790	95,455	93,668	92,648
As % of total rural labor force	9.5	9.4	18.8	23.8	22.9	—
As % of national labor force	7.0	7.1	14.0	17.6	16.9	16.3
Total output value (Rmb billion)	49.3	67.0	275.3	701.8	840.3	(846.1)
As % of national gross social product	7.2	7.8	16.6	23.5	24.3	(22.3)
As % of total rural gross social product	24.2	24.0	43.4	58.1	58.0	—

Note: Data on TVEs before 1985 are not, strictly speaking, comparable to those after 1985.
Sources: *Zhongguo Nongye Nianjian 1990* (Beijing, 1990); and for 1990, *1991 Statistical Yearbook of China* (Beijing 1991).

As can be seen from Table 2, the growth of TVEs from 1978 to 1988 exploded in numbers, mainly due to the inclusion of numerous small individually owned enterprises. Total employment by TVEs increased from 28.3 million in 1978 to 95.5 million in 1988, and output value from Rmb 49.3 billion to Rmb 701.8 billion. From late 1988 to late 1990, however, TVEs became the main target of economic retrenchment. To squeeze the rampant inflation, the government applied a severe credit crunch, leading to the closure of two million TVEs and widespread job losses. During the retrenchment period 1988–1990, the total number of TVEs in 1989 dropped 1% from 1988, but increased again in 1990 by 0.9%. In terms of employment, the retrenchment led to a loss of 1.8 million jobs in 1989, and a further 1.0 million in 1990. But their total output had not declined: it increased to Rmb 840 billion in 1989 from Rmb 702 billion in 1988. This implies that the credit crunch had less effect on the larger and better organized ones. In any case, it is precisely because TVEs can be easily set up and closed down that the yearly statistical aggregates cannot explain the exact impact of the retrenchment. The mortality rate of TVEs in a particular month or season could be much higher than that shown in the yearly figures. As the unemployed rural workers drifted to the cities, Beijing was forced to soften its anti-TVE retrenchment policy for fear of social unrest. This shift of policy in 1990 was clearly evident in the numerous speeches and national conferences, which started to stress the positive role of TVEs.[14]

As the Chinese economy rebounded toward the end of 1990, the TVE sector also resumed dynamic growth. In the first 10 months of 1991, this sector was reported to have registered a record growth of 20%, as against the 14% growth for total gross industrial output in the same period.[15] The Ministry of Agriculture had set an annual growth target of 11% for TVEs during the Eighth Five-Year Plan, 1991–1995. Clearly, this is an unrealistically low target for this dynamic sector.

Structure, Conduct, and Performance

TVEs, by their very diverse nature, are apt to give rise to a great deal of variation in terms of structure and performance. Furthermore, since TVEs are closely tied to specific rural communities, the conduct and performance of TVEs depend crucially on such variables as the level of economic development of their home-based rural communities as well as the degree of their natural and human resource endowment. Besides, the location factor is another important determinant.

Chinese scholars, mindful of the great diversity of TVEs in their vast country, have wisely approached the subject by selecting a number of prototype-TVEs from special localities as "models" for detailed analysis:

— *Su-nan Model*: This covers TVEs in the historically highly industrialized southern Jiangsu. Typically large and well-managed, TVEs here

---

[14]Li Peng, after paying a visit to southern Jiangsu, where many highly successful TVEs can be found, admitted that "insufficient emphasis has been laid on rural industry". Old guards like Bo Yibo were reported to be lobbying on behalf of the TVE interest group. See David Zweg, (1991). Rural industry: Constraining the leading growth sector in China's economy. In *US Congress Joint Economic Committee.* China's Economic Dilemmas in the 1990s. The Problems of Reforms, Modernization, and Interdependence, Washington, DC: US Govt. Printing Office. Vol. 1, p. 422.

[15]Rural firms grow 20% — with more to come", *China Daily*, Beijing, 20 November, 1991.

were started by business-minded township governments and then expanded with retained profits. They undoubtedly owned much of their success to their easy access to skills, technology, and markets from nearby industrialized Shanghai and Wuxi.[16]

— *Wenzhou Model*: Equally well-known are the TVEs from Wenzhou, which is a small trading city on the southeast coast of Zhejiang province. TVEs in this area were started by individual peasants as private enterprises, partnerships, or even joint-stock companies, with the township governments having played little role in their initial formation. Many TVEs raised their capital through a rudimentary financial market. TVEs have been successful here mainly because they were run much like business enterprises in an overall environment shaped by a strong commercial tradition.

Other special TVEs, which have received wide attention, include the *Gengche Model* in the low-income region of Northern Jiangsu with little start-up capital and no easy access to any urban center. Both township governments and individual peasants struggled to pool their collective and private resources and started their TVEs in a rather hard way. Then there are outward-oriented prototypes such as the *Jinjiang Model* in eastern Fujian and the *Zhujiang Model* in the Pearl River Delta region of Guangdong. Some TVEs in these two places were started by issuing shares to overseas Chinese and some by entering into various forms of joint venture arrangements (e.g., *Sanlai yibu*) with foreign partners for export processing.[17]

---

[16] For a good discussion of various TVE models in Chinese, see Chen Jiyuan (ed.) (1988). *Xiangzhen qiye moshi yenjiu* (A Study of Township and Village Enterprise Models), Beijing: Chinese Social Sciences Publishers. Specifically for the Su-nan model, see Tao Youzhi (ed.) (1988). *Sunan moshi yu zhifu zhidao* (Su-nan Model and the Road to Wealth), Shanghai Social Sciences Publisher. For a brief account in English of the TVE models, see Dong Fureng (1988). *Rural Reform, Nonfarm Development, and Rural Modernization in China,* Economic Development Institute of the World Bank, No. 38. Also, "Lesson from Sunan", *Far Eastern Economic Review* (4 June, 1987).

[17] For a more detailed discussion of the joint venture activities in Guangdong, see John Wong (1991). "Economic Integration of Hong Kong and Guangdong: Hong Kong's 'Outward Processing' in China", *IEAP Internal Study Paper* No. 2.

The World Bank in 1986–1987 in collaboration with the Chinese Academy of Social Sciences undertook a comprehensive study of TVEs in four selected counties, each representative of a particular pattern of TVE development. Thus Wuxi in Jiangsu is supposed to represent TVEs from a well-off industrialized region; Nanhai in Guangdong from the "opened" economic region; Jieshou in Anhui from the region of average level of development; and Shangrao in Jiangzi from the below-average region.[18] The World Bank findings provide as yet the best comparative analysis of the microeconomic behavior of TVEs in China up to 1987.[19]

The most salient feature of TVEs is their close links with specific rural townships, with the supply of capital, labor, and entrepreneurship predominantly local in origin. Local factors like appropriateness of township government policies or quality of township and village leadership are therefore crucial for the success of TVEs. This is one of the important themes brought out by the World Bank study.

Viewed from a different angle, the close symbiotic existence between township governments and their TVEs gives rise to limited factor mobility. Capital and labor were supposed to be tied down to specific TVEs. This rigidity clearly hampers the efficient operation of TVEs in regard to important decisions like investment and technological development, and can hinder the long-term growth of successful TVEs. It may also make it difficult for future TVE relocation or TVE merger. But it remains to be seen if such nominal barriers against factor mobility would in future effectively constrain the expansion of dynamic TVEs.

TVEs, being outside the planned state sector, can be fertile ground for entrepreneurship to thrive. The World Bank study illustrates this point with vivid examples of how enterprising township officials acquired the knowledge and production technology to start up their TVEs. On

---

[18] The report was published in a book: William A. Byrd and Lin Qingsong (eds.) (1990). *China's Rural Industry: Structure, Development, and Reform*, Oxford/New York: Oxford University Press for the World Bank.

[19] On 4 January 1991, the World Bank prepared an unpublished follow-up report on its 1986–1987 study: "China: Rural Enterprise, Rural Industry, 1986–90" (Country Operations Division, China Department, Asia Region).

internal operations and performance, most TVEs were observed to be comparatively efficient. Being smaller and more labor intensive, TVEs have higher capital productivity than the large state-owned enterprises. But the latter, being more capital intensive (or more fixed assets per worker), generally have higher labor productivity in aggregate terms. Furthermore, the more developed TVEs like those in Wuxi and Nanhai and tend to have lower capital productivity as they have gone into capital–labor substitution.

TVEs have avoided the "Iron Rice Bowl" syndrome so characteristic of the state enterprises. Most TVEs pay their workers on piece rates so that wages are directly linked to individual and enterprise performance. Labor relations in TVEs are usually good. Suffice it to say that many of the World Bank observations on the behavior of TVEs come as no surprise, given the ways in which TVEs operate.

The World Bank study has not focused very much on the shortcomings of the TVE sector. Critics of TVEs are ready to point out their many negative aspects: wasteful investment, shoddy products, high energy consumption, high pollution, low labor productivity, frequent tax evasion, and so on. Small industry everywhere has its inherent structural weaknesses, and TVEs in China are no exception. Under the market system, the weak ones are constantly weeded out, and hence the generally high mortality rate of small industry. In China the troubled TVEs, in theory, could find shelter in their local communities. But on balance, the law of the market still applies as a township is often too small to have sufficient resources to bail out a large ailing TVE.

The Challenge for TVEs in the 1990s

The various reforms in the 1980s had created a favorable preconditon for the dynamic growth of TVEs. Such a relatively easy "honeymoon" period for their initial growth was over, and the next phase of expansion for TVEs in the 1990s was widely expected to be more difficult. They had to overcome new and greater constraints. Their inherent structural short-comings became more apparent as TVEs became more mature or grew bigger. They had to come to grips with many structural problems internal to TVEs: weakness in the management structure, lack of technical progress, lack of trained manpower, lack of ancillary services, lack of formalized relations with the township government, lack of clear-cut property rights, and so on. Viewed from the opposite angle, such a less conducive evolving environment would result in the rise of more competitive TVEs in future.

As for the external constraints, the most crucial was for TVEs to sort out their potential "contradiction" with the agricultural sector. For many TVEs (except for those export-oriented TVEs in the coastal region), their rate of growth was conditioned by the rate of growth of agricultural productivity. TVEs could not continue to expand without rising agricultural surplus. This called for a kind of "balanced" intersectoral relationship between TVEs and the agricultural component of the township economy. Take the development of the non-export type of TVEs, the township is like a mini-economy for the operation of the famous dualistic Lewis-Ranis-Fei model, which depicts economic development as a process of transferring agricultural surplus in the traditional (rural) sector for industrial development in the modern (urban) sector. The Industrial Revolution of England and the development experience of Japan seem to bear out the working of his model; but for many LDCs, the same process of development had given rise to the urban-biased development pattern. The development of TVEs in China, in bringing industry to the rural areas (or industrialization within the traditional sector), had actually provided an important corollary to this two-sector model: instead of dualistic development for the *whole economy*, the Chinese experience showed dualistic development within the rural sector, thus avoiding the problem of urban-biased development. But, however, the model is viewed to operate, its implications stay: agriculture, while carrying the main burden of development in the initial phase of industrialization, cannot be squeezed all the time.

Some Chinese economists have argued that since agricultural surplus had been skimmed off to help develop TVEs in the initial phase (*Chou-nong bu-gong*), the reverse should be the case for the second phase, with industrial surplus being mobilized to aid agriculture (*Yi-gong bu-nong*). This means that township governments should use some of the tax revenue from TVEs to invest in agricultural infrastructure.[20] A strong agriculture would ensure the stable development of TVEs.[21]

From all indications, TVEs continued to outgrow and outperform the state sector in the 1990s, even though TVEs have not been competing with the state industry in a "level playing field". In the past, the expansion of the TVE sector meant the weakening of the state sector and hence a dilution of the socialist economy. Conservative leaders have accordingly come to fear that TVEs may ultimately be a capitalist Trojan Horse. But the future need not be a zero sum game situation whereby the growth of one is inevitably at the expense of the other. Liberals accordingly take the positive view that the dynamism of TVEs can act as a source of pressure for the state sector to step up reform and improve its own efficiency.

In the short run, TVEs can play a useful role in stimulating the state sector to revive itself. In the longer run, the development of TVEs obviously would represent a viable path for industrializing the Chinese countryside. And rural industrialization is the only hope for realizing the government's objective of lifting the standard of living of the rural masses.

---

[20] See, e.g., He Jiacheng, "TVE Development Problems and Policy Options", in the Chinese version of the World Bank study published by Economics Science Press, (Beijing, 1989). Also, Zhao Jianguo, *et al.*, *Zhongguo xiangzhen qiye de shijian lilun fazhan* (The Practice, Theory and Development of China's Township and Village Enterprises), Beijing, 1988.

[21] In Jiangsu, where many successful TVEs are found, rural industry had actually provided substantial subsidies to agriculture. In fact, investment and transfer payments from TVEs to peasants during 1978–1986 have greatly exceeded the total state investment in the province. "Lesson from Sunan", *Far Eastern Economic Review* (4 June, 1987), p. 79. The Chinese leadership was getting concerned over the adverse effect of the development of TVEs on agricultural production. There were frequent reports of TVEs drawing away the young and the best educated from the villages for industrial employment in the townships, leaving behind mainly women and old people to tend the farm. This might be one of the reasons behind Beijing's recent re-emphasis of rural development in the Central Committee meeting of the Communist Party in 1991. "Party decision stresses solid rural development", *China Daily* (2 December 1991).

Chapter 10

Why Deng was so Concerned About Agriculture

Introduction

In 1995, as the new market reform initiatives in the urban areas, sparked off by Deng Xiaoping's nanxun, were building up momentum and the industrial sector was booming, China's top leaders turned their attention to problems in the agricultural sector. One after another from Jiang Zemin, Li Peng, and Jiang Chunyun (Vice-Premier in charge of agriculture), made strong statements stressing the fundamental importance of agriculture in China's economy. They all called for concerted efforts to boost grain production.

Deng's warning was even more serious and ominous, as he was reported to have cautioned the top leaders that: "Should China encounter problems in the 1990s, it would happen in agriculture". Mao used to assert that "agriculture is the foundation of the Chinese economy, with grain as the key link in agricultural development" — *yi-nong wei-ben, yi-liang wei-gang*. Deng and other senior leaders who had worked with Mao, had all shared Mao's strong "peasant mentality".

Even Deng's successors like Jiang Zemin and Li Peng, who had lived through the serious food crisis of the Great Leap Forward period (1979–1982) had acute sensitivity toward problems of agricultural development and food production. In 1994, the primary sector (agriculture, fishery, husbandry, and forestry) still accounted for 20% of the nation's gross domestic product (GDP), as compared to 10% in 2011. In terms of labor force, 54% (35% in 2011) came from the primary sector. In terms of population distribution, 71% of the total population in 1994 were classified as rural, as compared to 49% in 2011. Thus, the rural sector was still politically, economically, and socially highly important, after decades of industrialization and urbanization.

But there were other problems that brought the issue of agriculture to the fore. To begin with, grain production in the early 1990s had been growing slowly, with percapita grain output actually declining for many years since 1990. Total gain output for 1994 dropped by 2.6%.

This prompted the famous American agronomist Lester Brown to sound an alarm that China was "starting to lose the capacity to feed itself". This highly publicized statement from Brown was actually made on the basis of sound socio-economic arguments. China's population in those days were still growing at fairly high rates, at around 1.1% a year (as compared to 0.5% in recent years), despite the introduction on the one-child policy. This, coupled with increasing consumption of meat and other protein foods (which required more grain and feed) along with the increasing loss of croplands to non-farming uses, would inevitably put high pressures of China's food production capacity. Indeed, China at that time experienced double-digit rates of inflation (24% in 1994), and rising food prices were a major cause of inflation. Hence, real official concern over the state of agriculture.

In response, the government had to publicly refute Brown's warning as too alarmist on the ground that bad weather was the main cause of the decline in the 1994 grain production. At the same time, the government also took some remedy measures to boost grain production. Apart from shrinking sown area and low agricultural productivity, the distribution system was a major problem. For years, the government kept on paying farmers "white slips" as IOUs from the Agricultural Bank in procuring the agricultural products at subsidized prices from the farmers; but this had created bad incentives for farmers to produce more and sell more to the state. So, the government had to overhaul this distribution system. In fact, Zhu Rongji had subsequently spent a lot of effort trying to work out a better procurement system without much success, as it was hard to satisfy the producer, the consumer, and the middle-man all at the same time. Eventually, the grain market had to be marketized.

The government's jitters about agriculture were initially caused by a small decline in grain production. But some aspects of rural or agricultural problems had since constantly cropped up. Almost in every year, the No. 1 Central Document was issued about agriculture and rural development. In the 1990s, the focus was mainly on maintaining the stability of agricultural production and distribution.

Underlying the government's continuing concern about agriculture was the fundamental policy dilemma of what to do with the diminishing economic and social role of agriculture in a rapidly industrializing economy. Agriculture will eventually have to yield to industrialization and urbanization. Through the 2000s, the political and social discourse on agriculture and rural problems was no longer about production and distribution, but in a broader context of san-nong: agriculture, the village and the rural population.

China Unable to Feed Itself?

China's total grain output in 1994 was 444.6 million tons, down 12 million tons (enough to feed about 30 million population) from the historical peak of 456.4 million tons for 1993. The 1994 production dip represented only a 2.6% shortfall from the 1993 level and actually stayed within the acceptable range of normal year-to-year fluctuation. Yet it had created a great political fuss from the top leadership.

Agriculture, along with inflation and corruption, suddenly became a hotly debated topic in the 1995 session of the National People's Congress, with delegates from the food-deficient provinces like Gansu, Jilin, Jiangxi, and Guangxi demanding the government to review its 1995 agricultural policy.[1] Jiang Zemin, Li Peng, Qiao Shi, and Jiang Chunyun (the Vice Premier in charge of agriculture at that time) all had made strong statements to stress agriculture as the backbone of the Chinese economy.[2] Was China facing an agricultural crisis or were the

---

[1] Rethink on farming demanded, *South China Morning Post* (Hong Kong, 13 March 1995); and Crops vs concrete crisis raises voices of concern, *China Daily: Business Weekly* (Beijing, 19–25 March 1995).

[2] In his address to the closing session of the annual national work conference on agriculture in late February 1995, President Jiang Zemin called on government and Party officials to pay their "utmost attention to agriculture and rural development". (Agriculture called top issue, *China Daily*, 28 February 1995.)

Premier Li Peng, in his Report on the Work of the Government to the 13th Session of the 8th National People's Congress on 5 March 1995, also singled out curbing inflation, increasing agricultural production, and reforming state-owned enterprises as three top priorities for 1995. (Li Peng's Report on the Work of the Government, *Beijing Review* 27 March–2 April 1995.)

top leaders just reiterating their usual rhetoric? What was the background to this?

During the past few months in 1995, problems of food and agriculture have been frequently headlined in China's media. These were then picked up by some foreign press as through a real food crisis in China was in the offing.[3] Confusion was further compounded by the public's general inability to separate the long-term problem of "food and population balance" (more a technological issue) from the short-term problem of production shortfall (more an economic policy issue). Back in September 1994, American agronomist-cum-environmentalist Lester Brown of the World Watch Institute first sounded the alarm that China was "starting to lose the capacity to feed itself" on account of its growing population, higher consumption of meat due to rising incomes, and increasing loss of croplands for non-agricultural uses — Brown's scenario is clearly reflected in Fig. 1.[4]

Brown's gloomy prediction for China could not have come at a worse time when the Chinese government announced at the end of 1994 that

---

Chairman of the National People's Congress Qiao Shi warned that agricultural development "held the key to China's entire reform programme this year." (China's top leaders underline agriculture as key to reforms, *Business Times,* Singapore, March 9, 1995.)

Jiang Chunyun, the new Politburo member in charge of agriculture, pointed out at the National Agricultural Conference in February 1995 that agriculture had become the "weak point in our national economy" and vowed to increase investment in agriculture and mobilize farmers' enthusiasm or production. (Farming gets new priority, *China Daily*, 25 February 1995.)

[3] See, e.g., "China Grain Crisis Seen Worsening", *International Herald Tribune* (Singapore, 20 March 1995); "Beijing facing agricultural crisis", *Straits Times* (Singapore, 9 February 1995); and "Chinese Communist Government is Deeply Vexed by the Agricultural Problem", *Xinbao* (Hong Kong Economic Journal, Hong Kong, 6 January 1995). The cover story of the *Newsweek*, 15 May 1995): "The Bad Earth — China's Looming Grain Crisis".

Officially, the Chinese government had never referred to any "agricultural crisis": it had merely admitted the existence of "an agricultural problem".

[4] Brown argued that with China's population growing by 14 million a year and increasing meat consumption amidst the rapid shrinkage of croplands, China by 2030 could face a grain shortfall of 384 million tons or at least 263 million, which would exceed the world's entire grain exports of about 200 million tons in 1993. Lester R. Brown (1994). Question for 2030: Who will be able to feed China? *International Herald Tribune and When China's Scarcities Become the World's Problem, ibid.*

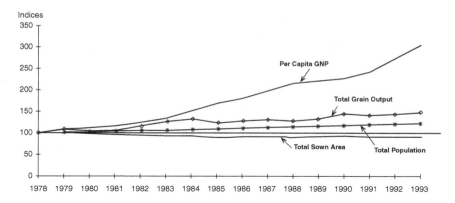

Figure 1. China: Grain output, sown area, population, and economic growth.

China's total population had reached 1.2 billion, a target that was originally projected for the year 2000. To add another omen, 1994 was a bad year for agricultural production due to bad weather. Grain harvests in several provinces, especially in southern China, plummeted, with regional shortages reported in several localities.[5] Not surprisingly, Brown's prediction received attention even within China.

A number of Chinese agronomists in Beijing have since refuted Brown's alarmist conclusion on the ground that his premises were wrong and data inadequate.[6] More significantly, Vice Premier Jiang Chunyun,

---

In early February 1995, as China's poor 1994 harvest was known, Brown repeated his arguments in another paper entitled "Who Is Going to Feed the Chinese", delivered at a high-powered international roundtable in Norway.

[5] Grain shortages were reported around the Lunar New Year in parts of Guangxi, southern Guizhou and Yunnan, central Henan and Sichuan, and western Shaanxi. The Ministry of Civil Affairs had to set aside a record 600 million yuan as special relief funds for those rural areas threatened by food shortages and soaring grain prices. ("Beijing sets aside record 600m-yuan famine relief fund", *Business Times,* Singapore, 29 March 1995.) Also, "New year's grain jitters", *China Trade Report* (Hong Kong, February 1995.)

[6] Both Dun Runsheng and Hu Angang rejected Brown's prediction on grounds of wrong statistics and wrong calculation, and asserted that China would pose no threat to future global food supply. ("Expert says China can feed itself", *China Daily,* 25 March 1995; and "China Poses No Threat To Future Global Food Supplies", *Beijing Review,* Beijing, 30 January–5 February 1995.)

China's "grain czar", came out openly to dispel public fears by saying that the unwarranted prediction by the "foreign agronomist" should "keep us on the alert but it does not mean that China's development has no hope". Jiang was confident that with the application of new technology and the reclamation of new land, China could still increase grain output by 50%.[7] If China was not worried over its capacity to feed itself, what then was the official concern on agriculture really about?

The official anxiety over agriculture could be traced to the drop in the foodgrain output in 1994, which in turn sparked off a sharp rise in foodgrain prices, fueling inflation, and heightening the official worry over possible social disorder. It was largely political and social in nature; and it was about inappropriate agricultural policy in the short run rather than the technological question of long-term food–population imbalance as construed by Lester Brown.

Underlying the government's jitters about agriculture was its fundamental policy dilemma of what to do with the diminishing economic role of agriculture, which nonetheless remained socially and politically important. The share of agriculture in China's Net Material Product declined from 36% in 1980 to 25% in 1993. In international trade, agriculture was also rapidly losing its comparative advantage to labor-intensive manufactures. In 1980, primary products constituted 50.3% of China's total exports; but the proportion fell to 18.1% in 1993.

Despite such a decline, agriculture in 1993 employed 56% of the total labor force. In 1993, 72% of the total population was classified as "rural". Hence, its social importance amidst its declining economic role.[8]

But the most interesting refutation came from Professor Zhou Guanzhao, President of the Chinese Academy of Sciences at that time, who complained that Brown's study had quoted him out of context. Zhou said he told Brown that China would have to import 400 million tons of grain in the next century *if* other parts of China also left huge tracts of fertile land idle or for conversion into industrial uses as in some of the booming coastal provinces. Zhou believed that it was still possible for China to become self-sufficient in grain during the next one to two decades by increasing per-unit grain yield by 20–30% through technological progress. ("Concerted efforts can gain more grain", *China Daily*, 16 March 1995.)

[7] "New man allays food supply fears", *China Daily* (16, March 1995).

[8] *1994 Statistical Yearbook of China.*

Since 1994, agriculture increasingly looked like a loser in economic reform, with the real incomes of peasants consistently lagging behind those of urban dwellers. The 1994 grain production setback and its resultant price hike provided further manifestation of the government's neglect of agriculture. Mounting peasant discontent was one of the several top priority areas which Jiang Zemin was expected to address in the post-Deng era.

The Politics and Economics of Grain Production

For a big country like China having 22% of the world's total population supported by only 7% of the world's cultivated land, grain production is always a business of precarious balance between deficit and sufficiency. Grain production has historically been one of the most important barometers of China's economic and social stability.[9] Mao Zedong used to assert that "agriculture was the foundation of the Chinese economy, with grain as the key link in agricultural development" — (*yi-nong wei-ben, yi-liang wei-gang*). Mao's assertion served to reflect the deep-seated "peasant mentality" of not just Mao's generation of Communist old guards, but also China's rulers through the centuries, whose "Mandate from Heaven" would be immediately withdrawn once they had failed to feed China's teeming millions. Thus, all Chinese rulers, past and present, took the following political motto seriously to heart: (*Wu-nong bu-wen, wu-liang ze-luan*) — "Without a strong agriculture, there will be no stability; without sufficient grain, there will be chaos".

Deng Xiaoping was no less pro-agriculture. He started his economic reform program first with rural reforms, with spectacular success. As can be seen from Table 1, total grain production increased by a hefty 50% from 305 million tons in 1978 to 446 million tons in 1990.[10] Since 1984,

---

[9] The Chinese statistical system adopted a broad definition of grain. Apart from such cereals as rice, wheat, and a variety of coarse grains like corn, barley, and sorghum, it also included soybeans and tubers. In 1993, 75% of the total sown area were devoted to food crops, with the three crops of rice, wheat, and corn in turn taking up more than 75% of the total sown area for food crops.

[10] For a further discussion of China's grain production situation since 1949, see John Wong (1992). Implications of the growth trends in Mainland China's grain production. *Issues & Studies,* 28(1).

Table 1. China's Grain Production 1978–1994.

	A Population (Million)	B Sown Area for Grain (Million ha)	C Total Grain Output (Million tons)	D Per-Capita Grain, C/A (kg per person)	E Unit Yield C/B (kg per ha)	F GNP per Capita (Yuan)
1952	575	123.9	163.9	285	1323	104
1965	725	119.6	194.5	268	1625	194
1978	963	120.6	304.8	317	2527	375
1979	975	119.3	332.1	341	2784	413
1980	987	117.2	320.6	325	2735	456
1981	1,000	114.9	325.0	325	2829	480
1982	1,016	113.4	354.5	349	3126	515
1983	1,030	114.0	387.3	376	3397	568
1984	1,043	112.9	407.3	391	3608	671
1985	1,059	108.8	379.1	358	3484	814
1986	1,075	110.9	391.5	364	3530	909
1987	1,093	111.3	402.9	369	3620	1042
1988	1,110	110.1	394.1	355	3579	1277
1989	1,127	112.2	407.6	362	3633	1430
1990	1,143	113.5	446.2	390	3931	1559
1991	1,158	112.3	435.3	376	3876	1758
1992	1,172	110.6	442.7	378	4003	2093
1993	1,185	110.5	456.4	385	4130	2663
1994	1,200	109.3	444.6	375	4068	—

Source: Statistical Yearbook of China 1994.

agriculture took a backseat as Deng's major attention was focused on industrial and financial reforms in the urban sector. After 1990, however, as production became stagnant, agriculture was back in the limelight, with the government holding an annual national agricultural conference to be attended by top government leaders.

In 1993, as the peasant grievances were boiling to a new high due to the government's procurement of agricultural products by paying "white slips" or IOUs, Deng Xiaoping was reported to have warned that

"Should China encounter problems in the 1990s, it would happen in agriculture".[11] Jiang Zemin made it a point to attend the 1993 National Conference on Agriculture and delivered a highly publicized speech. He acknowledged how "new contradictions and problems in the rural economy have been created in the process of developing the socialist market economy" and avowed higher government priority for agricultural development.[12]

Whereas much of the 1993 government policy statement on agriculture was largely rhetoric, the government's concern over the state of agriculture in early 1995 seemed quite real. Why? To begin with, while 1993 was a bumper year with a record output of 456 million tons, output in 1994 fell to 445 million tons, mainly because of floods in the south and droughts in the north, which affected about 61% of all cultivated lands.[13] But a mere production shortfall of 12 million tons or 2.6% decline was actually statistically within the normal range of annual fluctuation along the trend. In fact, technically speaking, the average deviation from the predicted trend should yield a variation of 13 million tons in both directions for 1994[14] (Fig. 2). In aggregate terms, the 1994 drop in output was, therefore, more in the nature of production stagnation, which should not spark off any real food crisis. Furthermore, China had over the years built up huge grain

---

[11] Deng's warning was made known by another senior leader Wan Li, who was also alarmed over the agricultural deterioration. "Wan Li Echoes Deng Xiaoping's Warning on Problems in Agriculture", *BBC Summary of World Broadcasts* (third series FE/1736, 9 July 1993).

[12] "Jiang calls for a new focus on agriculture", *China Daily* (19 October 1993).

[13] "Harvests last year still good despite extensive natural calamities", *Renmin Ribao* (People's Daily, Beijing, 11 January 1995).

Every year about half of China's cultivated area (or about 25% of total sown area) was affected by varying degrees of natural disasters, usually floods in the south and droughts in the north. However, the recurrence of such natural disasters had apparently made no significant impact on the overall national grain production, partly because half of China's cultivated land was under irrigation. The extent of natural disasters for 1994 was about 18% higher than in 1993, and hence the drop in grain output for 1994.

[14] From the grain production statistical series of 1978–1993 (which gives rise to the trend), the yearly variation in quite wide, e.g., 1980 was 3.5% down from the previous year, 1985 6.9% down, and 1991 2.4% down while 1979 was 9% up from the previous year, both 1982 and 1983 were 9% up, and 1990 9.5% up.

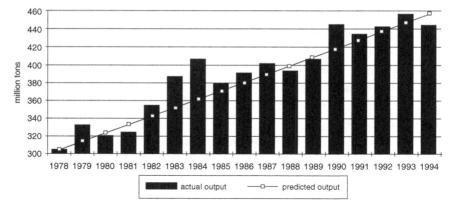

Figure 2.   China's grain production 1978–1994 (Trends (1978–1993): Y = 304.8 + 9.5X).

reserves, which in 1990 were reported to be 491 million tons or equivalent to China's consumption needs for 14 months.[15]

But the timing of the production decline was bad enough, as 1994 was a year of high inflation for China. In 1994, average food prices went up 31.8% over 1993, and average grain prices up 50.7%.[16] Accordingly, as reported by Premier Li Peng, the price increases of agricultural products

---

[15] The Food and Agriculture Organization (FAO) had recommended that producing nations should keep about 18% of their annual grain consumption as reserves, or about two months' consumption needs. China's stock was reported to be well above the world average level, partly because of China's self-reliance mentality.

For a long time, China considered its grain reserves data as top state secret, with strategic and commercial implications. But in November 1990, China disclosed for the first time that is national grain stock for 1990 was 491 million tons, well above the estimate of 82 million tons by the US Department of Agriculture. The bulk of the stock was kept by peasants, while the state grain bureau maintained a one-year supply for urban residents. (United States Department of Agriculture, Economic Research Service, *International Agriculture and Trade Reports: China,* July 1993).

[16] "Statistical Communique of the State Statistical Bureau of the People's Republic of China on the 1994 National Economic and Social Development", *China Economic News* (Beijing, 27 March 1995).

accounted for 13 percentage points of the 21.7% inflation in 1994.[17] The retail price for rice in the major cities more than doubled in 1994; and for Beijing alone, 150% higher.[18] Economists know very well that since food has low elasticity of demand and supply, a small production shortfall can lead to a much higher price increase. But still, why should a 2.6% decline in national grain output (which was in the nature of annual fluctuation) have triggered off such a disproportionate price hike as to be major cause of the 1994 inflation?

A number of aggravating factors have since been known. First, in a situation in which the overall supply of a commodity is adequate and yet its price has skyrocketed, the problem must be associated with inefficient distribution. Starting in early 1993, the Chinese government had been trying to remove the last vestiges of centrally planned agriculture by dismantling its 38-year old planned purchase and planned supply system for grain and edible oil, in which the state would purchase the quota at fixed or negotiated prices, and then transport, store, mill, and sell the grain to urban consumers. This resulted, in the transitional period, different provinces having different distribution systems, which were ill-equipped, on account of local trade barriers, to cope with regional shortages, which were accentuated by a sudden surge in demand due to the influx of migrant ("floating") population.[19]

Secondly, apart from inefficient distribution, the reform had aggravated the price hike. In late 1993, the government announced new reform measures of abolishing grain coupons and raising procurement prices in order to improve the incomes of the disgruntled farmers and to eliminate subsidies on inputs. This immediately caused farmers to withhold their marketable surplus in anticipation of higher procurement prices. These measures

---

[17] "Methods sought to curb inflation," *China Daily Business Weekly* (19–25 March 1995). See also, "Farming the key to inflation," *South China Morning Post* (Hong Kong, 5 January, 1995).

[18] "Experts note reasons for hikes in grain prices," *China Daily* (6 January, 1995).

[19] See Frederick Crook (1994). "Seeds of change. *The China Business Review.*

One of the key problems of distribution was that China had not developed a national grain wholesale market. The grain market was presently fragmented, reflecting administrative boundaries of the different local grain bureaux, and hence the problem of trade barriers. ("Experts note reasons for hikes in grain prices," *China Daily*, 6 January, 1995.)

were eventually implemented in June 1994 with an average 40% increase in the official procurement prices for grain. The state grain bureaux followed suit by raising their retail prices for commercial grain in their grain stores, which were supposed to be independent business units. As a result, speculation in grain was rife, further fueling the grain price hike.[20] And the inflation negated the government measures of raising the procurement prices for grain by making grain cultivation unprofitable.

Lastly, the aggregate grain statistics did not reveal the structural change in the actual supply and demand for grain. As a result of growing affluence in urban areas (the main markets for commercial grain), the demand for fine grain like rice and wheat, particularly for high-quality rice, has risen sharply in recent years. But the total rice output since 1990 has been on the decline every year, in part due to the shrinkage of cultivated acreage for rice; and wheat output in 1994 also fell by 7%.[21] In other words, the highly demanded grain experienced more than a 2.6% decline. The same was true of the government's grain stock, which appeared huge in aggregate statistics; but it actually comprised a lot of low-quality rice from the high-yielding varieties and coarse grain with lesser commercial demand.[22] Therefore, the government's huge grain stock was not effective in stabilizing grain prices.[23]

---

[20] In theory, the grain stores were supposed to buy grain when prices were low and sell it when prices were high, as ways of regulating the market. But the abolition of coupons had bred speculation. To maximize profits, many grain stores would sell subsidized grain to speculators; and this led to a public demand for the return of the coupon system. (Abuse of subsidies bred unrest in China's grain market", *Straits Times*, Singapore, 28 March 1995).

For a more detailed discussion of the complicated institutional arrangements of China's grain reserve management system and grain markets, see Cheng Yuk-shing and Tsang Shu-ki (1994). The changing grain marketing system in China. *China Quarterly* (140).

[21] "Our National Grain Production Situation and Some Proposals", *Renmin Ribao* (2 April, 1995).

[22] The demand for high-quality rice (usually of elongated type) by the more affluent urban residents was well known. Even for wheat, quality also counted. The traditional high-carbohydrate wheat varieties (which were also high yielding) were facing lower demand from urban residents because they were not good for baking bread and biscuits. Hence, China had to import a large quantity of wheat flour and Durum wheat (higher protein and more gluten), averaging at about 11 million tons a year during 1979–1992. ("Wheat production to focus on quality", *China Daily*, 25 March, 1995).

[23] See Cheng Yuk-shing and Tsang Shu-ki, *op cit.*

Apart from its inflationary impact, the grain production stagnation in 1994 had also brought to the fore two critical structural issues in China's agricultural development. First, since 1990, the total sown area for grain had been decreasing at the average rate of 1 % a year, mainly due to industrial and infrastructural uses.[24] For China, a 1% fall in the sown acreage means a whopping loss of 1.1 million hectares, or equivalent to Taiwan's total sown area! The government found that this problem was more disturbing, not just because the shrinkage has continued unabated, but also because China's total sown area for grain in 1994 fell below the "critical" level of 110 million hectares.[25]

Furthermore, it was generally the booming coastal provinces which suffered a higher loss of croplands because of their higher opportunity cost of land for non-farming usage. It followed that a lot of the lost agricultural land happened to be the more fertile land under rice cultivation. This in turn led to the cumulative decline in rice production. As a result, a new national grain distribution pattern was taking shape. In the past, the southern rice-growing provinces had surplus grain to be shipped over to the deficient northern provinces (*Nan-liang bei-yun*). The 1994 grain production setback saw, for the first time, a reverse movement of "northern surplus grain going south" (*Bei-liang nan-yun*).[26]

---

[24]The decrease in the total sown area for grain was 1 % for 1991, 1.6% for 1992, 0.1% for 1993, and 1.1% for 1994. (*Statistical Yearbook of China 1994*); for 1994, "The Sown Area for Grain in Mainland China Fell Below Warning Line", *Mingbao* (Hong Kong, 8 February, 1995).

[25]The 110 million hectares was more a "psychological" than a scientific number. In 1985, for the first time since the reform, the total sown area for grain fell 3.6% to below the level of 110 million hectares and grain production also fell sharply, by 7% in that year.

According to a report by the State Land Administration, in 1994 63.4% of the total lost land was used by township and village enterprises and 20% used for construction. ("Department draws plan to curtail land losses", *China Daily: Business Weekly*, 30 April–6 May, 1995.)

[26]"From Southern Grain Being Shipped North to Northern Grain Being Shipped South" *Renmin Ribao* (People's Daily, 27 March, 1995). Historically, more than 90% of China's rice was grown in the south. Since mid-1980s, however, many rice farmers in the south have shifted to other more profitable crops or simply left farming for non-agricultural pursuits. At the same time, as millions of migrant laborers from the north flocked to the south, the traditional south–north pattern of grain supply and demand had accordingly been upset. ("Grain production needs better macro control", *China Daily*, 13 April 1995.)

Secondly, *pari passu* with the steady loss of good croplands had been the rapid decay of the elaborate production support system in the rural areas, which Mao had painstakingly built up to mobilize resources for building such rural infrastructure as irrigation and for organizing production. Much of this had gone after the commune system was dismantled in the early 1980s. But a new, market-based modern agricultural extension service (which was critical for the agricultural take-off in South Korea and Taiwan) was not coming up fast enough. Worse still, the central government's agricultural policies were often not effectively carried out at the local level, because either the local Party mechanism had become defunct or the local officials were more interested in promoting the glamorous and more profitable industrial and commercial activities.[27]

Upon a careful analysis, therefore, the 1994 fall in grain output was not just the usual effect of bad weather, but also the combined outcome of policy and structural problems. Though there was no full-blown food crisis, the Chinese government had cause for real concern.

Policies to Treat Symptoms, not Root Causes

In the eyes of the government, the most serious manifestation of the agricultural problem was its direct implication for the rampant urban inflation. Hence, the government's high priority was to stabilize food prices with measures, which included a retreat to centralized agriculture. This was done by regulating food prices together with the reimposition of ration by grain coupons,[28] by retaking control of the domestic grain distribution system and improving the existing national farm-product wholesale

---

[27] Many local leaders take the view that industrial development was more important than agricultural development: "Why grow grain, you can always buy grain as long as you have money". *Ban-yue-tan* (Beijing, April 1995, p.30.) In the prosperous coastal provinces, which used to cultivate high-yielding grain, local officials were only keen to promote township and village enterprises (TVEs), which were the main source of their revenue; and agricultural output often constitutes a small part of their total agricultural and industrial output value. ("The Obstacles for Implementing Agricultural Policy in Mainland China", *Xin-bao*. Hong Kong Economic Journal, 23 January 1995.)

[28] Except Beijing, Tianjin, Nanning, Fuzhou, Guangzhou, and Xi'an, all the rest of China's 35 major and medium cities have re-introduced grain coupons (mainly for rice and wheat

markets and setting up new ones,[29] and by placing greater reliance on international grain trade (liberalizing imports and discouraging exports) as a means of increasing grain supply to the cities.[30]

In 1994, it was predicted that in the next five years, China would have to increase grain output to 500 million tons for its growing population, and more resources would have to be pumped into the agricultural sector. For 1995, the Ministry of Finance earmarked 69 billion yuan, up 11% from 1994, to boost agricultural production.[31] The amount, representing only about 2% of China's total capital investment, was obviously grossly inadequate for agriculture's actual need, even though the bulk of the agricultural investment came from bank loans.[32]

---

flour) since the winter of 1994. This allowed poorer urban residents to purchase a certain amount of grain from the state grain stores at prices lower than the market prices.

The government had emphasized that the revival of grain coupons was only a temporary measure, not a "signal of rolling back" economic reform. ("Revival of coupons seen as temporary", *China Daily*, 28 April 1995.)

[29] There were 10 major farm-product wholesale markets across China at that time; but farmers often faced serious market problems as these markets were often not functioning very well due to lack of market information for farmers, transportation difficulty, and local barriers. The Ministry of Internal Trade was planning to set up a state-owned grain storage network across the nation in order to better balance demand and supply. ("Grain mart reforms to sprout", *China Daily Business Weekly*, 19–25 February 1995.)

[30] Import of foreign grain was the most effective means of meeting supply shortages in the cities, especially since the prices for rice and edible oil in China were already above world prices. This explains why Guangdong province resorted to importing rice from Thailand rather than going back to the ration system to meet shortages. ("China: Cost of food surges", *South China Morning Post*, Hong Kong, 18 April 1995.)

In 1995, China was expected to be a net grain importer. China was a large importer of wheat and a significant exporter of rice and corn. But China was expected to be a net importer of rice in 1995. See United States Department of Agriculture, *Grain: World Markets and Trade* (Washington, DC. February 1995).

[31] Of this amount, 37 billion yuan was to be invested to promote agricultural production, and 12 billion yuan for basic construction in agriculture, forestry, and water conservancy. ("China to Boost Funds For Agriculture in 95", *Asian Wall Street Journal*, 24–25 March 1995.)

[32] Total agricultural investment included, apart from the budgetary allocation from the state, also bank loans, related spending by rural collective, and non-agricultural industries as well as by individual farmers. In 1994, the government allocated 48 billion yuan (10% more than in 1993) or about 8% of the state budget to agriculture departments. This

To cope with the growing loss of good croplands, the State Land Administration had set a ceiling for their conversion to non-agricultural uses, and started a national drive to demarcate highly productive farmland for protection, which covered 90% of the farmland in the coastal provinces.[33] However, effective implementation of this farmland protection scheme, like other such measures, much depended on local authorities. In this regard, the central government had instituted the "provincial governor responsibility system", which required individual provincial leaders to ensure that their food supply situation would not get out of hand.[34]

---

amount was small compared to 250 billion yuan of outstanding loans by banks to agricultural purposes in 1994. Chinese experts argued that the state should at least allocate 10% of the country's total investment to agriculture. ("Cash still a root problem in farming", *China Daily*, 2 May 1995.)

In 1980, 9.3% of China's total investment went to agriculture; but the proportion had gone down to 5% in 1984 and further to 1.9% in 1994. ("Agricultural investment: What should be the right proportion?", *Zhongguo cai-jing bao,* China's Financial and Economic News, Beijing, 11 March 1995.)

[33] The State Land Administration had stipulated that the occupation of farmland for non-agricultural purposes from 1991 to 2000 was to be controlled within 2 million hectares, thereby limiting the annual loss from now on to 200,000 hectares. ("Department draws a plan to curtail land losses", *China Daily: Business Weekly.* 30 April–6 May 1995.)

The problem of cropland shrinkage can of course be countered by reclaiming more wasteland as well as by increasing the multiple crop index. A Chinese study showed that over the next six years, it was possible for China to raise its multiple crop index by 3.5 percentage points to 158.9 and reclaiming 2.4 million hectares of new arable land. But both schemes involved expensive capital investment. It was also not a one-to-one loss compensation, as the land lost to non-agricultural uses often happened to be more fertile than the newly created cultivated land. ("Agriculture: Increased Output Hopeful Despite Difficulties", *Beijing Review*, 20–26, March 1995.)

[34] China had in existence for some time the "vegetable basket" system for individual mayors to take care of the vegetable supply in their own cities, and the "rice bag" system for individual governors to take care of the grain supply in their own provinces. As the agricultural problem got worse in 1994, the State Council had made clear that the provincial governor "rice bag responsibility system" would be vigorously implemented. In effect, the central government was just passing the buck to local authorities; but at the same time, it provided the necessary incentives and political pressures for local authorities to pay more attention to agricultural problems, which the central government might not be able to cope with. Under this system, provincial level leaders would be removed or transferred if their grain production ran into trouble. Premier Li Peng declared that if a provincial leader could

So much for short-term policy responses. For any effective long-term solution of the agricultural problem, the Chinese government would need to address two fundamental issues: (i) How to raise the incomes of the farmers? (ii) How to raise the productivity of agriculture? The former required good and sensible government policy initiatives while the latter was related to the long-term technological progress in agriculture. But the government did not appear to be tackling these root causes headon with full policy measure.

It is inevitable that agriculture in a rapidly industrializing economy will continue to lose its best resources, i.e., its good croplands as well as its young and better educated peasants to non-agricultural sectors. Any sound agricultural policy will have to delicately balance rural and urban interests. But still, the relative decline of agriculture should be properly managed without "squeezing" peasants too hard and too fast. The rising peasant discontent and the glaring rural-income gap provided a clear indication that the government had mismanaged the agricultural transition, with its present overall policy orientation too urban biased. [35] Since some 400 million people or 56% of the total labor force were still engaged in fulltime farming, such mismanagement politically and socially cannot be justified. Yet, the government only showed its worries and issued statements, without coming up with effective counter-measures.

Nor was it any easier for the government to vigorously push ahead with further technological transformation of agriculture. At that time, China's productivity levels for grain, as can be seen in Table 2, were already quite high by international standards (37% higher than world average, though

---

not solve the rural problem, he would not be a "qualified leader". ("China decided to implement the governors' rice bag system", *Lianhe Zaobao*, Singapore, 1 March 1995; "Who is going to feed the Chinese?", *Zhongguo shi-bao zhou-kan* (Chinese Times Magazine, Hong Kong, No. 174, 1995.)

[35] In 1993, some 830 incidents of peasant revolts involving more than 500 people — 21 of which involved more than 5,000 people, were reported, and armed police were called to quell 340 incidents. ("Rural Rumblings", *The China Business Review,* November–December 1994.)

In 1994, the average rural–urban income gap for China as a whole was 1:2.59, compared to 1:2.21 in 1991. ("Agriculture: The Unsolved Equation", *China News Analysis* (No. 1533, April 15, 1955.)

Table 2.   China's Grain Productivity in International Perspective.

	Grain Yield (kg per ha)		Productivity Growth (%) 1979–1981 to 1992	Index for 1992
	1971–1981	1992		
China	**3,207**	**4,397**	**137**	**100**
World Average	2,196	2,791	127	63
N. America Average	3,733	4,681	125	106
Europe Average	3,522	4,006	114	91
Developing Countries Average	1,901	2,502	132	57
East Asia				
Japan	5,252	5,847	111	133
South Korea	4,986	5,825	117	132
Southeast Asia				
Indonesia	2,837	2,908	138	89
Malaysia	2,828	2,784	98	63
Philippines	1,611	2,067	128	47
Thailand	1,910	2,024	106	46
Southern Asia				
India	1,324	1,969	149	45

Source: FAO Production Yearbook 1992, Vol. 46, Rome, 1993.

still 33% below that of Japan and South Korea). Any further yield increases would have to depend even more on the intensive use of such secondary inputs as chemical fertilizers, as in Japan and South Korea. This called for massive investment in rural infrastructure as well as greater efforts to expand agricultural research activities.[36] But neither was very

---

[36] It was of course cheaper and more cost-effective to increase grain yield through varietal (i.e., seed) improvement than by intensifying secondary inputs. But China in recent years had produced no significant technological breakthrough comparable to its remarkable achievement in developing the hybrid rice in the 1970s, and its seed technology gap was widening. For a more detailed discussion of this subject, see John Wong (1993). Technological transformation of Chinese agriculture: Key to long-term rural stability, *IEAPE Internal Study Paper*, No. 5.

forthcoming, given the fiscal plight of the central government and the sorrowful state of China's science and technology system in 1994.

It was anticipated that as the government's policy responses were largely of fire-fighting nature, operating to relieve symptoms rather than to treat root causes, China's agriculture would remain a recurrent problem to plague the post-Deng leadership in future. Another production dip following another bad weather would once again bring hue and cry from the top leadership.

According to two studies, science and technology (S&T) contributed only 35% of the agricultural growth in China during the Seventh Five-Year Plan (1985–1990); and the share had gone down to 28% during the Eighth Five-Year Plan period. In developed countries, S&T generally contributed some 60–80% of their agricultural growth. ("Let more science do the farming work", *China Daily*, 1 March 1995.)

At that time, China's socialist-based S&T system was under great stress as a result of the market reform. According to a survey conducted by the World Bank in 1994, agrotechnicians working above the county level scored only 50% in a test of technical competence, while 20% of the people in the research profession had no high education. (Imports tip the balance, *China Trade Report,* April 1995.)

According to Professor Lin Yifu of Beijing University and 455 other agronomists, it was possible for China to raise its grain yields drastically even if the acreage under grain crops does not expand, provided the government can provide 130 million yuan a year, for 20 years, for the seed-improvement program. In 1995, agricultural research in China represented only 0.1% of the output value of agriculture. It should at least be raised to 0.26%. (How Great is the Potential for Grain Production Increases?", *Jingji Ribao* (Economic Daily, Beijing, February 27, 1995.)

Part IV

Foreign Trade and Investment

Chapter 11

Progress in Foreign Trade Reform

Introduction

Deng Xiaoping always referred to "economic reform" as a double-barrel process for both "reform" and the "opening up", or gaige kaifang in one breadth. To Deng, economic reform was not just about the introduction of the market system or market reform, but also opening up China to the outside world for trade and investment. Thus, the first shot of the gaige kaifang saw the setting up of the special economic zone in Shenzhen in 1980 (initially for the purpose of attracting capital and investment from Hong Kong and Macau), which was quickly followed by Zhuhai, Shantou, and Xiamen during 1980–1984. In fact, it was this external aspect of the reform involving the open-door policy that had made greater and smoother progress in the 1980s than the internal market reform, which was a slow-moving process, fraught with many obstacles and resistances.

It was probably no co-incidence that in early 1992, Deng went south to Guangdong from Beijing to use Shenzhen and Zhuhai as a platform to air his frustration over the lack of market reform breakthrough on the one hand and implicitly also brandishing the success story of these special economic zones for the purpose of accelerating market reform. Indeed, on the eve of Deng's Nanxun, China's foreign trade reform had already achieved remarkable progress, leaving no doubt that the main thrust of the Nanxun was how to step up the reform of the domestic market. This chapter, circulated on 4 June 1992, was to review the reform progress of the foreign trade sector up to 1991.

During the period of 1978–1991, China's foreign trade had increased more than six folds from US$21 billion to US$136 billion, growing an annual rate three times that of world trade growth. This clearly pointed to the successful reform and restructuring of the foreign trade system.

139

The process of reforming the foreign trade sector comprises many phases. The major reform efforts in the first phase were devoted to changing the basic approach to foreign trade and dismantling the Soviet-style trade bureaucracy based on the state monopoly of foreign trade. As Marxists, all central planners do not subscribe to the theory of comparative advantage, which is the underlying principle of foreign trade. As such, all socialist economies based on central planning will take to the autarky model, or what Mao had advocated "self-reliance", treating foreign trade as only a marginal activity to complement the central plan by getting rid of surplus and making up for the shortfalls. This is of course a far-cry from the role of foreign trade in China's economy today, which is an important engine of economic growth.

The second phase of foreign trade reform started in 1984, with MOFERT (Ministry of Foreign Economic Relations and Trade) putting up a proposal to liberalize the overall foreign trade planning and administration, such as greater reliance on guidance plans and less on rigid mandatory plans, and the gradual use of indirect levers like tariffs and taxes to achieve the foreign trade objectives.

Before the reform, foreign trade was the monopoly of the state, with a dozen or so foreign trade corporations handling all transactions. Subsequently, provinces and localities were allowed to set up their own foreign trade corporations, and the state would no longer be responsible for their profits and losses. Still more, the contract responsibility system was introduced in 1988, with the state entering into contracts with foreign trade corporations for export targets and sharing foreign exchange.

Thus, on the eve of the Nanxun, China's foreign trade system had already undergone substantial liberalization in terms of organizing imports and exports and pricing of the traded goods as well as rendering its foreign exchange regime more realistic. All these were taking place gradually and by trial and error.

In fact, success in foreign trade reform had contributed to the rapid recovery and expansion of foreign trade in the aftermath of the Tiananmen. At the same time, the sharp expansion of foreign trade during 1989–1991 had also laid bare some of the structural problems of the half-reformed Chinese economy on the one hand (e.g., price distortion) and the need for further foreign trade liberalization, e.g., the various problems related to the foreign exchange regime and the foreign exchange retention system.

As discussed in the previous chapters, the prime objective of Deng's Nanxun was to complete the process of marketization and open up the Chinese economy further. And, in 1994, the government finally took steps to overhaul the foreign exchange regime. At the same time, efforts were also taken to prepare China for greater integration of the global economy by joining (or rejoining) the world trade body, the General Agreement on Tariffs and Trade (GATT).

Impressive Foreign Trade Performance

Since its adoption of economic reform and the open-door policy in 1978, China emerged as the world's 13th largest trading nation. In 1978, China's total trade turnover (imports plus exports) was US$21 billion or a mere 0.8% of the world share; but by 1990, it had increased sixfold to US$128 billion or 2.5% of the world share. In this short span of 12 years, China's foreign trade had experienced a hefty average annual growth of 16.5%, just about three times the rate of growth of world trade.[1] No other socialist economy had achieved such a high level of participation in the world economy in such a short period.[2]

In 1991, China's foreign trade further increased to US$136 billion despite slower world trade growth.[3] During this period, the trade had

---

[1] The trade data for this period was from the International Monetary Fund, *Direction of Trade Statistics* (relevant years).

[2] In 1978, China's exports were only 20% of the former Soviet Union's, and below those of Poland and Czechoslovakia. By 1990, China's exports had exceeded the Soviet level by 11%, and were more than four times higher than those of Poland and Czechoslovakia. Computed from trade data from IMF's *Direction of Trade Statistics 1991*.

[3] "Statistical Communique of the State Statistical Bureau of the People's Republic of China on the 1991 National Economic and Social Development", 28 February 1992, in *China Economic News* (Hong Kong, 9 March 1992). This was Chinese customs figure. Since 1979, China has had two sets of trade figures with substantial discrepancies: by the Ministry of Foreign Economic Relations (MOFERT) and by the General Customs Administration. The Customs figures were more comprehensive, as they record movements of all goods when they clear customs, regardless of whether this leads to payments to or receipts of income from, China's trade partners. The data by MOFERT recorded only movements of goods that lead to payment. This means that for export processing only the value-added, but not the full value of the imported raw materials and machine, was captured in the MOFERT data. Hence Customs data tend to be much higher than those from

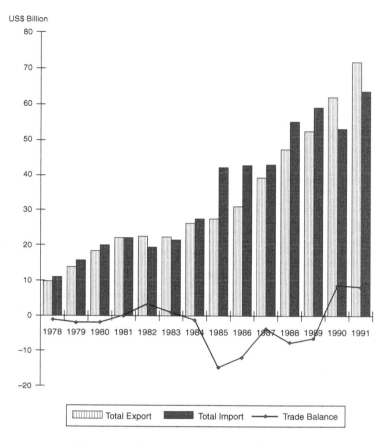

Figure 1.   China's Foreign Trade, 1978–1991.

Source: State Statistical Bureau, Beijing.

turned into a huge surplus for China with comfortable foreign reserves of US$45 billion, or about nine months of imports. All these pointed to the highly impressive performance of China's foreign trade sector since 1978, which coincided with the equally dynamic growth of the Chinese economy in the same period Fig. 1.

MOFERT, some 20–30% higher in recent years. (See Christopher M Clarke 1987). "Two views of China's foreign trade". *China Business Review*, July–August, pp. 15–16.

It was generally believed that the rapid expansion of foreign trade, in bringing about the needed industrial raw materials, advanced technology and equipment as well as the catalyst effect of stimulating production and efficiency, had played a crucial role in China's spectacular economic growth. During 1952–1977, the Chinese economy grew at the average annual rate of 5.7% while trade, at 8.5%. This yielded a trade gross national product (GNP) elasticity of 1.57. During the reform period of 1978–1989, the Chinese economy grew at the average annual rate of 8.7% while trade, at 13.3%. This yielded an elasticity of 1.52. But the simple elasticity approach merely implied that after the reform, higher trade growth was associated with higher economic growth, providing no exact causal relationship as to which leads to which and by exactly how much.

However, by constructing a general equilibrium model, economists can measure the sources of growth, i.e., for every unit of output growth, the proportion that had been contributed, respectively, by export expansion, import substitution, consumption, investment, and technological change. It was also possible for economists to compute the total linkages (forward and backward linkages) of the export sector by means of an input–output table. These have been commonly done for market economies.

The data problem apart, in view of the half-reformed nature of the Chinese economy with price distortion and price control, such technical exercises tended to yield imperfect and inexact conclusions for the Chinese case.[4] Rapid foreign trade expansion had led to fast economic growth, which in turn fueled further foreign trade expansion, feeding each other in an upward spiral manner.

It is nonetheless clear that China's foreign trade would not have achieved such staggering growth if its foreign trade system had failed to undergo reform and restructuring since 1978. Compared to the Maoist autarky period, China's foreign trade sector had changed almost beyond recognition, especially in terms of foreign trade organization, pricing of traded goods, developing a more realistic exchange rate regime with limited

---

[4]John C Hsu has argued that during 1979–1985, China's foreign trade growth has been "growth-led". The expansion of exports was due to GNP growth with the expansion of imports due to expansion of exports and external borrowing. (*China's Foreign Trade Reforms Impact on Growth and Stability*. Cambridge: Cambridge University Press, 1989, p. 26–27).

convertibility, and abolishing direct trade subsidies. Thanks to successful trade reforms, China today operates a less rigid and a more open trading system, which in turn has rendered the Chinese economy in recent years more export oriented. Only the progress of rural reforms can match that of trade reforms. As the American economist Nicholas Lardy puts it, foreign trade had started to "exert a greater influence on the [Chinese] domestic economy than at any other period in China's history."[5] Such increasing openness of the Chinese economy was manifested in the sharply rising trade–GNP(nominal) ratios, from 9.7% for 1978 to 28% for 1989.[6]

Yet, from an international perspective, China's trading system at that time was still not sufficiently liberalized. Its trade regime fell short of achieving "GATT compatibility", i.e., not yet consistent with the principles of the General Agreement on Tariffs and Trada (GATT). More specifically, its imports were still tightly controlled through high tariff barriers and complicated licensing arrangements. That is why China was locked in a prolonged trade friction with the United States, even though China under Washington's pressures signed a Memorandum of Understanding on 17 January 1992 to resolve the intellectual property

---

[5] Nicholas R Lardy (1992). *Foreign Trade and Economic Reform in 1978–1990*. Cambridge: Cambridge University Press, p. 1.

[6] The trader–GNP ratio was commonly used by economists to judge the degree of economic openness of a country. But using this measure obviously presented a great problem for China. Apart from the fact that China compiles its trade data in US dollars and its GNP in domestic currency, Chinese GNP when converted into US dollars was grossly underestimated. Hence this unusually large trade–GNP ratio of 28% for China.

If China's nominal GNP was to be revalued at international prices to reflect purchasing power parity (PPP), it would be much larger and the *real* trade-PPP-based-GNP ratio for 1988 would only be 3.8%. (For a discussion of Chinese real PPP-based GNP, see John Wong (1991). *What Is China's Real Per-Capita GNP?*, IEAP Background Brief No. 18. Though a PPP-based GNP inevitably exaggerated Chinese GNP, a much smaller trade–GNP ratio Deemed more realistic. As a large country, China was inherently more self-sufficient and thus less dependent on foreign trade. So far only its coastal provinces and cities were trade-oriented while its vast landlocked interior was still very much inward-looking. Viewed in this light, such a high trade–GNP ratio of 28% for China was unwarranted.

Regardless of whatever trade–GNP ratio to be used, the fact remains that the Chinese economy over the years had become much more open.

rights issue. From the American standpoint, Chinese trade regime needed further liberalization and its trade regulations greater transparency.[7]

What have been the major changes in China's trade system since 1978? How much has the foreign trade system been reformed? Are the reforms enough? What would be the likely direction of trade reforms in the 1990s? The following background analysis was aimed at providing the basis for understanding these issues.

Trade Liberalization Process

China's foreign trade liberalization process from self-reliance to export orientation consists of four waves of trade reforms. These reforms were primarily designed to address the domestic issues of foreign trade, mainly by liberalizing and rationalizing the overall foreign trade system.[8] In addition, China had also introduced significant changes in trade policy and trade practices that fall into the area of China's international economic relations or economic diplomacy, e.g., efforts made to meet the GATT requirements and to accommodate mounting US trade demands.

It is well-known that prior to 1979, China's foreign trade was organized on the socialist principle of central planning. All foreign trade was a state monopoly. As a residual part of the overall state plan, trade was merely a means of making up for domestic shortfalls and getting rid of unwanted surplus. For 30 years from 1949 to 1978, China sought to minimize participation in the world economy in accordance with Mao's celebrated "self-reliance" development strategy, which had no place for the law of comparative advantage. It may of course he argued that at the time of the Cold War, China, faced with the US-led embargo, had no real alternative to such a self-reliant development strategy. As a large economy with a relatively high degree of self-sufficiency, China could also better survive

---

[7] "1992 Trade Policy Agenda Report" of the Office of the U.S. Trade Representative (USTR), 2 March 1992, United States Information Service, Embassy of the United States of America, Singapore.

[8] Chinese writers also talk about only four stages in the reform process. See for example, Zhang Yi (1991). Initial achievements in the implementation of new foreign trade system in China. *Liaowang*: Overseas Edition, Hong Kong, No. 39.

with a minimal dependence on foreign trade. At the ideological level, Marxist theorists simply reject Ricardo's theory of comparative advantage, which runs contrary to Marx's theory of value. Chinese trade theorists had also cogently argued that higher dependence on capitalist economies would also mean higher vulnerability to external fluctuation. Furthermore, they readily accepted the argument of the Dependency school, which regards foreign trade as a form of capitalist exploitation of the Third World countries on account of "unequal exchange". But from economic standpoint, such economic self-reliance amounted to an extreme form of import substitution, which had been a major source of gross economic inefficiency of many developing countries. In China, as a result of operating the Soviet-type foreign trade system, its exchange rate was overvalued and its domestic currency inconvertible while its distorted domestic prices bore no relationship to world market prices.

The historic Third Plenum of the 11th Central Committee in December 1978 laid the political groundwork for China to adopt economic reform and the "open-door policy". The open-door policy was perceived as a means by which China could capture the international capitalist forces for its own economic growth. This touched off the first wave of foreign trade reforms along with the establishment in 1979 of the Special Economic Zones (SEZs).[9] Specifically for trade reforms, the main efforts at the first stage were directed at dismantling the state monopoly on foreign trade. Thus, provinces and localities were allowed to set up their own foreign trade corporations (FTCs), which could retain a certain portion of their foreign exchange earnings. In 1979, a dozen or so FTCs handled all foreign trade transactions; but their number increased to 6,000 in 1989.[10]

---

[9] In 1979, Guangdong started three SEZs: Shenzhen (which also includes the Shekou Industrial District), Zhuhai, and Shantou. Fujian soon followed suit by setting up a SEZ in Xiamen. Hainan Island became a SEZ only in 1988.

[10] World Bank (1990). *China: Between Plan and Market*. Study, Washington, DC. A World Bank Country, p. 79. Of these 6,000 FTCs, some 1,000 were reported to have been closed during the retrenchment in 1990. (Hong Kong Trade Development Council (1991). *China's Foreign Trade System*. Hong Kong, p. 24.

FTCs, originally the business arm of the Ministry of Foreign Economic Relations and Trade (MOFERT), were organized along product lines and existed at national, provincial,

In effect, the break-up of the state monopoly on foreign trade does not by itself bring about more efficient foreign trade operation. In fact, the proliferation of FTCs when domestic prices remained separate from world prices, actually aggravated the inefficiencies of the trading system at that time and resulted in serious trade (and also budget) deficits in the early 1980s. This led to the second wave of trade reforms along with the announcement to open 14 port cities and Hainan Island to foreign investment. In September 1984, the State Council approved MOFERT's proposal on "The Reform of the Foreign Trade System", which formed the basis of subsequent trade reforms. The main thrust of the reform efforts of this period was to liberalize the overall foreign trade administration and planning. Central to the new reform initiative was the separation of government agencies from the day-to-day management of trade, with greater reliance instead on indirect levers like tariffs and taxes to administer trade policy. The foreign trade planning system was also to rely more on guidance plans and less on the rigid mandatory plans. The state would not be responsible for the profits and losses of FTCs. The agency system (*daili zhi*) of conducting foreign trade was to be promoted. The idea was for the FTCs to provide diversified trade services to production enterprises.[11]

But a number of unforseen problems soon cropped up. As strong demand existed in China for such consumer goods as TVs and taperecorders, trade liberalization triggered off a rush to import them, leading to a quick drain on China's valuable foreign exchange — in 1985, China registered its largest ever trade deficit of US$15 billion. Further, as long as domestic prices remained distorted within China, traders had a stronger incentive to import than to export, or to export merely for the sake of collecting state subsidies. The financial responsibility system had indeed pushed traders to cover costs. But under disequilibrium domestic prices, profit-maximizing traders would have a lot of loopholes to exploit and they would only handle commodities like consumer durables for quick profits. China might have a

---

municipal, and county levels. At the national level, they were directly under MOFERT while at the provincial level, they were under the relevant Commission of MOFERT.

[11] See The MOFERT's Report on the Reform of the Trade System, approved by the State Council on 15 September 1984. (The World Bank (1988). *China: External Trade and Capital.* Washington, DC, p. 21.

strong comparative advantage for producing black-and-white TV sets; but when their domestic prices were set higher than overseas, traders would import them rather than produce them for exports. While individual traders profited, the country could not reap the gains of foreign trade. In fact, opportunities for rent-seeking activities (i.e., time spent by individuals to capture the unearned benefits or "economic rent" arising from price distortions caused by government control such as licenses and quotas) or outright corruption would abound in a situation with disequilibrium domestic prices. This had exactly happened: numerous independent FTCs in the SEZs with more lax import control exploited the liberalization measures for their own gains, culminating in the Hainan import scandal.[12]

To cope with the resultant foreign exchange crisis, the government in 1985 had to slow down or even reverse the liberalization process by adopting instead tougher measures of import control through the imposition of special adjustment taxes and stricter licensing arrangements over certain categories of imports. To accelerate exports, the government sought to offset the unfavorable ratio of domestic to world prices for export products by offering exporting firms various financial incentives, including tax exemption and rebates, higher foreign exchange retention, and more favorable internal foreign exchange conversion rates. Specifically, the foreign exchange retention right was a unique Chinese instrument of promoting exports. Since the start of the trade reform, China had put in place an elaborate foreign exchange retention system. In general, rights to foreign exchange generated by exports were shared among the central, provincial, and municipal governments; FTCs; and the production enterprises responsible for exports. The shares of these recipients may differ by commodities and have been varied several times over the years. Retained foreign exchange can be either used for imports permitted by the State or sold for specific purposes in the Foreign Exchange Adjustment center.

---

[12]The Hainan authorities were using foreign exchange obtained on the black market to import some 70,000 Japanese motor vehicles for Hainanese firms, which then resold the cars to buyers on the mainland for huge profits. (A crisis of plenty, *Far Eastern Economic Review* 1 August 1985.)

Subsequently, the importation of motor vehicles into China was banned outright for two years.

As long as the exchange rate of the renminbi was overvalued, a higher retention rate for the production enterprises would operate to offset partially the negative effect of the overvalued foreign exchange rate.[13] As a result of applying these carrot-and-stick measures, import growth in 1987 was held down while exports shot up, leading to a substantial reduction of trade deficits from US$12 billion to US$3.8 billion in 1986.

The main thrust of the third wave of trade reforms, which began in 1988, was the introduction of the foreign trade contract responsibility system. Under this system, all national and local FTCs would enter into foreign trade contracts with the state, i.e., MOFERT. Fixed and unchanged for three years, the contracts would specify: (i) an annual export earnings target for three consecutive years; (ii) the rates for sharing foreign exchange between the state and the local contracting party (or simply, the center and the provincial governments), with one rate (about 75–80%) for above target earnings; and (iii) the "net economic results" of the export activity, i.e., the central government would fix the maximum level of subsidies to the contracting party, which was in turn made responsible for all losses in excess of the contracting amount.

These reform measures were accompanied by appropriate administrative decentralization toward increased regional autonomy and greater integration of production and trade activities. More and more FTCs were set up under the auspices of local governments and some local enterprises were granted direct trading rights. However, decentralization also heightened inter-provincial economic rivalry, as provincial FTCs competed for the scarce raw material supply. The case in point was the "silk war" in the summer of 1988. Furthermore, this period of trade reforms coincided with wider economic reform measures undertaken at the macroeconomic level, which sparked off economic overheating and eventually a runaway inflation. Much to the credit of MOFERT, the government did not renege on the trade responsibility contract system or roll back trade reforms in the face of such great economic instabilities.

The fourth wave of reforms was associated with the abolition of direct export subsidies. Starting from 1 January 1991, the central government

---

[13] See Arvind Panagariya (1991). *Unraveling the Mysteries of China's Foreign Trade Regime: A View from Jiangsu Province*, World Bank Working Paper, WPS 801.

ceased to subsidize FTCs for their losses arising from discrepancies between domestic and world market prices, and these enterprises themselves would have to bear sole responsibility for their own profits and losses. This round of trade reforms (which at that time came much as a surprise to outside observers as the overall economic reform was put on hold in the aftermath of the Tiananmen[14]) was introduced shortly after the sharp depreciation of the *renminbi* in late 1990. This moved the official exchange rate much closer to the "shadow" or free market rate.[15] These changes have brought China more in line with universal practices. The ground was thus laid for China to implement the agency system, under which domestic prices of both imported and exported goods were linked to international prices via the exchange rate.

In short, China's foreign trade system since 1978 has undergone substantial reforms and changes. However, China's overall trade regime remains under tight government control. Imports of consumer goods are severely restricted — even some raw material imports require licenses. Import licenses were divided into three categories: (i) Category I include steel products, timber, civil aircrafts, petroleum, sugar, wool, etc., which were regarded as essential goods for economic development. MOFERT would issue licenses for their imports. (ii) Category II comprised many consumer goods such as washing machines, tape recorders, cameras, etc., and licensing for their imports comes from the provincial authorities. (iii) Category III was goods for which licenses were issued by MOFERT's Special Commissioners at major ports or coastal cities with foreign enterprises.

The system of import tariff was even more complicated. More than 2,000 items categorized into approximately 100 types of goods were subject to import duties, generally ranging from 8% to 180%.[16] On the export

---

[14] See Thomas Chan (1991). No more subsidies. *China Trade Report*, Vol. 29.

[15] In this round of reform, the practice of fixing different rates of foreign exchange retention for different localities was replaced by a uniform rate for the whole country. Under the new system, 20% of foreign exchange earnings from the export of general commodities would be turned over to the central government and 10% each to the local government and to the manufacturers. The rest would go to the foreign trade enterprises. ("Spokesman Announces Foreign Trade Reforms", *Xinhua* News Agency, Beijing, 23 January 1991.)

[16] Arvind Panagariya, *op cit.*

side, a large number of commodities are also controlled, including items for which China has no strong market power. Excessive control over imports and exports thus negates the efficiency gains which China is supposed to reap in opening up its economy to the international division of labor. There is clearly much room for further trade liberalization.

Issues and Implications of Reforms

It might be recapitulated that China's trade reforms were fundamentally motivated by two related objectives: (i) to raise the efficiency of its foreign trade mechanism and (ii) to realize the gains from international trade for its own economic growth. To fulfil these objectives, the reform process therefore started off by breaking up the highly centralized state monopoly on trade. In the area of decentralization China evidently achieved a great deal of progress during 1980–1992. It was possible for a foreign investor in Guangdong or Sichuan intending to import or export to apply direct to local authorities without having to refer to the central bureaucracy in Beijing.

To achieve the efficiency objective, the individual FTCs must shake off their old mentality of "eating from the same pot" and become independent financial units to be responsible for their own profits and losses. Thus, part of the reform efforts was aimed at instituting some measures of "hard budget constraints" in FTCs. The end to direct export subsidies in 1991 had been a significant reform landmark in this direction. Financial accountability in turn paved the way for FTCs to evolve into specialized agents providing trade services to production enterprises.

Obviously, China would not be able to capture the real gains from foreign trade if individual FTCs continued to operate in a macroeconomic environment marked by gross price distortions. A recurrent theme in the trade reform process had been how problems had frequently arisen when the overall economic reform failed to keep pace with trade liberalization. In fact, an "irrational" domestic price structure often created an opportunity for rent-seeking activities for the profit-maximizing FTCs, as actually happened in 1985. Trade reform was only half a loaf: domestic price reform must also follow suit. After all, getting the prices of traded goods right would raise the efficiency of the production units as well as provide a correct signal to FTCs.

But price disequilibrium also occurred at the international level. With the socialist trade system in operation for 30 years, domestic prices in China had become completely divorced from world prices. Such a divergence between domestic and world prices was far greater for imported goods than for exported goods, hence a full battery of domestic protection measures and exchange control before 1978. Since China was not purported to become a truly open economy with complete factor mobility, the realistic objective of trade reforms was to liberalize the trade regime so as to reduce (not to eliminate) the divergence between domestic and world prices only to an acceptable degree. This brings to the fore the importance of a more flexible and realistic exchange rate (i.e., the price of domestic currency in terms of a foreign currency) as a supplementary instrument of trade policy.

As noted earlier, Chinese domestic currency before trade reforms was overvalued and completely inconvertible. The official exchange rate at 2.46 RmB per US dollar was fixed in 1955 and remained unchanged for 20 years and then moved up further to 1.55 RmB in 1979. On the eve of the trade reform, the *renminhi* was clearly grossly overvalued. So Chinese export goods were sold at a financial loss to FTCs, i.e., the dollar value of the export goods when converted to Rmb at official rate was far below the Rmb price of the goods paid for by the trading corporation, which had to subsidize the losses from gains made from imports. The first step in the trade reform was for the government to give up its monopoly on the control of foreign exchange by introducing in 1979 the "foreign exchange retention system". This system existed until 1992; but over the years, the retention rates have been varied and structured (e.g., a preferential retention rate for above-plan exports) to suit specific policy objectives. The next important step was the creation of the rather innovative "foreign exchange adjustment centers" (FEACs or *waihui tiaoji zhongxin*) in several cities in 1986 for enterprises to sell their surplus foreign exchange retention rights. Actually back in 1980, foreign exchange adjustment centers started in Guangzhou and Shanghai, and enterprises with surplus foreign exchange were allowed to sell it through the local branch of the Bank of China. But they were not really foreign exchange markets where, buyers and sellers could come into direct contact. The first formerly sanctioned center was opened in 1985 in Shenzhen, to be followed by the Shanghai center in 1986.

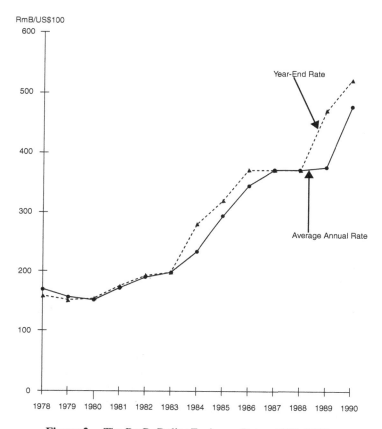

Figure 2. The RmB–Dollar Exchange Rates, 1978–1990.

Source: State Statistical Bureau, Beijing.

Initially, a wide differential between the official and parallel exchange rates occurred in the FEACs. In 1988, the Shanghai FEAC started to make the price of foreign exchange more transparent and subject it to the market forces of supply and demand. By early 1991, after two rounds of devaluation of the *renminbi*, coupled with the surge of China's foreign exchange reserves (Figs. 2 and 3), the gap between the official and parallel rates in all the FEACs had become fairly close.[17] The FEACs in China at that time

[17] By early 1992, the spread between the official and the average swap rate had narrowed to less than 10%. So long as the *renminbi* was not freely convertible, someone would be

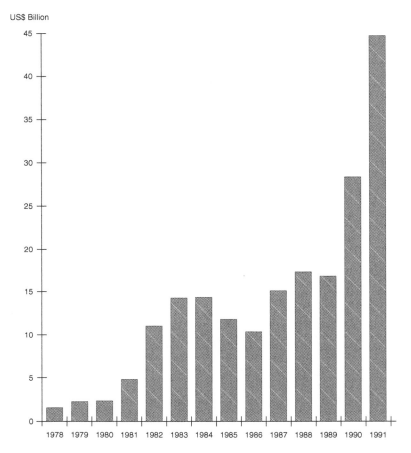

US$ Billion

Figure 3.   China's Foreign Exchange Reserves, 1978–1991.

Source: State Statistical Bureau, Beijing.

were operating more like market-based "swap centers", which basically absorbed the black market for foreign exchange. Initially only for joint ventures, FEACs have since 1988 become available to domestic enterprises. By virtue of the FEAC mechanism, China had been able to bring

willing to pay a premium for foreign exchange and hence the swap rate must be necessarily above the official rate. "Swap centers: Past, present, and future". *The China Business Review,* March/April, I992, p. 16.

its exchange rate regime to a realistic level along with a limited (albeit indirect) convertibility for the *renminbi*. In this way, China had successfully embarked on a transition toward a viable, managed exchange rate regime.[18]

In summary, China's trade liberalization had progressed as far as was politically and economically feasible. Nonetheless, compared to the other open and outward-looking Asia-Pacific economies at that time, it was predicted that China still had a long way to go in terms of trade liberalization. The future course of trade reforms was likely to concentrate on substituting indirect price levers for direct control, e.g., replacing import licensing with tariffs. Other new measures included granting more direct trading rights to production enterprises, a further lowering of import tariffs, and improving the transparency of its trade laws and regulations. But the next breakthrough in trade reforms would have to wait for the macroeconomic reform to catch up.

Lessons from Chinese Trade Reforms

Chinese trade reforms over the past decade have evidently been successful. Its booming exports and soaring foreign reserves spoke best for its past reform efforts. But economists argued that what was financially profitable may not be economically efficient. The reforms may have enabled the foreign trade sector to thrive or motivated trading enterprises to maximize exports. But this does not necessarily bring about higher economywide efficiency in terms of the best use of resources. So long as there were price distortions in the half-reformed Chinese economy (e.g., with many state enterprises continuing to survive on state subsidies), export earnings may not have reflected the true cost of domestic resources.[19] Thus, the net

---

[18] Deputy Governor Chen Yuan (son of Chen Yun) of the People's Bank of China said in Hong Kong in 1992 that he supported the idea of making the *Renminbi* a convertible currency. (China to make its currency convertible soon: Official, *Business Times*, Singapore, 8 May 1992.)

[19] For further discussion of this sophisticated topic, see Jeffrey Robert Taylor (1989). *Trade reform and efficiency of resource use in China*. Ph.D. Dissertation, University of Michigan, Ann Arbor.

results of the trade reforms should be weighed in the context of the overall economic reform progress.

What have been the main contributing factors to China's success in trade reforms? Certainly, they would not have been so successful without concomitant progress in domestic price reforms and market creation. Trade reforms and price reforms have fed on each other in the process. Tactically speaking, both owe their success to the pragmatic and gradualist approach based on trial and error. This was in sharp contrast to the general reform strategy adopted by the Soviet Union and other East European countries, which opted for a "big push" toward privatization rather than the Chinese way of gradual creation of markets. In China, the open-door policy started with the setting up of SEZs and other open cities where bolder reforms measures were experimented, their effects demonstrated, and their experience then popularized (e.g., the foreign exchange adjustment center was first tried out in Shenzhen).

But there was one exclusive factor for the Chinese success. China had been benefiting enormously from its connection with the overseas Chinese from Hong Kong, Taiwan, and Southeast Asia, who have invested in China and transferred their knowledge and experience of production organization and market development to the local Chinese. The Chinese on their part have also proved capable of adapting fast to foreign contacts, thanks to the fact that its foreign trade organizations have been staffed with the country's best talent and more flexible bureaucrats.[20] Not surprisingly, foreign trade was the first sector in China to revive and foster traditional Chinese entrepreneurship. In contrast, the entrepreneurial factor seemed missing in the European socialist countries.

---

[20] It is common knowledge that during the Cultural Revolution, the best brains joined the armed forces. But in recent years, schools of finance, economics, and foreign trade have attracted the best students.

Chapter 12

China and the GATT

Introduction

The basic rationale behind the Nanxun was to reinvigorate and expand domestic market reform while opening up China further to foreign economic activities, with the two being closely interrelated. Progress in domestic market reform, by rationalizing the prices of both the factor and output markets, would obviously stimulate trade and foreign direct investment. As the country's external operations had expanded, it would also get more integrated with the world economy. This follows that China needs to understand the basic rules of the game in the international economy, for China's benefits and China's protection.

Thus, as China's exports had grown rapidly, having emerged as the world's 13th largest trading nation in 1991, it would naturally want to seek institutionalized international protection against trade protectionism and also to benefit from such schemes as reciprocity and non-discrimination with its trade partners. For all these, China had to be a participant of the multilateral trade negotiation (MTN) process. In other words, China had to be a member of the GATT (General Agreement on Tariffs and Trade), then the world's umbrella organization for international trade. Thus, soon after the Nanxun, China mounted an intensive international trade. Thus, soon after the Nanxun, China mounted an intensive international economic diplomacy to join the GATT.

With the WTO (World Trade Organization) in existence since January 1995, not many people were familiar with its predecessor the GATT, which along with the IMF and the World Bank, was created at the Bretton Woods Conference in 1944. The GATT was supposed to promote global free trade through its many rounds of multilateral trade negotiation — it was the Uruguay Round at the time of the Nanxun, and at that time, the world was still engaged in the process of completing the protracted negotiation for the Doho Round.

Still more, not many people have known that China was actually a founding member of the GATT. When the Nationalist government retreated to Taiwan in 1949, it took with it the China seat in the GATT. A year later, however, Taiwan was forced to give it up. So China had to apply to rejoin, which it formally did in 1986, after having been actively involved earlier on in the Multifibre Arrangement (MFA) for textiles and clothing. Initially, China was contemplating of seeking re-entry by requesting the restoration of the old China seat through invoking the "Grandfather Clause" of the US law, as China was technically already a contracting party to the GATT. But Beijing had later decided to formally apply for membership on the ground that it had already extensively reformed its foreign trade sector.

In any case, most of the technical groundwork for China's accession was actually completed by 1989, and China was set to join. Unfortunately, the Tiananmen even had radically changed the whole scenario.

In the wake of the Tiananmen, the United States had put up a major stumbling block to China's accession on the technical ground that China's domestic market reform had not gone far enough to meet the "GATT compatibility". This had immediately raised the "admission price" of China's membership.

On the demand side, the post-Tiananmen Li Peng government was all the more determined to mend its diplomatic fences of which the GATT membership was high on Li's agenda. In the aftermath of the Tiananmen, the United States imposed a political barrier on the China–US trade by requiring the annual renewal of the MFN (most favored nation) clause. If China were a GATT member, that would make it technically difficult for the United States to continue with its annual MFN pressures on China — the MFN clause was removed only in 2000, i.e., by offering MFN to China on a "permanent" basis!

In the circumstances, China's negotiation for the GATT membership proved to be a complicated process, not so much because China had failed to comply with the technical standards like transparency in trade matters, the safeguard mechanism, export subsidies, and so on. China had in fact made great progress in liberalizing its over trade regime. The basic problem was because China's GATT membership was deeply entangled in the political tug-of-war between the United States and China, particularly in the early years of the Clinton Administration, which put China's human rights records as the center of US–China relations. But China continued to make efforts, first going after the GATT, then the WTO.

China's Determination to Rejoin GATT

In 1992, China's Vice-Minister of Foreign Economic Relations and Trade (MOFERT), Gu Yongjiang announced that China would soon "rejoin" the General Agreement on Tariffs and Trade (GATT).[1] In early March 1992, MOFERT's Director of the GATT Affairs Division, Li Zhongzhou, also optimistically predicted that China would "regain" its GATT status some-time that year. Returning from the GATT's 10th Session of the "Working Party on China" in Geneva, Li stressed: "The Chinese government attaches great importance to the issue and is sparing no efforts to comply with GATT requirements".[2]

The GATT, the International Monetary Fund (IMF), and the International Bank for Reconstruction and Development (IBRD or World Bank) are the three keystone international economic organizations created at the Bretton Woods Conference in 1944 with a view to remedying the economic ills that plagued the world economy in the 1930s. Specifically for the GATT (which came into being in 1948), its basic goal has been to foster an open trading system within its institutional framework, i.e., the GATT rules. In effect, trade liberalization has been promoted by the GATT through its various rounds of multilateral trade negotiation (MTN) based on three cardinal principles: (i) reciprocity; (ii) non-discrimination; and (iii) transparency. First, in negotiating trade barriers, the GATT relies on "reciprocity" to mobilize political support for the world-wide reduction of trade protection: nations reduce their tariffs in the knowledge that other countries are making equivalent cuts in theirs. However, developing countries which have

---

[1] "China may soon join GATT", *Lianhe Zaohao,* Singapore, 17 April 1992.
[2] "Trade reforms follow GATT rules", *China Daily Business Weekly,* Beijing 1–7 March 1992.

obtained special and different treatment within the GATT are exempt from making reciprocal tariff cuts.

Second, the GATT embraces "non-discrimination" or most favored nation (MFN) treatment (any tariff reduction granted by any contracting party should be accorded unconditionally to all other contracting parties) to prevent the cycle of selective retaliation and counter-measures which would have occurred under discriminatory trade. Since MFN rules prevent an importing country from using tariffs selectively, the country is less likely to raise its protective barriers and risk retaliation.

Third, in the 1930s uncertainty and lack of transparency in trade policies were a common source of trade frictions among countries. Foreign producers were often not sure what kind of trade barriers or customs regulations they would face at the border and their exports were accordingly discouraged. The GATT preferred bound tariffs to the less transparent quota system.[3] One of the MTN process was the Uruguay Round, which, started in 1986, but failed to come to successful conclusion, mainly because of the continuing dispute over the agricultural trade between the European Community and the United States.

By 1992, the GATT had 103 countries or territories as its signatories. Some "80% of the world trade was affected by, although not necessarily in conformity with, the GATT rules".[4] At the same time, China since its adoption of the "open-door policy" in 1978 emerged as the world's 13th largest trading nation, with its share of the world trade soaring from 0.8% in 1978 to 2.5% in 1990. It was clearly not good for the GATT as an umbrella World Trade Organization (WTO) to exclude permanently such a large and expanding trading entity as China with 1.1 billion people.

China was actually a founding member of the GATT. But when Chiang Kai-shek's Nationalist government retreated to Taiwan in 1949, it took with it the China seat in the GATT, only to give it up a year later. In 1986, China formally applied for membership in (technically "accession to") the GATT. Most of the technical groundwork for China's accession was reported to have been completed by 1989; but the last stumbling block

---

[3] For a simple discussion of the GATT in economic development, see World Bank, *World Development Report* 1987, chapter 9.
[4] *Ibid.* p. 154.

was put up by the United States, ostensibly for such technical reasons as insufficient transparency in China's trade regimes. In reality, the US blocking move stemmed from the same set of political and diplomatic forces that have adversely affected Sino–US relations since the Tiananmen event. Ironically, the US obstacle only served to stiffen the Chinese resolve to rejoin the GATT. If China were in the GATT, it would make it technically difficult for the United States to continue its diplomatic maneuver of applying the annual MFN pressures on China. In other words, China's ultimate success in the GATT would not only be a breakthrough in its international economic diplomacy but also signal a significant improvement in the existing Sino–US bilateral relations.

China's eventual accession to the GATT has never been in doubt. It was high time to take a close look at the possible implications of China's GATT membership, both for China and the GATT. China has stepped up trade reforms in order to meet the "GATT compatibility". Will China's membership continue to exert a strong influence on the process of China's trade reforms? An examination of the negotiation process can also provide a glimpse of China's behavior in international economic diplomacy.

Protracted Negotiation

The GATT is basically an organization for market economies which can more easily follow the free or fair trade rules. Because of central planning and government involvement in foreign trade, it is difficult to establish if a socialist economy has followed "fair" trade or not, e.g., it is not easy to tell if a socialist economy has practiced dumping. Thus, the East European countries had all gone through a rather long negotiation process before they were finally admitted to the GATT.[5] On account of its different trading system, China's application process from the outset is apt to be protracted regardless of the technicality of whether China's entry was a new application or merely a resumption of its old membership status. From the standpoint of Beijing, it is of great political importance to assert that there has always been one China, and that the PRC was technically

---

[5] It had taken Hungary four years, Romania three years, and Poland eight years to join the GATT.

and legally a member of the GATT from its very beginning. This claim would give China certain advantages (in terms of restructuring its foreign trade legislation to suit the GATT rules) by resorting to the legal technicality of the so-called "Grandfather Clause" of the US law, i.e., the "Jim Crow laws" passed in 1870 by various states in the US: "A person is entitled to vote if only he or his forefather voted in 1867". Applying to the GATT, the "Grandfather Clause" would allow an interim protocol to contain a "current legislation clause", to wit: "Application of Part II of the GATT to the maximum extent possible without violating current legislation." Roughly, this means that PRC was already a contracting party to the GATT as of 30 October 1947 when the GATT was founded. China could therefore keep its internal legislation in force on or before 30 October 1947 if China's application was merely a request for the restoration of the old China seat. Invoking the "Grandfather Clause" would thus greatly simplify China's need to introduce new foreign trade legislations but not entirely exempt China from reforming the foreign trade system.[6]

In early 1979, shortly after the establishment of the Sino–US diplomatic relations, China expressed its desire to join the IMF and World Bank. The admission procedures for these two international bodies had been relatively simple, for it had taken China only one year to be admitted. China needed only to release to the Bank some economic data which were previously held secret and to agree to follow certain procedures to meet the Fund's conditionality. Full participation in the GATT, however, had proved exceedingly troublesome for China, as it involved a fundamental change in the ways China organized its foreign trade.

China's first official contact with the GATT activities was in the early 1980s through its participation in the GATT negotiation concerning the Multifibre Arrangement (MFA), as China was then already an important exporter of textiles and clothing. In 1984, having successfully implemented its first round of trade reforms by decentralizing state control on foreign trade, China requested to be a permanent observer in the GATT's Council. In the meanwhile, as he GATT was getting ready to launch the

---

[6]For a more detailed discussion of the legal technicality, see Wang Yi (1986). "How China can make the most of the 'Grandfather Clause" in the GATT. *Guoji Maoyi Wenti* (International Trade Journal), Beijing, (6).

new Uruguay Round, most member countries came to recognize that such a large trading country as China should be part of the WTO. In January 1986, the Director-General of the GATT, Arthur Dunkel, was invited to China.[7]

On 14 July 1986, just two months before the Uruguay ministerial meeting, China formally applied to the GATT for the resumption of its status as a contracting party. At this juncture, although China's foreign trade organization had been substantially decentralized, its overall trade regime was still quite a distance from meeting the GATT requirements. China's foreign trade system during 1986–1987 remained under extensive state controls: (i) Roughly 70% of China's exports and imports were subject to either mandatory plans or guidance plans negotiated by central and local officials. (ii) About half of China's trade was subject to import or export licensing. Trade reforms had merely transferred the issuing authority from central to provincial levels without substantially dismantling the share of trade covered by licenses. (iii) The government subsidized the losses incurred by trading enterprises due to the discrepancy between domestic and world prices. (iv) The government set the official exchange rate for its non-convertible currency and strictly controlled the use of foreign exchange.[8] But the GATT application provided China the needed impetus as well as a clearer direction for its subsequent rounds of trade reforms, which in turn created pressure to reforming the price structure.

In response to a Chinese memorandum, the GATT set up a working party in May 1987 to formally examine China's trade regime and to develop the basic protocol for China's rights and obligations in the GATT. The negotiation process had to overcome two initial obstacles: (i) the legal

---

[7] In 1984, China invited Ake Linden, the legal adviser to the Director-General, to visit China to familiarize the Chinese government with the GATT requirements. A useful go-between, Linden paid another visit in 1985 to explain to China what it would mean to be a full GATT member while China through him put out its basic requests to the GATT. See Harold K. Jacobson and Michel Oksenberg, *China's Participation in the IMF, the World Bank, and GATT,* Ann Arbor, University of Michigan Press, 1990. This book provides a detailed account of China's negotiation process to join the GATT up to the Tiananmen event.

[8] The World Bank, China: External Trade and Capital, Washington, DC, 1988.

implications of China's entry status as a resumption of its "old seat" or as a new contracting party;[9] and (ii) the need for China to provide explanations to over 1,200 searching questions concerning China's trade system and trade practices.[10]

By the spring of 1989, the fact-finding phase was completed, with China having responded to all the questions. The GATT was about to work out the terms of protocol for China's resumption. In the meanwhile, China's foreign trade system had undergone a further round of reforms and liberalization, with foreign trade enterprises required to operate the contract responsibility system.[11] But the developed country members of

---

[9] If China were to resume its old membership, it would pose problems for countries like Australia, Japan, and the United States which had enacted certain laws in the interim that would have legal implications for China, e.g., the US 1974 Trade Act. It would be simpler if China were to come in as a new member and be exempted from certain obligations as provided by Article XXXV of the GATT.

When a new country accedes to the GATT, Article XXXV allows any member country to refrain from establishing GATT relations with that new member. Many member countries in fact invoked this Article when Japan joined the GATT, out of fear of Japan's potential economic strength. If China were to assume its old seat, Article XXXV could not technically be invoked because China would be in effect an old member. However, this might pose problems for the United States because of its need to invoke Article XXXV against China in order to satisfy the requirements of its 1974 Trade Act. In the circumstances, the United States might be prompted to block China from resuming its old seat. In this sense, China's claim of the "Grandfather Clause", as explained in footnote 6, would be "more important in theory than in practice". See Robert E. Herzstein (1986). China and the GATT: Legal and policy issues by China's participation in the General Agreement on Tariffs and Trade. *Law & Policy in International Business,* 18(2).

[10] In order to answer those questions, the Chinese government had to promote serious study and analysis of its foreign trade system and practices. This led to the publication over the last few years of many good articles on China's foreign trade in *Guoji Maoyi Wenti* (International Trade Journal) and *Guoji Maoyi* (International Trade). The former belongs to the University of International Business and Economics while the latter, to the International Trade Research Institute. Both organizations were under MOFERT.

Another fallout from the GATT application had been the rise of a large group of bureaucrats and experts with a good understanding of the international trade system and problems.

[11] At that time, China as in many other developing countries operated the import licensing system because of its shortage of foreign exchange. But, as defended by a Chinese economist, the commodity items subject to import licensing were very few, accounting for only

the GATT at that point were not so much worried about China's trade regime (which was in any case seen to be moving in the right direction toward greater market orientation) as about the technical areas like transparency in trade matters, the safeguard mechanism, export subsidies, and dumping. "Transparency" and "reciprocity" have already been explained earlier. "Safeguard action" allows a developed country to use as "a temporary measure" tariffs of quotas against labor-intensive exports (e.g., textiles) from LDCs. "Dumping" is defined as a sale for export at less than "fair value" or "normal value". Both export subsidies and dumping are treated as unfair competition by the GATT. To "safeguard" its domestic industries, the importing country was allowed to undertake anti-dumping measures by imposing "countervailing duties".

The application of these measures to China would naturally pose many problems. First, the legal regime in China had always been opaque as China was known to have changed tariffs, quotas, and licensing system unilaterally and without warning. China had no such American equivalent as the "Federal Register" to announce officially new laws and regulations. Secondly, as a half-reformed socialist economy with a dual-price system, China's subsidies were artificial and difficult to track. Thirdly, China being a large trading country, the potential benefit denied to China's trade partner as a result of non-reciprocity could be very substantial. Lastly, it would also be more difficult for a developed country to invoke safeguard action against China. This is because China, being a large economy, could threaten to retaliate by cutting down its imports. Nonetheless, for geopolitical reasons, most GATT members by mid-1989 "were willing to give China the benefit of the doubt in many areas of concern to them".[12]

However, much of China's international goodwill generated by its open-door policy and economic reform was lost overnight following the violent suppression of the student protest at Tiananmen in June 1989. In

---

2% of all items or 30% of all imports. Further, China had no import quotas for certain countries — hence, Chinese trade system was not discriminatory. Liu Guangzi (1989). The import licensing procedural agreement in the GATT in relation to China's import licensing system. *Guoji Maoyi Wenti* (International Trade Journal) (10).

[12] Penelope Hartland-Thunberg (1990). *China, Hong Kong, Taiwan and the World Trading System.* New York: St. Martin's Press, p. 95.

the aftermath of Tiananmen, Western countries were concerned that the Chinese government might even suspend economic reform. In particular, the United States Congress, making use of the human rights issue, had turned openly hostile toward China. The Bush Administration was accordingly under strong pressures to politicize the question of China's GATT membership and to delay the process by emphasizing such technical difficulty as lack of transparency in China's trade policies.

On the other hand, the post-Tiananmen Li Peng government was equally determined to mend its diplomatic fences by expanding its diplomatic activities.[13] The GATT matter was obviously high on China's diplomatic agenda. It has since come to light that the drastic trade reform on 1 January 1991 associated with the abolition of direct export subsidies, at the time while the overall economic reform was put on hold, was undertaken primarily to satisfy the GATT.[14] Toward the end of 1991, as China had settled its trade dispute with the United States over the intellectual property rights issue, China launched its final efforts to realize its GATT objective. In October 1991, Premier Li Peng was reported to have written to the heads of governments of the GATT contracting parties about China's case.[15] At the World Economic Forum in Davos in January 1992, Li repeated China's request for the GATT membership.

More significantly, China had adopted a number of specific measures to meet the GATT requirements: (i) The General Administration of Customs had introduced new import and export tariff regulations based on the harmonized commodity description and coding systems commonly used in world trade. (ii) The Customs Tariff Commission announced the reduction of tariff rates for 225 items (including raw materials and agricultural

---

[13] This was clearly shown in China's efforts toward making the Asian Games in Beijing a success, in addition to a string of state visits undertaken by Li Peng around 1990.

[14] *Xinhua* Newsagency, Beijing, 23 January 1991. With this reform, the government would cease subsidizing foreign trade enterprises for their losses arising from discrepancies between domestic and world market prices, and these enterprise themselves would have to bear sole responsibility for their profits and losses. Shortly prior to this round of trade reforms, the *Renminbi* was sharply devalued, thereby bringing the official exchange rate fairly close to the "spot" market rate.

[15] "Trade reforms follow GATT rules", *China Daily Business Weekly,* Beijing, 1–7 March 1992.

products), effective from 1 January 1992.[16] (iii) China had submitted to the GATT Secretariat 21 documents, including 17 formerly classified documents, on import and export administration (see Appendix 1). (iv) China had pledged to remove, during the first half of 1992, 16 product categories from a list of 53 subject to import licensing, and within two to three years to reduce further the number of licensed products by two-thirds.[17] (v) China after 1 April 1992 abolished "all import regulatory duties".[18]

China has indeed gone a long way in meeting the GATT compatibility in terms of both reforming its foreign trade regime and improving its foreign trade transparency. All the important GATT members except the United States on account of its domestic political problems, were reported to have responded to China's latest initiatives positively. To have its GATT endeavor finally materialized, China had to wait for the shift of the domestic political climate in the United States, perhaps after its presidential election.[19]

Pros and Cons for China

Apart from the political question of asserting what it considers to be its natural right to rejoin this international organization, China would eventually have to face the benefits and costs arising from the rights and obligations of its full GATT membership. Broadly speaking, by participating in the GATT, China could legitimize its ongoing economic reform program whilst strengthening the hands of the reformers in Beijing. We have seen how the GATT negotiation had actually spurred China's

---

[16] "New import and export tariffs are unveiled", *China Daily,* Beijing, 1 November 1991.

[17] The products to be removed from import licensing included: rolled steel, sugar, tape recorders, black-and-white TVs, watches, garments made of synthetic fibers, electronic microscopes, coffee, and coffee products. "Trade reforms follow GATT rules", *op.cit.*

[18] "Trade reforms follow GATT rules", *China Daily Business Weekly, op. cit.*

[19] It was reported that according to "internal Chinese documents", Beijing had reached an important understanding with Mr Baker, US Secretary of State, during his last visit to China in November 1991 that the United States would make a concession on the Chinese membership provided China could also allow Taiwan to join. Wu Yian, "Internal Documents on both the Mainland and Taiwan joining the GATT", *Jiushi Niendai* (The Nineties), Hong Kong, April 1992.

During the debate on the annual renewal of China's MFN in July 1991, the US Senate openly declared its support for Taiwan membership in GATT.

foreign trade reform progress. The GATT membership would also facilitate the integration of the Chinese economy into the global economic system. It may even be argued that China's eventual accession to the GATT would enhance China's international standing as a responsible trading country and thereby also increase its attractiveness to foreign investors. It may be noted that the GATT can deal only with merchandise trade, not trade in services or investment activities, which are on the agenda of the Uruguay Round at that time. But a GATT member, in abiding by the open trading system is likely to be more attractive to foreign investors.

More specifically, the GATT membership could provide China with better defense against certain protectionist and discriminatory policies in developed countries. As China has learned from its dealing with the MFA negotiation, the established multilateral framework under the GATT is far more effective than the troublesome bilateral negotiations which China had to go through with individual countries. Other standard advantages would include China's access to GATT's dispute settlement mechanisms against unfair trade laws from other member countries and China's opportunity to take part in the formulation of various world trade policies.

In real terms, China was not likely to reap much potential economic benefits from the GATT membership at that stage. The most important and visible benefit for a developing country to join the GATT is associated with the preferential tariff treatment under the Generalized System of Preferences (GSP) from developed countries. But China had already in the early 1980s gained GSP treatment from all developed countries with such a scheme, except from the United States. It was expected that China's accession to the GATT should make it easier but not automatic for the United States to extend such duty-free treatment to China. According to the 1974 US Trade Act, the GSP scheme could only be accorded to market-based developing countries which are also members of both the GATT and IMF. Thus China still has to pass the US domestic political hurdle by satisfying the US government (i.e., the US Commerce Department) that China belongs to the market economies.

China has all along argued that its ongoing economic and trade reforms have rendered the Chinese economy increasingly responsive to market forces. In any case, "China could rightfully note that the meaning of 'market economy' is unclear since almost all governments interfere in the marketplace to some extent".[20] Similarly, for the Most Favored Nation (MFN) status, China had already received MFN treatment, albeit on a year-to-year basis, from the United States since 1980. Although China's GATT membership does not mean it would automatically receive such treatment from the United States unconditionally, it would be much more difficult for the United States to maneuver the MFN as an effective foreign policy instrument against China that time. As noted earlier, one of the fundamental principles of the GATT organization is non-discrimination on which the MFN is based. In 1979, China signed a bilateral trade agreement with the United States, which made China eligible to receive the MFN treatment, but not unconditionally. The Jackson-Vanek amendment to the 1974 US Trade Act requires the US President to certify every year that China is not violating human rights by placing restrictions on emigration before MFN treatment is extended to China. The Jackson-Vanek amendment was originally aimed at the former Soviet Union.

If China were not to derive much real gain from its resumption of the GATT membership, it would not have to bear much cost either. The cost to China would be generally in the nature of short-term adjustment for the economy. In observing the GATT obligations such as reciprocity, China would have to liberalize the access to its domestic market by its foreign trade partners. The potential influx of more imported goods would have adverse effects on many state industries, which are not competitive.[21] But China could reduce such short-term adjustment cost with a gradual import liberalization, which should be acceptable to the GATT. Given the inevitability of China evolving toward the market system, there was really no

---

[20] See "The membership maze", *China Trade Report*, November 1987, p. 37.

[21] The case in point was China's automobile industry. At that time, China had over 2,600 factories producing motor cars or components. At the Changchun Automobile, the unit cost of producing a German Audi was Rmb 270,000 (roughly US$50,000), which was many times above the world cost. Wu Yian (1992). Internal document on both the Mainland and Taiwan joining the GATT, *Jiushi Niendai* (The Nineties), Hong Kong, April 1992.

significant long-term political and economic cost for China in its efforts to regain the GATT membership.

Wider Implications

The GATT itself was facing uncertain prospects. With the world economic growth slowing down, with the industrial countries resorting to managed trade, and with the United States ceasing to champion for global free trade, the Uruguay Round failed to come to any fruitful conclusion despite its six long years of MTN process.[22] Thus, China's accession to the GATT at that juncture did not seem to make much difference to the GATT body one way or the other.

The role of the GATT in the world community may fluctuate or even diminish in importance. But it could not be written off. With world trade being increasingly politicized, there is in fact a greater need for the GATT to play the ombudsman's role. Hence, the long-term significance of China's GATT membership should be viewed in the context of the potential impact on this WTO by this large and rapidly developing economy already experiencing dynamic trade growth at double-digit rates.

More specifically, China's GATT membership might have greater impact on the Third World. China would be expected to utilize its status as a developing country to negotiate better tariff deals and demand better market access to the developed countries. Here, the Chinese interests could coincide with those of other developing countries. But the latter could also see China as a potential threat to their own exports. The position of the Third World countries on the China membership was understandably mixed. On the one hand, they were apprehensive of China as a large and new competitor in the world market. On the other

---

[22] In this Uruguay Round, the developed countries have problems with the less developed countries over such issue as trade in services and intellectual property rights. But the Uruguay Round negotiation got hogged down mainly because of the dispute between the United States and the European Economic Community (EEC) over the issue of agricultural protection. See "Outlook Dims on Trade Talks", *International Herald Tribune*. Singapore, 20 April 1992 and "A GATT Solution Is There for the Having", *International Herald Tribune*, 22 April 1992.

hand, China would also be a new market for other developing countries; and China could also support the general stand of the Third World. Hence, no Third World country expressed open objection the Chinese membership. China's GATT membership should also help stabilize, if not depoliticize, the Sino–US economic relationship. And continuing Sino–US trade frictions are not good for the economic development of the Asia-Pacific region.

Of even greater significance was the concept of "Greater China" in the GATT. Backed by both UK and China, Hong Kong became a full member of the GATT in 1986. Taiwan, with open support from the United States, formally submitted its application to the GATT in January 1990. It was predicted that Taiwan will come in as a "customs territory" once China acceded to the GATT.[23] In 1991, the total exports of these three territories amounted to US$303 billion or 8.6% of the world total. This put "Greater China" as the world's fourth largest trading entity after the United Sates Germany, and Japan. Here lies the greatest implication of China's membership in the GATT.

Appendix 1

Documents Submitted by China to the GATT to Improve Trade Transparency

- Import and export tariffs in new harmonized system
- Summary surveys of China's 1989 customs statistics
- China's Customs Statistics Year Book 1990
- Almanac of China's 1991 foreign economic relations and trade
- Import regulatory duty rates
- Tariff reductions on 225 product lines in a harmonized system (effective on 1 January 1992)
- Circular No. 1 of the Ministry of Foreign Economic Relations and Trade (21 February 1991)
- The Law of Import and Export Commodity Inspection

---

[23] "Waiting for the call: Taiwan more confident on GATT application", *Far Eastern Economic Review,* 12 Martcch 1992, p. 47–48.

- Commodities subject to inspection (effective on 1 January 1991)
- Products subject to import and export licence under harmonized system tariff line
- Replies to questions from China's Working Party members
- Outlines of the 10-Year Programme and the Eighth Five-Year Plan for National Economic and Social Development
- Product categories subject to State pricing
- Sixteen product categories no longer subject to import licensing requirements
- Regulations for foreign exchange control
- Comparative manual of customs tariff numbers and items/rates of product taxes/VAT
- Directory of Chinese Foreign Economic Relations and Trade Enterprises 1989
- Foreign trade firms designated to import the first and second category products
- Products subject to mandatory import plan
- Products first and second tariff line categories

Note: China was reported to have submitted to the GATT Secretariat 21 documents, but only 20 of them appeared in the *China Daily*.
Source: "Trade Reform Follow GATT": *China Daily Business Weekly* (Beijing, 1–7 March 1992).

Chapter 13

China and the World Trade Organization

Introduction

For nine long years, China had been making hectic efforts to join (or rejoin) the General Agreement on Tariffs and Trade (GATT); but its GATT efforts were largely in vain. In January 1995, the GATT was superseded by the World Trade Organization (WTO). In a sense, being outside the GATT, China had also failed to become a founding member of WTO. Undaunted, China had continued to intensify its drive to gain accession to the WTO right after it came into being. Looking back, China's application for GATT/WTO had been the longest and the most complicated in the history of this world trade body at that point of time.

On 11 July 1995, China had succeeded in getting only "one foot in" after the WTO General Council, with European backing, granted China an "observer status". This led China's chief negotiator to openly criticize the US for thwarting China's WTO efforts. It had then become sufficiently clear that China's full accession would be decided not in Geneva (where WTO was based), but in Washington, D.C.

Increasingly, China's WTO membership had become a pawn in the political game between China and the US. China had a particularly frosty relationship with the US throughout President Clinton's first term in office, and the US public and its media, with the Tiananmen images still fresh in their minds, were generally not well-disposed toward China. Clinton himself was also obsessed with the issue of China's human rights. It needs to be added that the US had also basic economic interest in this matter as over 60% of China's manufactured exports were destined for the US market.

Officially, the US opposition to the China membership had to be based on technical and legal grounds. Previously, some developed country members were quite happy with the overall reform progress of China as a socialist market economy. The developed countries led by the US wanted to raise the "admission price" of the China membership by pushing up the technical requirements as a condition for its accession to the WTO. The basic rationale was that the WTO could impose more stringent requirements than the GATT, particularly in terms of tariff and non-tariff barriers. In 1994, China's average tariff level was still 22.5% high, compared to the average rate of 4.7% for the developed world. China could be allowed to pass if it were treated as a developing economy. However, the developed countries implicitly wanted China to be admitted as a developed economy.

By mid-1990s, China had already emerged as a potentially important trading power. When China first put in its application to the GATT in 1986, its total trade was only US$74 billion. By 1995, China became the world's 11th largest trading country, with its total trade at US$280 billion and growing at 17% a year. China at that time had also become a big market. Obviously, it was to the interest of all the developed economies, not just the US, to pry open the vast China market as much as possible as a condition for China's entry.

To many people in China, the price of the WTO membership was just too exorbitant if China were not treated as a developing economy. In actual fact, the balance of economic costs and benefits for China that stage of its development was not clear-cut and not conclusive. The WTO membership could bring in severe foreign competition against many of China's inefficient state-owned enterprises and its numerous small and medium enterprises. It could also adversely affect China's agricultural sector. If China were then a true democracy, there would surely be many special interest groups to lobby against China's WTO membership.

To the Chinese government, however, the WTO membership was just a matter of asserting its "natural right" to resume the China seat in this important international organization, particularly since Taiwan was also stepping up efforts to join. (China was then already in the World Bank and the International Monetary Fund (IMF). This was the political issue, and it explains why China had never let up its bid for the WTO membership.

At the same time, the government also understood the short-term costs and risks for China arising from the WTO membership. To minimize the potential short-term disruptive effects of the WTO membership, the government had to intensify its efforts for domestic economic reform, particularly in respect of the state-owned enterprise reform and the related banking reform. This strategy, in retrospect, had proved to be extremely beneficial for China, with the WTO membership actually operating as a catalyst for domestic economic reform efforts. It was actually the case that Premier Zhu Rongji had achieved a number of important reform breakthroughs before he let China take the last leap to join the WTO — certainly not a leap in the dark.

In November 2001, China finally signed the protocol to join the WTO. This was also the last month of the Clinton Administration, and China's membership could also be seen as Clinton's last diplomatic gift to China. By 2001, China's total trade amounted to US$510 billion, rising to be the world's 5th largest trading nation. Of even greater importance, the WTO membership sparked off double-digit rates of economic growth for China through the decade. This may be called the "WTO effect", which refers to the additional productivity and efficiency gains by China due to its greater integration with the global economy.

Ten years later, by 2011, China's total trade increased sevenfolds to reach US$3,642 billion to be the world's leading trading power. China's WTO benefits were beyond all expectations.

Still out of WTO

For nine long years, China had been making ardent efforts to join (officially, "re-join") the General Agreement on Tariffs and Trade (GATT); but Chinese efforts have been thwarted time and again. On 20 December 1994, China ended the 19th round of GATT talks in Geneva with yet another failure, thereby denying it the opportunity of becoming one of the founding members of the World Trade Organization (WTO), which superseded the GATT on 1 January 1995. The Chinese leadership was manifestly humiliated over this setback, especially since it considered having made the necessary reforms and changes to meet the GATT requirements. Beijing publicly announced that China would no longer offer to hold bilateral GATT talks on its own.[1]

---

[1] According to a senior Chinese official, the problem was due to the "blockade and excessive demands from a few contracting parties". The spokesman of China's Ministry of Foreign Trade and Economic Cooperation (MOFTEC) had openly accused these countries of breaking "their promises of support for China to resume GATT status". *Bering Review* (2–8 January 1995).

However, China soon renewed its campaign to join the WTO once it had settled its trade dispute with the United States over the protection of intellectual property rights, which brought the two countries to the brink of a trade war.[2] On 8 March 1995, Pierre Girard, Chairman of the WTO's China Working Party called an "informal" meeting in Geneva to reconsider the question of China's accession, and a second round of informal talks was convened on 11 July 1995. China was then still hoping that if it were to be admitted by the end of July 1995, it could still be regarded, retroactively, as one of the founding members of WTO.[3] However, this deadline was passed as the second informal round ended on 28 July 1995, again without breakthrough, leaving China's chief negotiator Long Yongtu bitterly criticizing the United States for blocking China's entry and for being "hypocritical" in its promise of support for China's accession.[4]

In the meanwhile, there had been a dramatic change in the politics and economics underlying China's application. Beijing's relations with Washington have since turned sour as a result of Taiwan's President Lee Teng-Hui's visit to the United States while Europe was adopting more "proactive policies" to improve its business ties with China, as was evidenced by European Commission Vice-president Leon Brittan's visit to Beijing and China's President Jiang Zemin's visit to several European countries in June 1995.[5] On 11 July 1995, the WTO General Council, apparently with strong European backing, made an unprecedented move of granting China an "observer status", which would allow China to take

---

For more details, see also "Somebody Deliberately Obstructing, Asking for Exorbitant Prices", *Jingji Ribao* (Economic Daily, Beijing, 2 January 1995).

[2] On 12 March 1995, the two countries signed a trade accord which would ease access to China's markets for US products (particularly agricultural products) in exchange for increased American support (to be more "flexible and pragmatic") for China's bid to join the WTO. "US., China Sign Pacts on WTO, Bilateral Trade", *Asian Wall Street Journal* (13 March 1995); and "US Backs China's WTO Bid", *International Herald Tribune* (13 March 1995).

[3] "WTO entry requires more time", *China Daily* (Beijing, 21–27 May 1995).

[4] "No breakthrough in WTO entry talks", *China Daily* (Beijing, 31 July 1995).

[5] EU's Ambassador Endymion Wilkinson in Beijing said: "We want China to join the WTO...". "EU trade plans will boost China's world involvement", *The Straits Times* (Singapore, 4 July 1995).

part in all meetings and decision-making processes, though without a voting right.[6] China thus succeeded in getting one foot in. But its full accession was to be decided, clearly not in Geneva but in Washington.[7]

In its attempt to gain accession to the GATT, China since 1986 engaged in a protracted process of negotiation, the most complicated and the longest in the history of this world trade body. Why was China so eager to join? What did Beijing hope to gain? Was the Chinese government fully aware of the costs and risks involved in being a member of such a multilateral trade process? What would be at stake, for both China and the world's major trading nations, if China were to remain outside the WTO?

A Zigzag Process of Negotiation

The GATT, the International Monetary Fund (IMF), and the International Bank for Reconstruction and Development (IBRD or World Bank) are the three pillars of the international economic system created at the Bretton Woods Conference in 1944 to speed up post-war economic recovery and development. Specifically for the GATT (which came into being in 1948), its basic goal has been to foster an open trading system within the GATT rules. In effect, trade liberalization has been promoted by the GATT through its various rounds of multilateral trade negotiation (MTN) based on the principles of reciprocity, non-discrimination, and transparency. The eighth and the last MTN process was the Uruguay Round, which was concluded in December 1993. China took part in the Uruguay Round from the start and was a signatory to its final agreement.

China was actually a founding member of the GATT. But when the KMT (Nationalist) government retreated to Taiwan in 1949, it took with it the China seat in the GATT, only to give it up a year later. In 1986, China formally applied for membership in (technically, "accession to") the GATT. In response, the GATT set up a working party in May 1987 to

---

[6] "Mainland gets foot in WTO". *South China Morning Post* (Hong Kong, 12 July 1995).

[7] In the latest round of talks in July 1995, "China was making a concerted effort to be flexible, but was not meeting with any responses from the US. The US still has a tendency to be negative...". See "Beijing slams Washington for snubbing trade scheme", *South China Morning Post* (Hong Kong, Weekend edition, 5 August 1995).

formally examine China's trade regime and to develop the basic protocol for China's rights and obligations in the GATT. By the spring of 1989, the fact-finding phase was completed,[8] and the GATT was about to work out the final terms of protocol for China's resumption of the GATT seat.

However, much of China's international goodwill generated by its open-door policy and economic reform was lost overnight following the violent suppression of the student protest at Tiananmen in June 1989. In the aftermath of Tiananmen, the United States put up the last stumbling block. In particular, the Bush administration, yielding to strong pressures from the Congress, politicized the question of China's GATT membership and sought to delay China's accession process. At that time, many Chinese leaders had apparently failed to realize that China's accession to the GATT was no longer a mere technical matter of meeting the GATT requirements.[9] When its GATT endeavor was rebuffed in 1992, the Chinese leadership was flabbergasted and tried to set a self-proclaimed deadline (by March 1993) for China's final accession.[10]

In 1993, following Deng Xiaoping's tour of South China, the Chinese economy (now officially called "socialist market economy") was opened up further to foreign trade and foreign investment, and was also further

---

[8] This included overcoming two initial obstacles: (i) The legal implications of China's entry status as a resumption of its "old seat" or, as a new contracting party; and (ii) The need for China to provide explanations to over 1,200 searching questions concerning China's trade system and trade practices. For a detailed discussion of China's GATT negotiation process, see John Wong (1993). "China and the GATT", *IEAPE Background Brief*, (No. 38).

[9] Thus China's Vice-Minister of Foreign Economic Relations and Trade (MOFERT), Gu Yongjiang in early 1992 announced that China would soon "rejoin" the GATT. See "China may soon join GATT", *Lianhe Zaobao* (Singapore, 17 April 1992). Later in March 1992, MOFERT's Director of the GATT Affairs Division, Li Zhongzhou, also optimistically predicted that China would "regain" its GATT status some time in 1992. Returning from the GATT's 10th Session of the "Working Party on China" in Geneva, Li stressed: "The Chinese government attaches great importance to the issue and is sparing no efforts to comply with GATT requirements". "Trade reforms follow GATT rules", *China Daily Business Weekly* (Beijing, 1–7 March 1992).

[10] Partly as a result of frustration and partly as a negotiation tactic, China had in fact on record set another deadline. In December 1993, a trade official warned that Beijing would scrap its bid to rejoin the GATT if it did not get in by 1995. "China Gives GATT a 1995 Deadline", *International Herald Tribune* (20 December 1993).

liberalized (e.g., putting an end to state planning for foreign trade). At the same time, China adopted a higher profile in international economic diplomacy, leading to a renewed interest to rejoin the GATT. In 1994, the completion of the Uruguay Round lent further momentum to China's GATT efforts, which were mounted along with its other objective of keeping its MFN (most-favored nation) status with the United States.

In the meanwhile, the major GATT contracting parties led by the United States had also raised the "price" for China's re-entry. Previously, the developed country members might have been happy with the overall reform progress of China *as a socialist economy*. Now they had pushed up the technical requirements as a condition for the Chinese accession, demanding from China much tougher prerequisites like a single national trade policy (i.e., China's interior provinces to be as open as its special economic zones), full transparency, and a firm commitment to full market economy. WTO imposes even more stringent requirements than GATT.

According to the US Government Accounting Office, Washington wanted China to comply with the following before entering the WTO:[11]

— Greater transparency in trade laws.
— A timetable for tariff reductions.
— Equal treatment for foreign and domestic goods and services.
— Phasing out of state-fixed prices.
— Mechanisms to protect WTO members against sudden surges of Chinese exports.
— Removal of certain non-tariff barriers.
— A timetable for the phased elimination of certain industrial subsidies.
— Expanding the trading rights of Chinese companies and eliminating designated trading of certain products by certain firms.
— Demonstration of ability to apply WTO obligations uniformly across regions and provinces.
— Demonstration of ability to protect intellectual property rights.

---

[11] See "China Is Poised to Renew Campaign to Join the WTO", *Asian Wall Street Journal* (28 February 1995).

The terms and conditions laid down by the WTO for China were open to interpretation. China would insist that it could fulfil the WTO obligations as manifested in the measures it had already taken to protect intellectual property rights. China could also argue that the required reforms and changes had already been underway and were about to achieve their objectives: e.g., most consumer prices, except some for political and social reasons, were no longer fixed by the state. As for the elimination of non-tariff barriers, China would plead for a reasonable transitional period to allow itself to adjust.

Take the crucial question of tariff and non-tariff reduction. Following the reduction of tariff rates for 225 items on 1 January 1992, China cut the rates again for 3,371 items (which represented 53.6% of the total tax items) on 31 December 1992, and further for another 2,898 items on 31 December 1993.[12] This had brought down China's average nominal tariff from 39.9% to 36.4%.[13] In terms of weighted average, China's tariff level in early 1994 was 22.5%, compared to the average rate of 4.7% for developed countries and 14% for developing countries.[14] For non-tariff barriers, China on 1 July 1995 freed up 367 import items from quota and licence controls, following similar exercises on 283 items in December 1993 and on 208 items in March 1994.[15] Furthermore, China promised to bring its

---

[12] "New import and export tariffs are unveiled", *China Daily* (Beijing, 1 November 1991); and Xong Zhenyan, "What China has done to rejoin GATT", *International Business* (Beijing, January 1995).

[13] "Some People Deliberately Stand in the Way: Others Demand Exorbitant Price", reported by Yang Guangzhi in Geneva, *Jingji Ribao* (Economic Daily, Beijing, 2 January 1995).

[14] Zhu Tong, "GATT Membership", *China Mail* (Hong Kong, 1 March 1994).

It appeared that China's trade officials have failed to monitor the progress of tariff reduction systematically and its impact. China's high ranking trade officials have never put on record saying what China's average level of tariff protection was at a particular time. Many Chinese reports on this subject often failed to distinguish nominal tariff from effective tariff, and simple average tariff rate from the weighted average rate. Thus, another source put China's average tariff rate in 1994 as "19%". ("China ready to carry out demands of GATT", *China Daily*, Beijing, 2 December 1994.)

[15] "Beijing removes barriers on 367 imports", *The Straits Times* (Singapore, 18 July 1995).

At that time, in the latest liberalization, the new list reduced the number of raw materials imports subjected to quotas and licences from 26 to 16, and that of machinery and electronics from 18 to 15. The 1993 liberalization covered rolled steel, steel billets,

average tariff rate to below 30% by the year 2000, and the import items under quantity restriction from 1,247 to 240.[16] By 2000, the Chinese *Renminbi* was also freely convertible.

This, along with other changes like abolishing mandatory planning in foreign trade and direct export subsidies, indicated that China had in fact liberalized its foreign trade regime a lot, and was heading in the right direction. In a sense, China "has already achieved much of what it earlier thought it needed to do for GATT membership".[17] As a London-based business journal put it, "the (Chinese) government has met standards far more rigorous than those achieved by other developing countries".[18] For instance, China's average tariff rate was lower than that of India and China's treatment of foreign investment far more liberal than that in India. South Korea was admitted to the GATT in 1967 but its financial sector at that time in many aspects was not much more open than China's.[19]

But being "GATT-compatible" for China was not exactly the same as being "WTO-compatible" because of the generally stricter WTO entry conditions and additional requirements. From the standpoint of the Working Party (which was to prepare the final protocol governing China's accession), China had clearly not fulfilled the WTO conditions as they have demanded, especially in terms of full transparency, adequate

---

coffee, and aircrafts for civilian uses while the 1994 liberalization covered commodities like grain, TV sets, chemical products, and integrated circuits. See "What China has done to rejoin GATT", *International Business*, (January 1995).

Evidently due to their confusion over the trade classification system, the Chinese authorities at each policy announcement have never given a clear picture as to what proportion of commodity items have actually been liberalized. There were no official figures as to how many items were subjected to quotas and licences.

[16] This plan of import liberalization was contained in the package proposal China presented to the GATT on 31 August 1994. See "What China has done to rejoin GATT", *International Business* (January 1995).

[17] "Beijing Is Coy on Joining Trade Group", *International Herald Tribune* (24 April 1995).

[18] "Gatting there", *Business China* (London, 7 March 1994).

[19] As argued by Nicholas R. Lardy, China was already more integrated into the world economy than Japan, Taiwan or South Korea were at comparable stages of their economic development. "By some measures, China is more open than these economies even on a contemporary basis", (*China in the World Economy*: Washington, DC, Institute for International Economics, 1994), p. 110.

safeguard measures, and easy market access. Besides, China's tariffs at that time were undoubtedly high, even by the average standard of developing countries. China therefore needed to effect more changes.

In other words, China could be deemed to have fulfilled those requirements only if China were to be treated as a developing economy, with an allowance for a reasonable timetable to complete the transition. Thus whether or not China should be allowed to join the WTO in terms of a developing country had since become the bone of contention between China and the Working Party dominated by the United States. Apart from its different interpretation of China's WTO compatibility, the Working Party viewed China as a dynamic trading power, whose exports have grown at an annual rate of over 17% since its open-door policy in 1978, quite uncharacteristic of a developing economy. Representing the interests of the major developed economies, the Working Party naturally wanted to pry open the vast China market as much as possible, so that these developed countries could better position themselves to capturing China's future development benefits.

China was, of course, an out-and-out developing country. The Chinese government accordingly regarded the price set by the Working Party for China's WTO membership as "too exorbitant". It had cogently argued that only by insisting on the entry requirement of a developing country status can China be able to reform its economy to meet the WTO obligations. According to Minister of Foreign Trade and Economic Cooperation (MOFTEC) Wu Yi, while China would continue to adopt a "flexible but firm" policy, it would considers the developed country terms for China's WTO membership "absolutely unacceptable".[20] Hence, there was continuing impasse of China's WTO membership.

---

[20] China's official stand on its WTO entry was, as repeatedly uttered by Minister Wu Yi, "firm but flexible". First, for those things which China was doing, China would continue. Second, for those China was ready to do, China would carry them out as soon as possible. Third, for those which China was able to do in future and cannot be done now, China would set a timetable to realize them step by step. Fourth, for those China finds unacceptable, China would never go ahead regardless of external pressures. Transparency, safeguard measures, and unified trade policy belonged to the first and second categories. Further reduction of tariff and non-tariff barriers belonged to the third, as China would set a timetable to do it. The condition for China's entry as a developed country belonged to

Perceived Benefits and Their Uncertainty

WTO membership was still high on China's trade diplomacy agenda. Apart from the political question of asserting its "natural right" to resume the China seat in this important international organization and the need to join before Taiwan did, China's decision to join WTO must be based on rationally weighing the rights and obligations (or benefits and costs) of its WTO membership. The benefits to China were well known to Chinese policy makers: they were usually quite general and were of long-term nature.

To begin with, it was commonly thought that the Chinese return to the world's multilateral trade system would expedite China's economic restructuring, particularly the deepening and widening of its foreign trade reform. If China had been admitted to the GATT a few years back, it would have certainly produced much greater impact in terms of legitimizing its ongoing economic reform program and strengthening the hands of the reformers in Beijing. At that time, its WTO membership was unlikely to spur the reform progress much further in the short run, as the Chinese economy had already gone through extensive reform, with the remaining reform programs constrained by mainly domestic rather than external political considerations.

WTO membership would also facilitate the integration of the Chinese economy into the global economic system. The Chinese economy (especially, its coastal region) was already quite well integrated with the international economy in terms of foreign trade and foreign investment. Specifically, China had become the world's 11th largest exporting country (from the 32nd position in 1978) despite being outside the GATT. Similarly, China's WTO membership was supposed to enhance China's attractiveness to foreign investors. But again, China in 1993 was the world's most favored destination for foreign capital without being in the GATT.

---

the fourth category, which was considered by Wu as "absolutely out of the question" for China. "China and the Multilateral World Trade System by MOFTEC Minister Wu Yi", *Guoji Shangbao* (International Commercial News, Beijing, 9 December 1994).

The most important and visible benefits for a developing country to join the GATT/WTO are associated with the preferential tariff treatment under the Generalized System of Preferences (GSP) from developed countries. But China had already in the early 1980s gained GSP treatment from all developed countries with such a scheme, except from the United States. China's accession to the WTO this time should make it easier but not automatic for the United States to extend such duty-free treatment to China.[21] Similarly for the MFN status, China's WTO membership did not mean it would automatically receive such treatment from the United States unconditionally.[22] In any case, the MFN was no longer such a central issue for China since President Clinton delinked it in 1994 from the politics of human rights.

What then were the potential gains for China? For so many years, the Chinese government had been pushing hard to realize its "cherished GATT/WTO membership", despite repeated rebuffs. More than half of the 130 or so legislations which China enacted since the reform were related to commercial laws aimed at integrating China with the global economy, or making China more GATT/WTO-compatible. Evidently, in the perception of the Chinese leadership, there must be substantial gains for China from its WTO membership. As MOFTEC Minister Wu Yi stated: "We do not have any unrealistic illusions about the multilateral trade system but, after weighing the pros and cons, we still think it is best for China to participate in this system".[23]

---

[21] According to the 1974 US Trade Act, the GSP scheme could only be accorded to market-based developing countries which are also members of both the GATT and IMF. But the US government could still block it by arguing that china is not a "full market economy". See "The membership maze", *China Trade Report* (November 1987).

[22] One of the fundamental principles of the GATT organization is non-discrimination on which the MFN is based. In 1979, China signed a bilateral trade agreement with the United States, which made China eligible to receive the MFN treatment, but not unconditionally. The Jackson-Vanek amendment to the 1974 US Trade Act requires the US President to certify every year that China is not violating human rights by placing restrictions on emigration before MFN treatment was extended to China. The Jackson-Vanek amendment was originally aimed at the former Soviet Union. See "Susan Mac Cormac," "Eyeing the GATT", *The China Business Review* (March–April, 1993).

[23] Wu Yi, "China and the World's Multilateral Trade System", *Wen Wei Po* (Hong Kong, 1 January 1995).

Wu Yi was probably thinking in terms of the general benefits connected with a well-functioning multilateral trade system. WTO membership was expected to provide China with a better defense against certain protectionist and discriminatory policies from developed countries, e.g., dispute settlement mechanisms against unfair trade laws from other member countries.[24] As China had learned from its dealings with global trade issues like the Multifibre Arrangement negotiation, the established multilateral framework under the WTO would be less troublesome than alternative bilateral negotiations. But the multilateral system is not always effective and its benefits are by no means certain, because large developed countries, particularly the United States, can resort to domestic laws for unilateral "arm-twisting". The recent US–Japan trade dispute over automobile components was a case in point.

More specifically, the WTO membership would give China easier access to the markets of the developed countries for such labor-intensive manufactured products as clothing and footwear, which were subjected to high tariffs as well as stringent non-tariff barriers.[25] According to a World Bank study, 60% of China's manufactured exports to the US in 1990 and 41% to the EC faced non-tariff barriers, compared to 29% and 42%, respectively, for all developing countries. Chinese exports could well have increased by 38% at 1988 prices if protection levels in developed countries against Chinese products had been lowered in accordance with the Uruguay Round liberalization.[26] Therefore, Chinese manufactured exports

---

Speaking at the "China Summit" Conference in April 1995, MOFTEC Minister Wu Yi still reiterated China's willingness to shoulder the obligations of the global multilateral trade system, after China's last efforts to join GATT were rebuffed in December 1994. "Wu Yi says STATE ready for WTO obligations", *China Daily* (Beijing, 11 April 1995).

[24] The United States filed 57 anti-dumping cases against China, 39 of which were made since 1990. "Dumping measures mask US protectionist acts", *China Daily Business Weekly* (Beijing, 11–17 June 1995).

[25] For example, Chinese clothing products were subjected to the high tariffs of 23% in Europe and 49% in Australia, well above the average tariff rate of developed countries. For non-tariff barriers, about half of Chinese exports were subjected to quotas in the US market. "China Has Much to Gain, But Also Risk, With WTO", *Asian Wall Street Journal* (2–3 December 1994).

[26] World Bank, *China: Foreign Trade Reform: Meeting the Challenge of the 1990s* (1993).

should benefit more from trade liberalization than an average developing country.

Weighing the Costs and Risks

While the WTO membership would yield some real gains to China, the costs to China could also be considerable, generally associated with short-term adjustments. The actual adjustment cost to China depended on the exact terms of China's membership protocol, i.e., whether China be regarded as a developed or a developing economy. Whatever the terms for China's entry, however, China would have to observe such WTO obligations as reciprocity by liberalizing its domestic markets further. The potential influx of more imported goods would undoubtedly have adverse effects on many sectors and industries which were not competitive. Worse still, as one China expert put it, "Chinese people love foreign products, period".[27] Not surprisingly, Beijing insisted on the developing country terms of entry so as to allow for a gradual import liberalization.

Most of the risks associated with the WTO membership were sufficiently well known to Chinese officials and economists, who, because of the long GATT negotiation process, had adequate time to study the following pros and cons of the various issues involved.[28]

To begin with, it was commonly argued that China's WTO membership would bring in such severe foreign competition as to undermine its many inefficient state-owned enterprises (SOEs) and its numerous township and village enterprises (TVEs), which operated on outdated technology and

---

[27] This canny observation was made by J.P. Morgan's China expert Huan Guocang, and is quite obvious to all Chinese. "China Has Much to Gain, But Also Risk, With WTO", *Asian Wall Street Journal* (2–3 December 1994).

For different cultural traits, Japanese and Korean people take pride in consuming their domestically produced goods (hence making it difficult for foreign companies to break into their markets) while Chinese people have a habit of showing off their consumption of foreign goods, from cigarettes to liquor.

[28] In the past few years, China's foreign trade journal *Guoji Maoyi* (International Trade) was full of articles and papers by China's economists on the potential impact of GATT membership. But they mostly repeated general views, and none performed a technically competent exercise of quantifying the extent of the GATT impact on specific industries.

management.[29] While this argument had its general validity, it was too all-embracing to be meaningful, simply because there was also no lack of SOEs and TVEs which were competitive and export-oriented.[30] Obviously, those SOEs or TVEs which cannot withstand stiff foreign competition, would have to go under. Some amount of industrial shake-up was part of the inevitable structural adjustment process for a growing economy. It was therefore more useful to examine the potential impact of the WTO membership on individual sectors or industries as follows:

— In the agricultural sector, the agricultural product markets have long been subject to varying degrees of government control, e.g., state procurement and state distribution channels. WTO membership would accelerate further liberalization as well the reorganization and development of China's agricultural trade, e.g., the wholesale market, the futures market, commodity exchange, and so on. In the rural areas (with 70% of China's population), peasants would continue to display a high degree of self-sufficiency in grain, poultry, vegetables, tobacco, and so on, thereby limiting the development of the rural agricultural trade. Changes and adjustments would be mainly confined to the agricultural product markets in urban areas.

— Since the degree of international free trade in agricultural products under WTO was still low and the fact that the share of agricultural products in China's overall foreign trade was also low (less than 20%), the overall WTO impact on the agricultural sector in the short run was expected to be limited, one way or the other. Broadly speaking, China had high comparative advantage for corn, soybeans, and a variety of fruits, livestock, and aquatic products. But China has low comparative advantage for certain kinds of grain like good-quality

---

[29] For SOEs, see, e.g., Chen Zhanping and Liu Luwu, "Problems faced by state enterprises and their solutions after China's GATT re-entry", *Guoji Jingmao Xiaoxi* (International Trade News, Beijing, 23 March 1993). For TVEs, see Ma Zheshi, (1994). Way out for China's township and village enterprises after GATT re-entry. *Caimao Jingji* (Finance and Trade Economics), Beijing, No. 4.

[30] For further discussion on the "dynamic" aspects of the TVEs, see John Wong, Rong Ma and Mu Yang (eds.) (1995). *China's Rural Entrepreneurs: Ten Case Studies*. Singapore: Times Academic Press.

wheat, and vegetable oil as well as for many processed agricultural products and packaged foods and drinks. This should provide good markets for agricultural exporting developed countries like the United States and Australia, especially since China was not likely to seek "special exceptions" to protect its agriculture. [31]

— By comparison, the WTO impact on the manufacturing sector would potentially be greater, though vary. As can be expected, most domestic enterprises in the textile and clothing sector producing for the low- and mid-price ends of the markets would remain competitive. But many joint ventures and wholly owned foreign enterprises in China producing clothing for the upper markets could feel the pressure of increased imports, which were subjected to non-price competition like quality, style, packaging, and brand names, rather than China's low labor-cost advantage. In the long run, the WTO membership would hasten the restructuring and upgrading of the textiles and clothing industries toward more capital-intensive and higher value-added activities, as it was done in Japan and the East Asian Newly Industrialized Economies (NIEs). [32]

— In the more capital-intensive sectors, China's WTO membership would lead to an increased import of electrical and electronic goods, steel products and non-ferrous metals, chemical products, and medical equipment. At that time China was a large exporter of low-tech engineering and electronic products, and these enterprises should benefit from a greater export opportunity. But many domestic medium- and high-tech enterprises, especially those in the computer and information

---

[31] For more detailed discussion of the potential impact on agriculture, see Shen Anran and Liu Liedong (1993). "Impact and Countermeasures to the Reentry of GATT on China's Cereals, Oils, and Food Trade", *Guoji Shangbao* (International Commercial News, Beijing); Cheng Quoqiang (1993). "China's Agriculture: Opening to the Outside and Protection", *Zhongguo Nongcun Jingji* (China's Rural Economy, Beijing, No. 7; and "Rejoining GATT and China's Grain and Edible Oil Trade", *Jiage Lilun yu Shijian* (Price Theory and Practice, Beijing, 20 June 1993).

[32] See Jiang Xiaojuan (1994). GATT accession presents challenge, opportunity to textile and clothing industries, *Zhongguo Fangzhi Bao* (China's Textiles News); JPRS-CAR-94-054, 19 August 1994.

industries,[33] would be hard pressed or simply outcompeted by foreign products of higher quality and better technology, once their tariff and non-tariff protection were lifted.[34] Likewise, the impact on China's nascent automobile industry would also be serious, with greater import of foreign automobiles being foreseen. However, the automobile industry, at that time slated to be a pillar industry for the future, was expected to receive appropriate measures of tariff and non-tariff protection as an "infant industry".[35]

— In the service sector (which was the weakest link of the Chinese economy), the WTO membership could lead to a large influx of higher quality and more efficient foreign economic services from banking to aviation, unless China would take appropriate protection measures.[36] China was planning to open up five important service industries to foreign business: (i) finance, (ii) insurance, (iii) accounting, (iv) advertising, and (v) medical insurance services. In all these areas, developed countries have a strong comparative advantage over their Chinese counterparts, and China was expected to be a significant net importer of services for many years to come.

— Take banking and finance. Opening up more financial services would facilitate China's financial sector development as well as its internationalization through greater competition and transfer of financial management know-how. However, China's state-owned financial institutions would not stand up well to the onslaught of foreign financial services, especially since the required institutional and legal framework for the market-based financial activities in China was

---

[33] Chinese computer manufacturers were facing problems despite rapid market demands. In 1994, the sales of personal computers reached 700,000 units, with only about 100,000 made locally and another 200,000 locally assembled. ("China's Computer Crisis", *International Herald Tribune*, 18 August 1995.)

[34] Sun Pengzhang (1993). Outlet for the electronic industry in the coastal areas — Impact of GATT membership resumption and counter-measures, *Guoji Maoyi* (International Trade, Beijing, No. 5).

[35] Xie Zhenglin (1993). An analysis of the expected profit rate on motor vehicles after rejoining GATT, *Zhongguo Wujia* (China's Price, Beijing, No. 6).

[36] "GATT re-entry would usher in overseas competitors: Influx of services seen", *China Daily Business Weekly* (Beijing, 22–28 May 1994).

not firmly in place.[37] Above all, the resultant financial liberalization would make it difficult for the Chinese government to intervene with administrative means for macroeconomic control, or to stem capital flight. In short, there could be a significant negative WTO impact on the service sector; but at the same time, China was likely to adopt appropriate safeguard measures to reduce such a risk.

It can thus be seen that China's WTO membership could incur significant economic and social costs on many segments of the economy, even if China were to be admitted as a developing economy. Ironically, if the Chinese political system is as truly democratic and pluralistic as in the United States, China's decision to join the GATT/WTO would have faced enormous domestic political obstacles by tough lobbying from different industry groups (e.g., the 20 million or so TVEs)! The argument for the WTO membership to the Chinese was essentially like the free trade argument to the Americans, which was good economics in the long run but bad politics in the short run.

As the Chinese government had already made up its mind to join the WTO (on acceptable terms), it was rather immaterial to harp on its potential negative impact. MOFTEC Minister Wu Yi had already made clear her view: "I do not agree with the viewpoint which believes that China's GATT re-entry would cause severe damage to China's economic development and the viability of its enterprises".[38] Wu had taken all the possible adjustment costs, as discussed above, in her stride. Given the inevitability of China's evolution toward the market system, much of the short-term adjustment costs associated with the WTO membership would in any case coincide with the foregone costs of China's final transition to a full market economy.

Better for China to be In Than Out

China's eventual accession to the WTO was never in doubt. It was clearly an anomaly for the WTO as a global trade body to continue excluding

---

[37] Ha Jiyun (1994). An analysis of the impact of China's return to GATT on the banking industry, *Guoji Maoyi Wenti* (International Trade Problems, Beijing, No. 134.

[38] Wu Yi (1994). "China and the multilateral world trade structure", *Guoji Shangbao* (International Commercial News, Beijing).

China, the world's 11th largest trading nation, on which also hinge the world's two other great trading entities of Taiwan and Hong Kong. Hong Kong was already a GATT member in 1986. Taiwan's WTO membership was contingent on China's. This trio in combination (the so-called "Greater China") chalked up total exports of over US$300 billion in 1994, the world's third largest after the United States and Germany. Much was therefore at stake if China continued to be left out of the WTO.

As Singapore's Senior Minister Lee Kuan Yew put it, "the US and EU will lose in strategic terms if China operates outside GATT and goes it alone".[39] China's industrialization and export drives can be slowed but cannot be stifled. Thus, Singapore and many Asia-Pacific countries took the view that it would be better for the world's multilateral trade system to embrace China at the early stage so as to encourage China to be a cooperative and constructive member, and to accelerate "China's ability and willingness to play by global rules".[40] The same view was gaining acceptance in the European Union (EU).[41]

Such good political sense sooner or later also prevailed in Washington. China's accession to the WTO could significantly improve the overall Sino–US relations by removing one of the major irritants. And a stable Sino–US relationship was crucial for the continuing economic growth and prosperity for both China and the Asia-Pacific region.

---

[39] Mr Lee explains: "This means China will not pay copyright royalties or observe patent rights. The US and EC will give up exports and investments in the largest growing economy in the post-Cold War world". "China has its role to play", *International Business* (Beijing, January 1995).

[40] In his keynote address at the Asia Society International Corporate Conference in Beijing on 13 May 1995, Singapore's Prime Minister Goh Chok Tong also said: "China should be helped to join the World Trade Organization (WTO), not have its application blocked. Membership at the WTO will commit China to observing and enforcing international rules on trade. It will also help open up China's market". "Global Economic Trends and Developments: The China Factor in the World Economy" (Press Release by Singapore's Ministry of Information and the Arts, Release No. 14/May 1995).

[41] "EU trade plans will boost China's world involvement", *The Straits Times* (Singapore, 4 July 1995); and "EU will endorse China's WTO bid", *China Daily* (Beijing, 8 July 1995).

Chapter 14

Southeast Asian Ethnic Chinese Investing in China

Introduction

This paper was originally written for an international conference in Korea. It was not formally published before; and it had not been widely circulated, even though the topic is of strong academic interest and certain practical importance.

The term "ethnic Chinese in Southeast Asia" by itself was intriguing enough; but it was also politically sensitive and complicated at that time. Academically, it was an extremely difficult subject for research by scholars. Individually, it might be possible to identify an ethnic Chinese in the region; but it would be politically incorrect to label him or her as an "overseas Chinese" in the old sense of this term. Many Southeast Asian countries have long ceased to treat their ethnic Chinese as foreigners or "overseas Chinese." Hence official records on the economic activities of ethnic Chinese in Southeast Asia were scarce and incomplete.

At the same time, it is well known that China's success in its economic reform and the open-door policy in the early phases had owed a lot to the capital, technology and entrepreneurship of the ethnic Chinese from Greater China (i.e., Hong Kong, Macau and Taiwan) and Southeast Asia (or the ASEAN countries today). The foreign direct investment in China from the Chinese diaspora in the region had frequently been highlighted in Western media — e.g., it was called the "Bamboo Network" by the American business magazine Forbes. This is almost like saying that people have all known about this and seen it; but it is difficult to pinpoint and to quantify. There was a lot of anecdotal evidence; but there were no systematic official figures about this phenomenon. The usefulness of this paper is the way it had put together all available information at that time and built up a reasonably coherent picture of this topic.

After a brief introduction of China's open-door policy, this paper discusses the complex changing relations between China and Southeast Asia from the period of the Cold War to their normalization of relations in the 1970s. As China embarked on economic reform and the open-door policy in the 1980s and looked south towards the region, Beijing found that the Cold War legacies had cast a long shadow on China's relations with individual countries in the region.

Beijing had also found that "ethnic Chinese" was a politically and socially sensitive subject. Thus, this chapter also goes into the discussion of the supranational concepts of "Greater China" and the "Chinese economic circle."

For the actual foreign direct investment (FDI) in China from different countries, one has to refer to the official statistics from China, which only captures the country sources, not by ethnicity. Right from the beginning, more than half of China's FDI emanated from Hong Kong — 56% of China's total FDI for the period of 1983–1991 as compared to only 1.7% for the five ASEAN countries (Indonesia, Malaysia, the Philippines, Singapore and Thailand). This clearly does not conform to the prevailing view at that time of many "overseas Chinese" investing in their ancestral land.

What actually happened is also well known. The FDI of many ethnic Chinese to China, particularly those from Indonesia and Malaysia, routed through Hong Kong. The Taiwanese did the same in the 1980s. Of the share from Southeast, Singapore's FDI accounted for the bulk of it (1.2%), to be followed by Thailand, 0.3%. For Singapore's share, most came from the government-linked companies. Furthermore, most ethnic Chinese from Southeast Asia tended to invest in Fujian, which is the original home for many overseas Chinese in Southeast Asia.

Above all, instead of identifying which ethnic Chinese from which country was investing how much in China — an impossible undertaking, this chapter has captured some large business enterprises (basically owned by ethnic Chinese) from five ASEAN countries, which had invested in China. They include the Salim group and the Lippo group of Indonesia; the Lion Corp. and the Kerry group of Malaysia; the SM Prime Holdings of the Philippines; UOB and OCBC of Singapore; and the CP group of Thailand. Needless to say, they have all been doing well in China, riding on the continuing boom of the Chinese economy all through these years. To them, business is business.

Still, it is undeniable that the overseas Chinese diaspora has contributed a lot to China's economic rise, especially for its early phases. This is something that the overseas Indian diaspora has not done, at least not on the comparable scale, to India's recent economic rise.

The table has turned today. China is now the world's second largest economy, and its economic relationship with its ASEAN neighbors has also been radically altered. China has become ASEAN's leading trade partner, with their two-way trade in 2012 rising to a staggering US$401 billion. Over the years, China has become a capital surplus economy. It is becoming an increasingly important player in the FDI scene, with its cumulative FDI in ASEAN reaching US$19 billion. FDI either from Southeast Asian ethnic Chinese to China or China to ASEAN is actually a win-win outcome for both sides.

China's Open-Door Policy

The Chinese economy has experienced spectacular growth since it started economic reform and open-door policy some 20 years ago. Real growth during 1978–1997 was at an annual rate of 9.8%. In 1978, China's nominal gross domestic product (GDP) was only Rmb362.4 billion (US$44 billion) or about 70% of that of South Korea. By 1997, China's nominal GDP had grown to Rmb7, 477.2 billion (about US$900 billion), which was ranked the world's seventh largest.[1] According to the World Bank, it took Britain about 58 years to double its per-capita income from 1780–1838, 34 years for Japan (1885–1919), and 11 years for South Korea (1966–1977), but only 9 years for China (1978–1987) and another 9 years to double again (1987–1996).[2] By 1997, China, with per-capita gross national product (GNP) of US$860, had "graduated" from the category of low-income countries into that of lower middle-income countries.

---

[1] State Statistical Bureau, *A Statistical Survey of China 1998* (Beijing, 1998).
[2] World Bank, *China 2020* (1997).

Why has China been able to achieve such dynamic growth for a sustained period? In terms of simple technical explanations, China's high growth, viewed from the demand side, stems from its high levels of domestic investment, which has been matched by equally high levels of domestic savings. China's gross domestic investment during 1981–1991 averaged 30.5% of its GDP, and increased to 40.2% during 1992–1997 while gross domestic savings averaged 30.8% and 41.3% for the respective periods.[3] As in the other East Asian economies, high savings and high investment created a "virtuous circle of growth": high savings, high investment, high export growth, high GDP growth, and then high savings.

High savings and high investment alone would not have generated such sustained dynamic growth. To be sure, before 1978, China, operating under the Mao's self-reliant economy, also had high savings because of controlled consumption, and high investment because of socialist planning. But between 1952 and 1978, China's average annual growth was only at 5.7%, which was achieved with gross inefficiency and with a great deal of ups and downs. After 1978 when Deng Xiaoping started economic reform and the open-door policy, China's economic growth really started to take off by chalking up consistently near-double digit rates. Economic reform, by introducing market forces to economic decision making, has brought about greater allocative efficiency and provided the necessary incentives to production. The open-door policy, by reintegrating China into the global economy, has enabled China to plug into the international capitalism for additional capital, technology and markets, as well as exposing China to external competitive pressures. In short, both economic reform and the open-door policy (which China has carried out in a gradual and pragmatic manner with eminent success) have not only provided China with new sources of economic growth (or new "inputs") but also greater economic efficiency (higher "total factor productivity").[4]

---

[3] Asian Development Bank, *Asian Development Outlook 1998* (1998).

[4] In accounting for the 9.4% growth of 1978–1995, the World Bank has identified 8.8% for physical capital growth, 2.7% for human capital (years of education per worker) growth, and 2.4% for labor force increases, and explained 1.5% of GDP growth as due to sectoral reallocation (e.g., from low productivity agriculture to higher productivity industry), leaving

Specifically for the open-door policy, its implementation symbolizes China's sharp turnaround from an inward-looking economy under Mao to one that actively participates in the world economy. But unlike the former Soviet Union and other East European socialist economies, China's "economic door" was opened cautiously and step by step through several distinct phases. After President Nixon's visit to China in 1972, China started to gradually abandon its self-reliant development strategy by importing whole plants and equipment from the developed countries, especially in the late 1970s. But ideologically, foreign capital, regarded as "international monopolist capitalism", was still treated with suspicion. It was not till Deng Xiaoping's return to power, as epitomized by the convening of the historic Third Plenum of the Party's 11th Central Committee in December 1978, that China was politically ready to interact with international capitalism.

In more concrete terms, the open-door policy was associated with the establishment of the special economic zones (SEZs) and the opening up of coastal cities to foreign investment. In 1979, Guangdong set up the three SEZs of Shenzhen, Zhuhai, and Shantou, and Fujian's Xiamen followed suit (and Hainan became a SEZ in 1988). In the same year, the Joint Venture Law was promulgated to make it possible for foreign direct investment (FDI) to flow into the designated SEZs. Initially, FDI projects consisted mainly of hotels and tourism-related ventures, and a variety of light industrial processing, mainly for exports. China also allowed foreign investment connected with oil exploration activities in the South China Sea. But such FDI in China soon ran out of steam since FDI in manufacturing was not promoted, especially those activities geared to China's domestic markets.

It was only after 1986, with the promulgation of "The 22 Articles" and related implementing regulations that China started to facilitate FDI in import-substitution manufacturing activities. Still, China was not conspicuously successful in its FDI promotion efforts mainly because the overall investment climate, fraught with red tape, over-regulation, and

---

a large unexplained residue of 29%. A substantial part of this residue is understandably the total factor productivity (TFP) associated with economic reform and the open-door policy. (*China 2020*, *op cit.*).

price distortion, was not favorable. Furthermore, China had to compete head-on with the open, outward-looking Southeast Asian economies for similar FDI.

The real breakthrough in China's open-door policy came in 1992. Following Deng Xiaoping's celebrated tour of South China in February 1992, China was to transform itself into a "socialist market economy" and to throw its "economic door" wide open to foreign trade and foreign investment. Not just the designated SEZs and selected coastal cities but many interior regions were now open to FDI. Within a few months after Deng's tour, some 1,784 localities were open to FDI compared to 117 in 1989. FDI was now permitted in sectors and industries previously closed to foreign capital. These include areas such as foreign trade, domestic commerce, insurance, finance, aviation, and infrastructure.[5]

The results of this sudden liberalization were breathtaking. For the whole period of 1979–1985, China attracted a total of only US$4.7 billion of FDI, and a total of US$18.6 for the second phase of 1985–1991. But the influx of FDI began skyrocketing immediately after Deng's push: A total of US$11.0 billion FDI for 1992 alone, US$27.5 billion for 1993, US$33.8 billion for 1994, and rising to a hefty US$45.3 billion for 1997 (Table 1). In sum, for the past 20 years of 1979–1997, total FDI in China amounted to US$220 billion, making China the second largest recipient of international investment capital in the world after the United States. In all, more than 200 of the world's largest global multinationals have invested in China.[6]

What has been the exact economic contribution of FDI? China's total fixed investment during 1980–1997 amounted to about Rmb14,000 billion or US$1,680 billion. The US$220 billion FDI works out to be just 13% of China's total capital formation. It has been commonly recognized that a substantial portion, as much as one-third of China's total FDI had actually been China's own capital "round-tripped" back to China through Hong Kong in order to capture the various incentives afforded to foreign

---

[5] See John Wong (1993). *Understanding China's Socialist Market Economy*. Singapore: Times Academic Press.

[6] "Nation attracts foreign funding", *China Daily* (5 October 1998).

Table 1.   Foreign Direct Investment in China (US$ Million)

	1979–1982	1983–1991*		1992		1993		1994		1995		1996		1997	
	Actual Amount Invested	Actual Amount Invested	%	Actual Amount Invested	%	Actual Amount Invested	%	Actual Amount Invested	%	Actual Amount Invested	%	Actual Amount Invested	%	Actual Amount Invested	%
Total	1166	22182	100%	11292	100%	27771	100%	33946	100%	37806	100%	42135	100%	45260	100%
ASIA PACIFIC	NA	15627	70.4%	9900	87.7%	23333	84%	28267	83.2%	30235	80%	32714	77.6%	33222	73.4%
Hong Kong	—	12456	56.2%	7706	68.2%	17445	62.8%	19823	58.4%	20185	53.4%	20852	49.5%	20852	46%
Taiwan	—	466	2.1%	1053	9.3%	3139	11.3%	3391	10%	3165	8.4%	3482	8.3%	3290	7.3%
Japan	—	2705	12.2%	748	6.6%	1361	4.9%	2086	6%	3213	8.5%	3692	8.8%	4330	9.6%
South Korea	—	—	—	120	1.1%	382	1.4%	726	2%	1047	2.8%	1504	3.6%	2140	4.7%
ASEAN	NA	(371.5)	(1.7%)	(271.6)	(2.4%)	(1005.9)	(3.6%)	(2240.6)	(6.6%)	(2625)	(7%)	(3184.3)	(7.6%)	(2610)	(5.8%)
Indonesia	—	5.4	0.03%	20.2	0.18%	65.8	0.2%	115.7	0.3%	111.6	0.3%	93.6	0.2%	2610	5.8%
Malaysia	—	5.1	0.02%	24.7	0.22%	91.4	0.3%	509.4	1.5%	259.0	0.7%	460.0	1.1%	NIL	NIL
Philippines	—	20.7	0.09%	16.6	0.15%	122.5	0.4%	201.0	0.6%	105.8	0.3%	55.5	0.1%	NIL	NIL
Singapore	—	266.0	1.2%	125.9	1.1%	491.8	1.8%	1179.6	3.5%	1860.6	5.0%	2247.0	5.0%	NIL	NIL
Thailand	—	74.3	0.33%	84.3	0.75%	234.4	0.8%	234.9	0.7%	288.0	0.8%	328.2	0.8%	NIL	NIL
USA	NA	2246	9.9%	519	4.6%	2068	7.4%	2491	7%	3084	8.2%	3444	8.2%	3240	7.2%
Others	NA	3938	17.8%	873	7.7%	2370	8.5%	3188	9%	4488	11.9%	5977	14.2%	8798.4	19.4%

Note: * The date for 1983–1991 is actually from 1985–1991.
Sources: Statistical Yearbook Of China (1985–1997); China Monthly Statistics.

investors. If this were duly taken into account, FDI as a source of capital for China has not quantitatively important.

However, the most significant economic role of FDI to China, as to many developing countries, is not so much to meet its capital needs as to fulfil the other more important economic functions like employment creation, technology transfer (including modern management), and the development of export markets. With high levels of domestic savings, China did not really need a lot of FDI to meet its capital requirements as much as it would need from FDI its overall catalyst effect of promoting industrial development. Indeed, about a quarter of million of foreign-funded enterprises (FFEs) are now operating in China, providing employment to 17.5 million people. In 1997, China's total exports reached US$183 billion (the world's 10th largest), and these FFEs were responsible for 41% of China's total exports.[7] Viewed in this broader context, Deng's open-door policy, despite its hesitant start in the 1980s, has been a great success.

China's Complex Relations with Southeast Asia

The bulk of FDI in China so far has emanated mainly from the Asia-Pacific region, particularly Hong Kong, Taiwan, and Macau, and some Southeast Asian economies, where ethnic Chinese play an important economic role. Such extensive involvement of the "overseas Chinese" in China's open-door policy has thus raised the prospects (and fears) of China becoming the focal point of the growing "overseas Chinese economy." This chapter concentrates on the investments in China by the Southeast Asian ethnic Chinese. But a simple understanding of some key historical and political forces that have shaped the overall relations between China and Southeast Asia is crucial for appreciating the problems that operate to constrain the ethnic Chinese efforts in developing economic links with China.

"Southeast Asia" as a broadly defined geographical region lies to the south of China, separated by a vast expanse of the South China Sea. Hence, traditionally the Chinese referred to "Southeast Asia" as

---

[7] "Deng's policy made quality of life better", *Hong Kong Standard* (23 September 1997).

Nanyang, literally meaning "south sea." On account of history, migration, and geopolitics, China's relations with countries in Southeast Asia — in this chapter, we shall focus on Indonesia, Malaysia, the Philippines, Singapore, and Thailand, which were the original founding members of the Association of Southeast Asian Nations or ASEAN (1967) — are naturally extensive and deep-rooted. China's early contacts with individual Southeast Asian states can be traced back to ancient times. At the time of the Sung Dynasty (960–1280), Imperial China had already established firm tributary relations with many Southeast Asian states, culminating in the famous expeditions by Admiral Zheng He in the Ming Dynasty (1368–1644). But it was only after the 19th century that China's commercial relations with *Nanyang* began to grow markedly, along with the steady inflow of Chinese migrants (mainly from Fujian and Guangdong) into the region. Since then, not only have overseas Chinese played a pivotal role in the economic development of their host countries in *Nanyang* but they have also remained a crucial parameter in the political and economic relations between these countries and China.[8]

Following the establishment of the People's Republic of China in 1949, the traditional pattern of China's relations with the individual ASEAN states was radically altered, with complex ideological and political elements coming into play. The New China, marked by a strong revolutionary impulse and armed with a proselytizing Maoist ideology, was soon perceived by some ASEAN states as a threat, real or imagined, to their own security. This gave rise to more than two decades of what may be called "Cold War relations" between the two sides with numerous political twists and turns. It was not till the early 1970s with the advent of *détente* in the region (sparked off by President Nixon's visit to Beijing) that individual ASEAN countries started their long and often tortuous course of normalization of relations with China.

Among these five original ASEAN countries, Indonesia has had unique "Cold War experiences" with China. Indonesia was the first country in the region to recognize the New China soon after it was proclaimed

---

[8] See John Wong (1987). China's emerging economic relationship with Southeast Asia. *Southeast Asian Studies,* Kyoto, 25 (3).

on 1 October 1949. During the period of his "Guided Democracy", President Sukarno had developed a very intimate relationship with Beijing in common pursuit of the so-called "Bandung spirit" (i.e., non-alignment policy). In fact, China and Indonesia came close to forming a sort of "Beijing-Jakarta Axis." But little did Beijing realize that its apparent solidarity with the Sukarno regime was actually built upon a rather soft foundation, which had all along been plagued by the continuing rivalry between the Indonesian Communist Party or PKI and the Indonesian army.

In the event, the Indonesian coup *Gestapu* brought the so-called Beijing-Jakarta alliance to a violent end in September 1965. The coup provided the army under General Suharto the much-awaited chance to seize power and liquidate the PKI by force. It also led to an abrupt suspension of relation with China, which was openly accused by the Indonesian army of being behind the coup. It had taken China and Indonesia a quarter of a century to resume formal diplomatic relations, which came in 1990. The Indonesian government under Suharto had never developed warm relationship with Beijing. Not only that, anti-China feelings among certain Indonesian elite have lingered on to this day — the latest eruption being the May 1998 riots.[9]

By comparison, the Philippines and Thailand had taken a different approach to China. Both had stronger historical ties with, and geographically closer to, China. After 1949, their relations with China were engulfed in the rising tide of the Cold War, which swept the region in the 1950s and the 1960s. Accordingly, both the Philippines and Thailand on the one hand, and China on the other, developed misperception of each other's intentions and at times even indulged in harsh propaganda against each other.

As a truly close anti-Communist ally of the United States during the Cold War period, the Philippines had refused to have any form of contact with any Communist country. Thus, prior to 1971, the Philippines had no official records of trade with China. Similarly, Thailand, being the host to the anti-Communist Southeast Asian Treaty Organization (SEATO), was also a firm supporter of the American "containment

---

[9] For this and the subsequent paragraphs, see John Wong (1984). *The Political Economy of China's Changing Relations with Southeast Asia.* London: Macmillan Press.

policy" against China, and all forms of contact, including trade, with China were officially banned under Field Marshal Sarit Thanat's 1958 Decree No. 53. Yet, Thailand's *rapprochement* with China moved fast as soon as the geopolitics in the region started to shift after the Nixon's *détente* with Beijing. In less than three months after the fall of Saigon (May 1975), the Philippines and Thailand had normalized relations with China. Since then, both countries have enjoyed stable political and economic relations with China with hardly any significant ripple — except perhaps for the recent Sino-Philippine spat on the Scarborough Reef in the South China Sea.[10]

Again in a different way, both Malaysia and Singapore had their own distinctive experiences with China. In the early 1950s, Malaysia was the direct target of armed communist insurgency, which received open support from China. This had given rise to years of mutual suspicion, recrimination, and antagonism between the two sides. But Malaysia was the first ASEAN country to begin thawing its Cold War relations with China — in fact, Malaysia established full diplomatic relations with China in 1974, ahead of the Philippines and Thailand. Malaysia was also pragmatic enough, even at the peak of the Cold War, to separate trade from politics, and had always maintained uninterrupted commercial ties with China.

Singapore was part of Malaysia until their separation in 1965. All along, two conflicting forces had influenced Singapore's overall relations with China. As a globally oriented city-state, heavily dependent on trade for its economic growth, Singapore would be keen to cultivate good relations with any country of any ideological shade for the promotion of trade, provided Singapore's own security would not be compromised. This had shaped Singapore's commercial angle on China, and has since remained a guiding principle for Singapore's foreign economic relations to this day. On the other hand, Singapore, dominated by ethnic Chinese population (about 76%), had to be extremely wary of the political sensitivity of its ASEAN neighbors in its dealings with China. Politically, as far as

---

[10] See SHEE Poon Kim and ZOU Keyuan (1998). The Scarborough Reef: Political, strategic, security and legal implications for Sino-Philippine relations. *EAI Background Brief No. 22,* East Asian Institute, Singapore.

relations with China are concerned, Singapore would not want to move ahead of the other ASEAN states. This also explains why Singapore had chosen to be the last ASEAN country (i.e., after Indonesia) to formally recognize China, long after Singapore had exchanged trade representatives with Beijing.

For these five ASEAN states, their past dealings with China have, in varying degrees, influenced their present relations with China. Generally speaking, the Sino-ASEAN economic relations can be both the complementary and competitive. The Philippines and Thailand, having no big historical baggage on China (except perhaps for their previous Cold War rhetoric), have not allowed the "competitive aspects" to become serious obstacles in their economic relations with China. Their trade with China has been able to grow steadily over the years, and they have turned a blind eye to their ethnic Chinese citizens investing in China.

Malaysia and Singapore have been even more pragmatic in their response to China's open-door policy. Even during their worst Cold War days, they managed to continue their trade relations with China in the absence of a formal diplomatic framework. Accordingly, Malaysia and Singapore have all along constituted the mainstay of ASEAN's trade with China — e.g., Singapore alone accounts for about one-third of China's total trade with ASEAN annually. It should therefore come as no surprise that both Malaysia and Singapore have taken a positive attitude toward China's economic opening, which is regarded as potentially a new engine for the region's economic growth in future. The Malaysian and Singapore leadership openly shares this view.[11]

Indonesia, however, has openly felt uneasy with the rise of China. Indonesia is still plagued by its lingering suspicion of China due to their past unhappy relations. The Indonesian military takes the view that a resurgent China could pose a security threat to the region's stability. Some Indonesian elite have also argued that China's economic upsurge in the early 1990s has led to the diversion of foreign investment from ASEAN into China, as indeed Indonesia's FDI in 1993 did decline while China's FDI for that year had shot up. Jakarta is particularly sensitive to the

---

[11] See the interview with Dr Nordin Sopiee, an advisor to Dr Mahathir, by the *Asian Wall Street Journal* (17 May 1994).

question of Indonesian Chinese investing in China.[12] The view that China's economic growth has threatened Indonesia in terms of taking away Indonesia's export markets and FDI, does sound like a "bogey" argument. But the deep-seated anti-Chinese sentiment among many Indonesian people is real, as it has unfortunately been manifested in the frequent anti-Chinese riots.

Ethnic Chinese in Southeast Asia

China's dynamic economic growth over the past two decades along its increasing economic integration with the Asia-Pacific region has given rise to some supranational concepts like "Greater China" or "Chinese Economic Circle", which are getting popular in Western and Japanese journalism. "Greater China" refers to the ethnic Chinese economic entity existing outside the political boundary of China but with close linkages to China's economy. The narrow definition of "Greater China" commonly refers to Taiwan, Hong Kong, and Macau, which are technically "Chinese territories"; but its broader definition includes all economic activities and commercial interests of "overseas Chinese" (*hua-qiao*) or "foreign Chinese" the world over, particularly those in Southeast Asia.

China, mindful of the potential political controversies surrounding such concepts, has officially shunned such term as "Greater China."[13] Beijing is fully aware of its negative political undertone, which could spark off unwarranted fear of Chinese expansionism in the Asia-Pacific region. Ethnic Chinese in Southeast Asia, in particular, strongly dislike such a politically sensitive term because it could create a wrong impression that ethnic Chinese have not been well integrated into Southeast Asian societies, and that their loyalty is suspect. They are equally sensitive to the cultural and social term like "Chinese diaspora", which, in highlighting

---

[12] "China: A threat to Southeast Asia's industrialization and social harmony?" *Asian Economic Commentary* (A monthly review by Merrill Lynch, Singapore, July 1993).

[13] China's former Foreign Minister Wu Xueqian, speaking at an Asian forum at Stanford University, stated that China did not support the idea of "Greater China." *Lianhe Zaobao* (Singapore, 15 May 1995).

the common Confucian origin of the ethnic Chinese around the world, could also smack of unwarranted cultural chauvinism.

How many ethnic Chinese are there outside China? There are actually no reliable figures because of the definition problem.[14] Most estimates of the so-called "overseas Chinese" come from Taiwan, Japan, and the West, not China. The estimated number of "foreign Chinese" outside China in the early 1990s ranged between 55 and 60 million, which would include about 26 million in East Asia, 24 million in Southeast Asia, and 5 million in America and Europe. Table 2 gives a breakdown of ethnic Chinese in Southeast Asia.

According to China's new citizenship law, passed by the National People's Congress in September 1980, China does not recognize dual nationality for any Chinese national. Apart from those from the Chinese "inhabitants" of Taiwan, Hong Kong, and Macau, the "foreign Chinese" overseas or outside of the "Greater China" are legally not regarded as "Chinese". Accordingly, the ethnic Chinese in Southeast Asia are "Chinese" only in the ethnical, cultural, or social sense. In fact, thanks to the accelerated assimilation to their host societies over the past 50 years after the birth of New China, many ethnic Chinese in the region have become socially and culturally much less "Chinese", e.g., the *peranakan* in Indonesia, the *baba* in Malaysia, and a large proportion of Chinese-Filipinos and Thai-Chinese.[15] This leaves economic characteristics as the major common denominator among the people of the Chinese descent in the region, i.e., their predominance in retail trade and their possession of a disproportionate share of wealth.

The strong commercial presence of ethnic Chinese minority in Southeast Asian societies was in part a product of Western colonialism. The early Chinese immigrants were usually put in the intermediate position under the Western colonial social structure (e.g., the Dutch "Culture

---

[14] For a further discussion of the problems relating to the definition of "overseas Chinese" and the concept of "Chineseness", see Wang Gungwu, *Community and Nations: Essays on Southeast Asia and the Chinese* (Singapore and Sydney, Heinemann Educational Books and Allen & Unwin, Australia, 1981); and *China and the Chinese Overseas* (Singapore, Times Academic Press, 1991).

[15] For detailed discussion of ethnic Chinese in Southeast Asia, see the recent excellent study by the Australian Department of Foreign Affairs and Trade: East Asia Analytical Unit, *Overseas Chinese Business Networks in Asia* (Commonwealth of Australia, 1995).

Table 2.   Distribution Of Ethnic Chinese In Southeast Asia, 1991

	Ethnic Chinese (million)	Total Population (million)	% of Total Population	% of Total Ethnic Chinese
SOUTHEAST ASIA				
A				
Indonesia	**7.2**	**181**	**4.0%**	**29.7%**
Malaysia	**5.8**	**18.2**	**31.9%**	**23.9%**
Philippines	**0.9**	**63.0**	**1.4%**	**3.7%**
Singapore	**2.1**	**2.7**	**77.8%**	**8.7%**
Thailand	**5.8**	**57.2**	**10.1%**	**23.9%**
Sub-total	*21.8*	—	—	**89.9%**
B				
Brunei	0.04	0.29	13.8%	**0.2%**
Cambodia	0.36	7.1	5.1%	**1.5%**
Laos	0.05	4.1	1.2%	**0.2%**
Myanmar	1.3	42.0	3.1%	**5.4%**
Vietnam	0.7	72.0	1.0%	**2.9%**
Sub-total	*2.5*	—	—	**10.1%**
Total	24.3	—	—	**100%**

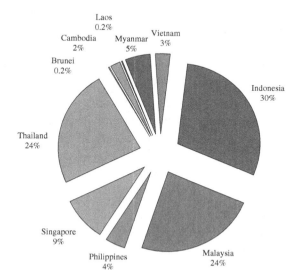

Sources: East Asia Analytical Unit, Department of Foreign Affairs and Trade, *Overseas Chinese Business Networks in Asia* (Commonwealth of Australia, 1995).
World Bank, World Development Report 1993 (1993).

System" for Indonesia), being segregated from both the ruling colonial elite and the indigenous population. While the ethnic Chinese were barred from participating in the modern sector activities like plantation agriculture, mines, finance, and export trade, which were dominated by the Europeans, they were also prohibited from owning and cultivating land. The openings left for the ethnic Chinese were in retail trade, money lending, and other middleman roles, which unfortunately did not endear them to the local population. After independence, the nationalists in Southeast Asia tended to view the ethnic Chinese as handmaidens of Western colonialism and continued to restrict the economic opportunities available for them. In the circumstances, many ethnic Chinese, driven by the need for survival plus their flair for risk taking and entrepreneurship, and their ability to network for mutual support among relatives and clan members, have made a success in commerce.[16]

But the remarkable commercial expansion of the ethnic Chinese in these five ASEAN countries had owed a great deal to the region's strong and almost uninterrupted economic growth since the early 1970s, as shown in Table 3. Furthermore, these ASEAN economies are well known for their open economic structures and extensive economic freedom, which are in turn backed by their pro-business governments. Under such favorable institutional conditions, sustained economic growth was apt to generate widespread economic opportunities for all social classes, including the Chinese minorities. In fact, many ethnic Chinese, on account of their high business acumen and superb entrepreneurial skills, have managed to overcome various built-in political and social discriminations by developing symbiotic relations with local indigenous elite to exploit business opportunities. This practice is now widely attacked as a form of crony capitalism, responsible for the recent financial crisis!

Investing in China

Suffice it to say that during the period of ASEAN's economic take-off, many ethnic Chinese were able to prosper and accumulate a lot of wealth,

---

[16] East Asia Analytical Unit, *op cit.* Also, J.A.C. Mackie (1992). Overseas Chinese entrepreneurship. *Asia-Pacific Economic Literature.*

Table 3   Economic Performance of Asia Pacific Economies

	Population (Millions) 1995	GNP per-capita, (US$) 1996	PPP estimates of GNP per-capita, (US$) 1995	Real Economic Growth (%)						Consumer Price Inflation (%) 1998ᵇ	Annual Export Growth (%)		Mfg export as % of total exports 1993	Export as % of GDP Ratio 1995	Gross Domestic Savings as % of GDP		Gross Domestic Investment as % of GDP	
				1960–70	1970–80	1980–90	1996	1997	1998ᵃ		1990–95	1997			1981–90	1995	1981–90	1995
China	1,200.2	620	2,900	5.2	5.8	10.2	9.6	8.8	7.8	1.0	19.1	20.9	89	21.3	30.8	42.2	30.5	39.5
Japan	125.2	39,640	22,110	10.9	5.0	4.0	3.9	1.0	-3.7	0.5	8.7	19.8	97	8.7	32.1C	31.7	31.7	28.5
NIEs																		
South Korea	44.9	9,700	11,450	8.6	9.5	9.4	7.1	6.0	-5.0	8.2	12.8	5.3	93	27.5	32.4	37.0	30.6	36.6
Taiwan	21.3	12,400	13,200	9.2	9.7	7.1	5.7	6.7	4.7	1.7	NA	5.3	93	38.5	32.9	26.3	22.8	24.5
Hong Kong	6.2	22,990	22,950	10.0	9.3	6.9	4.9	5.3	-4.0	4.3	15.9	4.0	93	120.9	33.5	34.5	27.2	33.1
Singapore	3.0	26,730	22,770	8.8	8.5	6.4	7.0	7.2	0.8	0.6	17.6	1.6	80	141.3	41.8	55.9	41.7	33.9
ASEAN – 4																		
Indonesia	193.3	980	3,800	3.9	7.6	6.1	8.0	5.0	-15.0	56.7	11.7	8.4	53	22.9	30.9	36.0	29.3	38.3
Malaysia	20.1	3,890	9,020	6.5	7.8	5.2	8.6	7.0	-6.0	5.4	20.0	12.4	65	86.8	33.2	37.2	30.6	40.6
Philippines	68.6	1,050	2,800	5.1	6.3	1.0	5.7	4.3	-2.0	9.2	16.2	22.7	76	23.6	22.2	14.7	22.0	22.3
Thailand	58.2	2,740	7,540	8.4	7.2	7.6	6.4	0.6	-5.0	10.2	18.6	24.1	72	33.8	27.2	34.2	30.7	40.0

Notes: NA denotes "Not Available". ᵃEstimated growth for 1998. ᵇAsiaweek estimates. ᶜFigures from 1983 to 1990.

Sources: The World Bank, *World Development Report 1997* and *World Development Indicator 1997*; International Monetary Fund, *International Financial Statistics Yearbook 1997* and *World Economic Outlook: Interim Assessment December 1997*; Asian Development Bank, *Asian Development Outlook 1997 and 1998*.

which could be freely moved around for international investment due to ASEAN's open economic structures. Thus, when China declared its open door policy in the early 1980s, ethnic Chinese promptly responded and came in droves to invest in China. As shown in Table 1, Hong Kong, Taiwan, and Macau together have been consistently responsible for 70% of the total FDI in China. This has led many writers and commentators to conclude that most of the FDI in China has come from the "foreign Chinese", even though Hong Kong is such an open financial center, no capital movement can be identified. But the share of total FDI in China *directly* from ASEAN was initially small, at only 1.7% before 1992. After Deng's tour of South China, ASEAN's share steadily grew to 7.6% in 1996, mainly because of Singapore's heavier involvement (e.g., the Singapore Suzhou project).

This means that during the first phase of China's open-door policy when the overall investment environment was still not conducive, very few ethnic Chinese from Southeast Asia had actually invested in China, and their investments mainly went to their native towns/villages (usually on a very small scale or even as a token) in Guangdong and Fujian, making use of their local connection. After Deng's tour of South China in 1992, as China's overall investment climate had dramatically improved and other parts of China were also opened up for FDI, more Southeast Asian ethnic Chinese started to invest in China in pursuit of new opportunities.

Only Guangdong and Fujian, which are the two provinces to receive the largest share of ethnic Chinese capital from all sources, published the breakdown of FDI *directly* from ASEAN. As shown in Table 4 for FDI in Guangdong, and Table 5 for FDI in Fujian, the total amount of ethnic Chinese capital from the four ASEAN countries of Indonesia, Malaysia, the Philippines, and Thailand has remained miniscule for all these years. This should serve to dispel the often mistaken impression of certain ASEAN governments that the opening up of China has sucked away a lot capital from their own ethnic Chinese citizens, which would have otherwise been invested at home.

The great unknown, of course, lies in the exact proportion of Hong Kong and Macau FDI in China, which actually originated from ASEAN. Understandably, a lot of Southeast Asian capital flowing into

Table 4 Foreign direct investment in guangdong province (1985–1996) (US$ million)

	Y1985		Y1987		Y1989		Y1991		Y1992		Y1993		Y1994		Y1995		Y1996	
	CAPITAL	%	CAPITAL	%	CAPITAL	%	CAPITAL	%	CAPITAL	%	CAPITAL	%	CAPITAL	%	CAPITAL	%	CAPITAL	%
EAST ASIA																		
Hong Kong	846	92.0%	—	—	1483	61.8%	1623	62.8%	3454	71.0%	7372	76.4%	8704	76.0%	8990	74.3%	9388	67.5%
Macau	—	—	884	72.6%	61.8	2.6%	102	3.9%	170	3.5%	282	2.9%	374	3.3%	265	2.2%	381	2.7%
Japan	34.8	3.8%	187	15.4%	398	16.6%	312	12.1%	534	11.0%	598	6.2%	748	6.5%	834	6.9%	818	5.9%
South Korea	—	—	—	—	—	—	1.3	0.05%	4.5	0.1%	8.7	0.1%	13.7	0.1%	23.2	0.2%	88.5	0.6%
Taiwan	—	—	—	—	22.7	0.9%	115	4.5%	130	2.7%	267	2.8%	438	3.8%	360	3.0%	474	3.4%
ASEAN																		
Indonesia	0.1	0.01%	—	—	—	—	0.4	0.01%	3.1	0.1%	5.5	0.1%	8.7	0.1%	45.0	0.4%	7.5	0.1%
Malaysia	—	—	0.01	0.001%	—	—	0.5	0.02%	4.4	0.1%	3.7	0.04%	25.5	0.2%	12.9	0.1%	41.8	0.3%
Philippines	0.4	0.04%	—	—	—	—	0.2	0.01%	2.6	0.1%	4.4	0.05%	2.4	0.02%	1.5	0.01%	27.8	0.2%
Singapore	4.3	0.5%	4.8	0.4%	23.8	1.0%	17.1	0.7%	22.7	0.5%	31.2	0.3%	178.6	1.6%	229	1.9%	418	3.0%
Thailand	4.9	0.5%	0.7	0.1%	1.7	0.1%	2.4	0.1%	32.6	0.7%	40.3	0.4%	34.3	0.3%	31.9	0.3%	85.4	0.6%
UK	2.2	0.2%	5.5	0.5%	41.7	1.7%	12.9	0.5%	30.9	0.6%	199	2.1%	190	1.7%	163	1.4%	396	2.9%
USA	20.3	2.2%	38	3.1%	110	4.6%	120	4.6%	78	1.6%	359	3.7%	186	1.6%	477	3.9%	565	4.1%
Others	6.5	0.7%	97	8.0%	256	10.7%	276	10.7%	396	8.1%	562	5.8%	543	4.7%	668	5.5%	1207	8.7%
Total	919	100%	1217	100%	2399	100%	2583	100%	4861	100%	9652	100%	11447	100%	12100	100%	13899	100%

Source: Statistical Yearbook of Guangdong (1985–1997).

Table 5 Foreign direct investment in fujian province (1985–1996) (US$ million)

	Y1985		Y1987		Y1989		Y1991		Y1992		Y1993		Y1994		Y1995		Y1996	
	CAPITAL	%	CAPITAL	%	CAPITAL	%	CAPITAL	%	CAPITAL	%	CAPITAL	%	CAPITAL	%	CAPITAL	%	CAPITAL	%
EAST ASIA																		
HK&Macau	153	44.2%	90.0	41.1%	204	52.2%	423	58.4%	960	65.5%	1638	56.4%	2117	57.0%	2527	61.0%	2484	58.9%
Japan	75.9	22.0%	80.7	36.8%	9.4	2.4%	4.6	0.6%	75.6	5.2%	65.0	2.2%	77.9	2.1%	61.7	1.5%	83.3	2.0%
South Korea	—	—	—	—	—	—	2.9	0.4%	1.2	0.1%	4.0	0.1%	7.0	0.2%	1.3	0.0%	1.3	0.0%
Taiwan	1.2	0.4%	0.8	0.4%	—	—	—	—	—	—	—	—	—	—	—	—	—	—
ASEAN																		
Indonesia	10.0	2.9%	0.3	0.1%	1.2	0.3%	0.2	0.02%	—	—	27.8	1.0%	—	—	18.9	0.5%	15.0	0.4%
Malaysia	0.6	0.2%	0.3	0.1%	0.4	0.1%	0.3	0.04%	1.2	0.1%	23.7	0.8%	45.3	1.2%	59.5	1.4%	57.9	1.4%
Philippines	4.9	1.4%	3.0	1.4%	1.2	0.3%	6.0	0.8%	—	—	86.2	3.0%	—	—	73.9	1.8%	14.8	0.4%
Singapore	7.3	2.1%	5.3	2.4%	1.6	0.4%	9.3	1.3%	30.2	2.1%	77.4	2.7%	147	4.0%	160	3.9%	159	3.8%
Thailand	—	—	—	—	1.7	0.4%	4.5	0.6%	3.7	0.3%	7.0	0.2%	11.6	0.3%	22.2	0.5%	1.3	0.03%
UK	—	—	3.3	1.5%	—	—	12.6	1.7%	9.6	0.7%	3.6	0.1%	68.5	1.8%	47.7	1.2%	13.3	0.3%
USA	40.7	11.8%	3.5	1.6%	8.6	2.2%	1.6	0.2%	7.4	0.5%	35.7	1.2%	47.0	1.3%	55.2	1.3%	95.6	2.3%
Others	52.1	15.1%	31.7	14.5%	106	27.0%	259	35.8%	376	25.7%	938	32.3%	1191	32.1%	1113	26.9%	1289	30.6%
Total	345	100%	219	100%	391	100%	724	100%	1466	100%	2906	100%	3712	100%	4140	100%	4213	100%

Source: Statistical Yearbook of Fujian (1985–1997).

China has been routed via Hong Kong and Macau. It is well known that many large investment projects in China by Southeast Asian ethnic Chinese are first incorporated in Hong Kong, which are then treated by China as officially "Hong Kong investment." But again, not all the capital required in these projects has come directly from Southeast Asia, and a great part of it was in fact raised in Hong Kong or even in China.

The fact that Southeast Asian ethnic Chinese have actually not invested a quantitatively significant amount of capital in China does not diminish their real contribution to China's success in its open door policy — quite the contrary. As asserted earlier, the main economic role of FDI, for China as for other developing economies, does not lie in its capital contribution, but more in its total catalyst economic effects, which are often not clearly reflected in the macroeconomic statistics. On account of their cultural and linguistic affinity, the "foreign Chinese" from all places have effectively transferred valuable business skills to the Mainland Chinese. Thus, the noted China scholar-businessman William Overholt once described the phenomenon of overseas Chinese executives training Mainland Chinese executives in capitalist methods as "the biggest business school for managers ever created in the world."[17] Ethnic Chinese all over the world have no doubt contributed to the revival of China's traditional entrepreneurship, which has in turn been instrumental in the economic transformation of China in recent years.

Ethnic Chinese Business Groups

It is admittedly difficult to track the activities of hundreds of ethnic Chinese who have invested on a small scale in their native towns in Guangdong and Fujian, or in the SEZs. But it is easier to trace the investment activities of the large business groups by ethnic Chinese. The recent decades have witnessed the emergence outside of China a growing number of transnational ethnic Chinese business conglomerates operating on mutual trust and rapport and sustained by the extensive Chinese business network of *guanxi* around the world. These rising "Chinese multinationals", which include those set up by Chinese from Hong Kong, Taiwan,

---

[17] Quoted in Andrew Tanzer (1994). The bamboo network. *Forbes*, 140.

Southeast Asia, or even China, have started to make an increasingly important impact on the international business scene of the Asia Pacific region.[18]

In 1994, the Chinese-language edition of "Asiaweek", *Yazhou Zhoukan*, listed the largest 500 companies reportedly controlled by "overseas Chinese" in Asia — 282 of which were from Hong Kong and Taiwan with the rest from the ASEAN region.[19] Of these 500 corporations, slightly over half were based in Hong Kong and Taiwan, with the rest in the ASEAN region. Together, they boasted a combined market capitalization of US$425 billion and total assets of US$539 billion.

According to Japan's Fuji Research Institute (ethnic), Chinese-owned firms accounted for 81% of the local market capitalization in Singapore, 81% in Thailand, 73% in Indonesia, 61% in Malaysia, and 50% in the Philippines.[20] The American *Forbes* magazine has also identified 38 ethnic Chinese billionaires outside China, each with a huge business conglomerate: 4 from Indonesia, 3 from Malaysia, 3 from the Philippines, 5 from Thailand, and 4 from Singapore, in addition to 15 from Hong Kong and Taiwan.[21]

These super-rich ethnic Chinese have certainly amassed a vast amount of wealth and business interests.[22] But their existence has also created the myth, often much exaggerated in the international press, that ethnic Chinese have dominated the Southeast Asian economies. The case in point is the oft-quoted statement that the Indonesian Chinese who "constitute about 3–4% of Indonesian population but control 70% of the Indonesian economy." Apart from the fact that hundreds of thousands of ethnic Chinese in Southeast Asia are still hawkers, street peddlers, and small shopkeepers, such domination of any Southeast Asian economy by Chinese minorities are politically and economically well-nigh impossible

---

[18] See Friedrich Wu and Sin Yue Duk (1994). Overseas Chinese capital in Asia and the Hong Kong-Singapore nexus. *JETRO China Newsletter*, (113).

[19] *Yazhou Zhoukan* (25 September 1994).

[20] "Osaka groups seek overseas Chinese ties." *The Nikkei Weekly* (Tokyo, 30 May 1994).

[21] "The Bamboo network", *Forbes* (18 July, 1994).

[22] According to Professor Gordon Redding of Hong Kong University, the Chinese diaspora is about 4% of China's population but generate a total income equivalent to two-third of China's GNP. "China's diaspora turns homeward", *The Economist* (London, 27 November 1993).

because (i) the state sector in the region is still predominant and (ii) a large number of indigenous elite have also controlled a large share of wealth.[23]

Nonetheless, the increasing commercial presence of a large number of cross-border ethnic Chinese business conglomerates in the Asia-Pacific region has led to growing interests among Western and Japanese scholars on this new phenomenon of "Chinese multinationals." In studies after studies, the family- or clan-based *guanxiwan* (human relations network) of the "Chinese multinationals" has been singled out as their dominant organizatonal and behavioral characteristics — so much so that the overseas Chinese business connection is often dubbed the "Bamboo Network."[24] According to the well-known American management guru Peter Drucker, the 21st century may well see many more of such Chinese multinationals characterized by their distinctive Chinese business culture, such as networking as a clan.[25] They could potentially pose a great challenge to Japanese and Western multinationals.

Table 6 lists a selected sample of large Southeast Asian ethnic Chinese business conglomerates with extensive business activities in the region. In varying degrees, they have directly or indirectly invested in China, as they must have, because China has become such an attractive emerging market in recent years. Some, like Thailand's Charoen Pokphand (CP) group and perhaps also Indonesia's Lippo group, are more heavily involved in their China operations — particularly for the CP group, which in 1994 was considered the "largest single foreign investor in China", operating virtually in every Chinese province and autonomous region except Tibet.[26] Others like the Salim group have much smaller involvement in China.

---

[23] See, e.g., George J. Aditjondro (1998). The myth of Chinese domination. *Jakarta Post.*

[24] Muray Weidenbaum and Samuel Huges (1996). *The Bamboo Network: How Expatriate Chinese Entrepreneurs Are Creating a New Economic Superpower in Asia.* New York: Martin Kessler Books, The Free Press. See also the Australian study by the East Asia Analytical Unit, *op cit*; and John Kao, The Worldwide Web of Chinese business, *Harvard Business Review* (March–April, 1993).

[25] As Peter Drucker remarks, the Japanese owe their success to their ability to run the modern corporation as a family. The Chinese owe their success to their ability to run their family as a modern corporation. The new superpower: The overseas Chinese, *Asian Wall Street Journal* (21 December 1994).

[26] The Charoen Pokphand conglomerate set up its first feedmill joint venture in Shenzhen in 1981. It has now diversified into motorcycle manufacturing and real estate. See "An

Table 6. Selected Southeast Asian ethnic Chinese business conglomertes

	Original Founder	Successor	Estimated Assets 1993 (US$)	Estimated Assets 1996/1997 (US$)	Main Business Activities	Investments in China
Indonesia						
Salim Group	Liem Sioe Liong (Sudono Salim)	Anthony (3rd son, age: 48)	3.0 billion	4.5 billion	• Manufacturing • Commerce • Real Estate • Hotel & Tourism • Transportation • Finance	• Invested in Suzhou Industrial Park • Infrastructure donation in Fuqing and investment in silk and shoe industries • Cement factory and bonded zone in Wuhan • Property development in Tianjin
Sinar Mas Group	Eka Tjipta WIDJAJA (Oei Ek Tjhong)	Oei Hong Leong (China Strategic Investment)	2.7 billion	3.7 billion	• Edible oil • Chemicals • Finance • Real estate • Industrial • Trade • Golf course mgt	• Pulp and paper-mill in Ningbo • Rubber factory in Hangzhou • Pharmaceuticals, dairy products, TVs, textiles & garments brewery in Fujian • Salt company in Shanxi • Coal pipeline Shanxi to Shangdong
Gajah Tunggal Group	Sjamsul Nursalim (Liem Tek Siong)	—	NA	1.3 billion	• Tyres manufacturing • Banking • Insurance • Real estate • Hotels • Shrimp farms	• Tyres factory in Anhui • Real Estate in Shanghai
PT Astra International	William Soeryadjaya	Theodore Permadi Rachmat (54)	NA	1.0 billion	• Automobile • Heavy equipment • Wood-based industry • Agribusiness • Electronics • Financial services	Details not known

Table 6.   (*Continued*)

	Original Founder	Successor	Estimated Assets 1993 (US$)	Estimated Assets 1996/1997 (US$)	Main Business Activities	Investments in China
Lippo Group	Mochtar Riady	James (age: 40)	1.8 billion	1.0 billion	• Banking • Insurance • IT • Textiles • Electronics • Real estate	• Ports, roads, hotels and retail centres in Fujian
Barito Pacific	Prajogo Pangestu	—	2.5 billion	2.0 billion	• Hardwood & plywood • Agribusiness • Banking • Chemicals • Real estate	Details not known
Malaysia						
Hong Leong Group	Quek Leng Chan	—	2.1 billion	4.0 billion	• Real estate • Manufacturing • Construction • Motorcycle assembly • Finance • Banking & insurance • Publishing	• 6 Dao Heng Bank branches • A hotel in Fuzhou • Motorcycle assembly and garment factory in Fuzhou
Genting Bhd	Lim Goh Tong	—	2.1 billion	5.2 billion	• Casino • Real estate • Power • Paper-making	• Palm-oil bulk breaking plant in Guangdong

As Singapore's Senior Minister Lee Kuan Yew has put it, the loyalty of these overseas "Chinese multinationals" belongs overseas, not to China.[27] For them, business is business, and their *modus operandi* is always based on profit maximization. But in doing so, they have prospered themselves and also created prosperity in China.

New Patterns of Relations

The Asian financial crisis has hit all businesses in Southeast Asia, with no exception for the ethnic Chinese business interests in the region. But the Indonesian Chinese business groups were the hardest hit, not just because the Indonesian economy has plunged deeper than the ASEAN economies, but also because of the widespread anti-Chinese violence, which led to indiscriminate destruction of wealth and assets owned by the ethnic Chinese throughout Indonesia. It may take some time for the ethnic Chinese business groups in Southeast Asia to recover, as the regional economic crisis is still raging on with no end in sight. By then, the post-crisis Asia-Pacific economies might have drastically changed.

Ironically, the present economic crisis has yielded unexpected bonuses to those Southeast Asian ethnic Chinese who have invested in China. Prior to the crisis, they have commonly considered investment undertaking in China risky relative to their home base. But the crisis has since reversed such risk premium the other way round, with many ethnic Chinese now finding China as a safe haven for their investments on account of China's stable economic conditions and the strong *Renminbi* — which has sharply risen against all Southeast Asian currencies. Many Southeast Asian investors, including Thailand's CP group, are reported to have liquidated some of their business interests in China and repatriated the funds to rescue their ailing home operations caused by the financial crisis.[28]

---

emerging giant from Thailand", *The Economist* (26 November–2 December 1994). Also, the Australian study.

[27] "The Loyalty of Overseas Chinese Belongs Overseas", *International Herald Tribune* (23 November 1993).

[28] The CP group is reported to be selling 40% of its motor-cycle manufacturing joint venture in Shanghai and scaling back its far-flung operations in China because of the financial

When the Southeast Asian ethnic Chinese have eventually recovered from their present economic woes to be ready for their next wave of overseas expansion, they will find the economic landscape in China significantly different. China is the one economy in the Asia-Pacific region, which has been left "largely unaffected" by the present financial crisis.[29] With good economic fundamentals and less vulnerability to external economic crisis, the Chinese economy will understandably come out of the Asian financial crisis faster and stronger, particularly if Premier Zhu Rongji can succeed in getting his domestic economic reform programs on track. Unlike many smaller ASEAN economies, China is a huge economic entity on its own, which has sufficient internal dynamics to maintain reasonable economic growth even as the international economic environment has turned highly unfavorable. Hence, China is set to play a greater political and economic role in the post-crisis region.

As the Chinese economy continues to grow and develop, the ethnic Chinese, be they from Southeast Asia or from the "Greater China" of Taiwan and Hong Kong, are expected to play a different and perhaps economically less crucial role in China's future economic development. In fact, China's foreign investment scene in recent years has already undergone significant changes, rendering it less dependent on ethnic Chinese capital and technology. First, China has been gradually implementing the "national treatment" clause for FDI by removing many special concessions for foreign investors and special privileges for its SEZs, where investments by ethnic Chinese investments are extensive. Secondly, China in recent years has been strengthening its legal and regulatory framework for FDI, which will increasingly operate to cancel out the inherent cultural advantages of the ethnic Chinese investors.

---

difficulties in its home business in Thailand. ("Thai conglomerate to sell 40% of motorcycle venture", *The Nikkei Weekly*, 23 March 1998.)

Likewise, the Salim group has sold its extensive overseas assets in order to repay the huge Indonesian government loans made to its affiliated company, the Bank of Central Asia. The group has sold some of its assets in Hong Kong (e.g., the 5% of its stake in First Pacific) to settle its debt at home; but it is not known if it has similarly liquidated its assets in China. ("Salim sells offshore assets to pay loans", *South China Morning Post*, 26 August 1998.)

[29] Nicholas R. Lardy (1998). China and the Asian contagion. *Foreign Affairs*, p. 78.

The use of *guanxi* would be less effective once the legal environment becomes more certain and more transparent.

Furthermore, as the Chinese economy has taken off, the Chinese government has made no secret that they want to attract more capital- and technology-intensive FDI, and that their investment promotion is increasingly targeted at the large multinationals from the West and Japan. Small and medium ethnic Chinese investors can still find their niche in China's foreign investment sector, e.g., the interior areas of China. But ethnic Chinese investors may not be able to wield the kind of dominant influence on China's foreign investment scene as they have in the early stages of China's open-door policy.

With continuing dynamic growth, the Chinese economy will also be increasingly integrated with the Asia-Pacific region.[30] At present, China itself has already started to invest overseas primarily for resource acquisition and technology transfer. In the years to come, China is likely to trade more with and invest more in other Asia-Pacific economies. Ethnic Chinese in the region, with their valuable entrepreneurial skills and established *guanxiwen*, could become useful partners for China's economic expansion in the region by forming a new symbiotic relation with mainland Chinese business interests, as they have done so for the Japanese, Korean, and Taiwanese businesses in the past.

---

[30] For a further discussion of this subject, see John Wong (1995). China in the dynamic Asia-Pacific region. *The Pacific Review*, (84).

Index

About the Author

John Wong is currently Professorial Fellow and Academic Advisor to the East Asian Institute (EAI) of the National University of Singapore. He was formerly Research Director of EAI, and Director of the Institute of East Asian Political Economy (IEAPE). He obtained his Ph.D. from the University of London in 1966.

He taught Economics at the University of Hong Kong from 1966 to 1970 and at the National University of Singapore from 1971 to 1990. He had also taught at Florida State University briefly as a Fulbright Visiting Professor. He had held visiting appointments with Harvard's Fairbank Center, Yale's Economic Growth Center, Oxford's St. Antony College, and Stanford University, Economics Department. In 1996, he held the Chair of ASEAN Studies at the University of Toronto.

He has written/edited 34 books, and published over 500 articles and papers on China and other East Asian economies, including ASEAN. In addition, he has written over 90 policy-related reports on China's development for the Singapore government.

He has served and is still on the editorial board of many learned journals on Asian studies and economic development. He has done consultancy work for the Singapore government and many international organizations, including UN ESCAP, ADB, UNIDO, APO and ADI.

Printed in the United States
By Bookmasters